THE END OF MAGIC

D1545188

The End of Magic

ARIEL GLUCKLICH

New York   Oxford
Oxford University Press
1997

Oxford University Press

Oxford   New York

Athens   Auckland   Bangkok   Bogota   Bombay   Buenos Aires
Calcutta   Cape Town   Dar es Salaam   Delhi   Florence   Hong Kong
Istanbul   Karachi   Kuala Lumpur   Madras   Madrid   Melbourne
Mexico City   Nairobi   Paris   Singapore   Taipei   Tokyo   Toronto

and associated companies in
Berlin   Ibadan

Copyright © 1997 by Ariel Glucklich

Published by Oxford University Press, Inc.
198 Madison Avenue, New York, New York 10016

Library of Congress Cataloging-in-Publication Data
Glucklich, Ariel.
The end of magic / Ariel Glucklich.
p.   cm.
Includes bibliographical references and index.
ISBN 0-19-510879-5 — ISBN 0-19-510880-9 (pbk.)
1. Magic—India.—2. Superstition—India;   I. Title.
BF1622.I5G58   1997
133.4'3'01—dc20   96-8916

1 3 5 7 9 8 6 4 2

Printed in the United States of America
on acid-free paper

For Rony Oren and Wendy Doniger

ꙅ PREFACE ꙅ

The word *magic* works far too hard. We reach for it frequently, to describe wildly different things: A moon-swept landscape is magical, and so are the first stirrings of love in spring. Glenn Gould's performance of the *Goldberg Variations* is certainly magical, but so is a Hopi ritual, a Hindu mantra, and a Ndembu cure. Buried under its immense load, the word *magic* has lost its clarity and vigor. It somehow expresses our sense of awe while retaining more technical meanings derived from ethnography, as well as from European history of ideas. Some people use the word *magic* to describe occult events, which they consider possible though rare. Others, usually lacking any such beliefs, study magic as a social, psychological, or cultural fact.

This confusion may seem like a trivial problem to specialists in anthropology and religion. A problem of commonsense getting in the way, some might say. But commonsense can deceive the wariest expert. It paralyzed me for a while in Banaras, first in 1992, then in 1993–1994. I came to collect modern forms of magic in this sacred city in order to compare them with ancient textual descriptions. But it quickly became obvious that without a clear and definite understanding of magic, I would have to include everything I saw in such a project. By one criterion or another, every act—from boat building to rickshaw maintenance—was somehow magical. The project was becoming too bulky and too vague. So I continued to collect cases and descriptions of practices that seemed magical, still casting my net as wide as possible. But meanwhile I also began to reflect on the nature of magic in general, on its meaning to the people of Banaras. *The End of Magic* is the result of this reflection. It is a necessary introduction to my more ambitious study of magic in India, which I have yet to write. The title announces the end of magic, but only as a phenomenon defined by well-enshrined prejudices. The reader who sticks with the argument woven into the narrative of the book will emerge with a new understanding of magic and an appreciation for those who practice it. Students of religion will be prepared to study the historical expressions of magic, in India and elsewhere.

I owe an extraordinary debt to Om Prakash Sharma for his knowledge, kindness, and hospitality. And if words of gratitude buried in the pages of books are often the currency of scholarly debt, in some cases that is not enough. This is one such case.

I could not have gone to Banaras without the help of Lee Siegel, Wendy Doniger, Carl Ernst, and Kenneth Zysk, who helped me wrench a Fulbright grant (1993–1994) against the odds. Others have helped this book *in utero* by reading drafts of chapters or sections, by commenting during lectures, helping with translation, and in various other ways. I am especially grateful to Amiya Kesavan, Sanjiv Sharma, T. N. Madan, Robert Svoboda, Shoshank Singh, Veneeta Sharma, Aditya Behl, Avner Glucklich, Deborah Gordon, and Leonard Levy (who will make a writer of me yet). Cynthia Read was supportive throughout the transmigratory pains of the book's incarnations, and her anonymous readers at Oxford University Press were extremely helpful. Finally, my deepest thanks to Leslie Levy, Natalie, and Elon, who suffered most for this book.

⚘ CONTENTS ⚘

৯ CASES ৲

THE END OF MAGIC

What Is Magic?

"And already the knowing animals are aware that we are not really at
home in our interpreted world."

RILKE, *Duino Elegis,* first

Omji's small apartment is located directly across from the Durgā Temple, just as the magician from Hawaii had said. The instructions were
vivid: "Ask your driver to take you to the Durgā Temple—the one near
Banaras Hindu University. When you get there, stand with your back
to the temple gate; you will see a taxi stand, and behind it a two-story
building. Sharma lives upstairs. You can't miss it." The magician ne-
glected to say that the taxi stand is seldom visible through the chaos of
cars, scooters, and bicycles. Nor did he mention what a spectacle one
makes by following these instructions. The merchants behind their trin-
ket and bengal stalls and the beggars lining the temple gate see a foreigner approaching the sacred temple purposefully, then turn his back
on it and stare across the road. Suddenly he lurches back into the traffic
and crosses the road, leaving the merchants to yell at his back: "Oh
Baba!—Durgāji is this way!"

I first met Om Prakash Sharma (Omji) in February 1992 when he
opened the door to a tiny, dark apartment. Omji was of average size,
with a graying crew cut and sparkling eyes above his full jowels. He
was wearing a white cotton undershirt and brown polyester trousers;
his feet were bare. Omji remembered the man from Hawaii as the one
who had made a cigarette disappear but smiled when he heard I was
not interested in that kind of magic, only in sorcery and healing.[1] He

may have suspected I was after Tantric eroticism but decided to wait and see. The front room was nearly bare; on one side there was a table with four chairs, on the other a bed. Two images of the goddess Kālī hung on the walls, and the photograph of a renouncer with burning eyes—Omji's guru, I assumed. Two men were sitting at the table watching me intently. This must have been a common sight for them: an American scholar with some vague introduction appearing at the doorstep of this man. Omji showed me to the chair in which he had been sitting and introduced the two men as professors from Banaras Hindu University, a sociologist and an economist. During the course of the next hour, in conversation with these three, it became painfully clear that I could not explain the search for magic. The subject of magic made me—as it makes everyone else—sound ignorant.

This was confirmed later that evening. "I think this rising full moon over the Ganges is magic," a neighbor at the Ganga View Hotel announced hours later, after hearing about my problems at Omji's house. She was a well-dressed German tourist on the way from a guru's ashram in Lucknow to Nepal for a trek, and she could afford to raphsodize about magic. The huge ochre moon lit up the river and silently bounced off the city. I said that unless you use the terms figuratively, beauty and magic were not the same thing. The tourist answered that she had not been referring to the beauty of the view but to her feelings about it, though she could not explain them. Earlier, the economist at Sharma's house had said something totally different about magic. He had heard of lamas in Tibet who could train themselves to walk on water. "That is magic!" he stated.

We use the word *magic* so often that it means too much, and therefore hardly anything. Anthropologists assign very specific meanings to *magic,* but most people say that something is magical if it is extraordinary, if it defies commonplace experience or even the laws of nature. I think both the hotel guest and the economist had this in mind, though one was speaking of her personal sense of awe, while the other spoke of supernatural acts. But the sociologist in Omji's apartment countered that reports of supernatural facts were grossly exaggerated; no such thing has really ever taken place. "In fact, anything you would consider magical—supernatural or extraordinary—is by definition false, based on rumors and utterly nonexistent. And so," he concluded, chuckling, "our American friend here is wasting his time. He is chasing ghosts." This was followed by a burst of laughter from both the sociologist and the economist. But Sharma was very earnest. "Oh, but I have seen such things with my own eyes. Once, when I was young, I saw a Tantric holyman make a bad tooth disappear from the mouth of a man and appear inside a folded handkerchief on the table. This was not a rumor!"

"O.K." said the sociologist. "I will grant the fact you saw something with your own eyes and maybe—just maybe, mind you—it was not sleight of hand. Or let's say you saw a lama walk on water. In that case there must be some physical explanation, and the fact that we do not have it now does not mean that in ten or twenty years some physicist or engineer will not be able to explain it. So it is not magic; it is simply a preexplained scientific phenomenon. So either way, I'm right, and magic is just some intellectual illusion. Or else," he added after a pause, "it is a psychological need finding a symbolic outlet in obscure and useless rituals. And there you have it: Is there any other possibility?"

The conversation drifted in other directions after this rhetorical question, and I spent that February evening arguing over word meanings on the hotel verandah. People in Banaras—and everywhere else—perform certain acts that they consider magical and somehow extraordinary. They use special words for these extraordinary rituals and phenomena—*jādū-ṭonā*, *ṭoṭakā*, *mūth*, *tantra-mantra*—and I could not accept the sociologist's verdict that they were just suffering from an "intellectual illusion" or a social neurosis.[2] There had to be something true or valid about the wisdom, or at least the persistence, of ideas that have survived for so many millenia. But at the same time I could not bring myself to accept the occult. Disappearing teeth and floating lamas and rains stopped on demand are hard to accept. In short, I was in a bind. Some time later, this dilemma became crystal clear in the case of a botched divination.[3]

A BOTCHED DIVINATION

I took a friend—Lorilai—to see a holy man who is known as the Lame Baba. A small, powerfully built renouncer whose left leg is partially paralyzed, the baba heals people and helps them with financial and other problems. He is renowned in the area for seeing things in the thumb of his young assistant. That afternoon the boy spotted us approaching first, and he ran enthusiastically to announce our arrival and make the preparations. The courtyard was actually a small cattle farm on the bank of the Ganges. At the center, near the cow shed and haystack, was a small shrine where the renouncer sat shaded by a huge neem tree. The boy brought him a small oil lamp in which a quantity of lampblack was mixed with jasmine oil and then applied to the boy's thumbnail thickly and evenly with a marigold petal. The nail became a shiny black mirror, and my friend was invited to see her parents in their Louisiana home. But she could see only her own face.

"You must try to concentrate!" she was firmly told, and now she could also see the windows of the shrine behind her.

Lorilai was stubborn and honest. She refused to patronize the diviner by lying, so a heated argument followed. "Here is your father," the baba insisted, "and next to him is your mother. See? She is a very tall woman, no?"

My friend, who at five feet eight inches seems very tall to Indians, shook her head. "No! Actually my mother is only five feet four inches—much shorter than me."

The baba became exasperated; the boy was angry. No one would back down. Then everyone turned to me, and I was commanded to look at the thumb and settle the matter once and for all. I tried to bow out in a ridiculous manner: "I have never met her parents, so I could not identify them in the nail." Lorilai was shocked. The others also refused to accept this, so I looked at the thumbnail and said I could not make out its contents. We decided to call the affair a draw, and I promised to return.

Was this a case of magic? Neighborhood people would certainly say so. And if it failed, magic can fail just like a television or a phone. The power was simply off that day. Did Lorilai think it was magic?

"It was certainly not magic," she claimed angrily as we walked back. "It was sheer fraud, or at the very best, self-deception."

"So you think they saw what you saw and knew it was a simple reflection but decided to call it something else?"

"They must have seen what I saw, that's obvious. Why they said what they said, I can't say."

At this point I needed to know what Lorilai meant by magic, so I asked: "If they had come up with astoundingly accurate information about your parents, then you would regard this as magic?"

"Yes!"

"Why?"

"Because then it would have been true."

"True for them?—wasn't it after all in this case?—or true for you?"

"Well, I don't think there is any difference. I know that amazing divinations or predictions and other miracles are possible. I have seen them. Those are magic. What we saw here was fake magic."

Here is the problem, then, clear as a shiny fingernail: Lorilai believes that a universal, objective standard of truth exists and can be used to measure practices that claim to be magical. That standard is not scientific in the strict sense—after all, it accepts miraculous phenomena as possible. Lorilai believes in magic but needed to see it to believe it. In contrast, I took a relativistic position: There is no one objective and universal standard of truth. The truth of the baba—though I would not buy bonds with it—is a legitimate subjective truth.[4] My personal beliefs about extraordinary phenomena have no bearing on his truth. Even if the baba accurately guessed the mileage on my Chevy at home, his success would still not give me an objective gauge for saying that this was magic. Magic, I claimed at that time, is intrinsically subjective—sometimes apparently successful, sometimes a failure—but always extraordinary to its beholders. Unfortunately, this may be a cozy relativism, a scholar's hideout and a way to avoid the question that interests everyone else: Is there such a thing as real magic?

For several weeks that winter of 1992, I watched people who practiced magic and considered it both true and extraordinary. But having returned home to find money for a proper search, I knew there would be no sense in packing again unless some of the confusion was sorted out. There was no point in looking for magic in a distant country if by "magic" one meant only what Indians regard as magic. That was too easy, even trivial—except perhaps to sociologists. There had to be something that would satisfy Lorilai and those who "believe in magic" but would not outrage the publishers of *The Skeptical Inquirer,* who support themselves by debunking the occult.

Three questions about magic dominated my efforts to sort out the subject: What is magic, what does magic do, and why do people believe in magic in the face of experience?

WHAT IS MAGIC?

The word *magic* has been used for a very long time and has had both positive and negative connotations. Taking it from ancient Persia, where the Magi were a class of priests—Herodotus regarded them as a tribe—the Greek turned the word into *mageia*. It later became *magia* in Latin. Both words had pejorative connotations that endure to this day in Protestant beliefs and rational scientific attitudes. According to both, magic implies gross superstition and a decadent hodgepodge of ideas taken capriciously from any source. *Webster's New Collegiate Dictionary* defines magic as the use of means, such as charms or spells one believes to have power over natural forces. Magic is also defined there as an extraordinary power that derives from seemingly supernatural sources. These definitions accurately describe what most people think of magic. Anthropological and other professional definitions have essentially just expanded this common view. There are several good scholarly definitions of magic, but among the more recent John Middleton's is considered authoritative:

> Most people in the world perform acts by which they intend to bring about certain events or conditions. . . . If we use Western terms and assumptions, the cause and effect relationship between the act and the consequence is mystical, not scientifically validated. The acts typically comprise behavior such as manipulation of objects and recitation of verbal formulas and spells. In a given society magic may be performed by a specialist.[5]

Like all definitions, this one has its problems, the worst being its use of the term *mystical*. Mysticism is the direct experience of the divine resulting from an arduous and highly disciplined contemplation. It has little in common with the hustle and bustle of magical activity. But regardless of such problems, Middleton's definition can be used to identify the following case as magical.

ॐ ॐ ॐ

Case Intro.1

Dirt from the Tracks

Harry Middleton Hyatt recorded—literally—the following conversation with a woman in Norfolk, Virginia:
"Well now, a lady got my hair one time and she stopped it in a bottle and she buried it. So it almost run me crazy but I went to a man. He made her bring de hair back. She'd brought it face to face and give it to me and told me why she did it, because she thought I had nothing to do but sit on de porch and read papers and I was in better circumstances den her. So dis man asked me what did I want done with her. I say, "Well, tain't worth while to kell her, but jest send her away from Portsmouth.". . .

He got three pinches of dirt out of her left track, right in the hollow of her foot and put it—made a little cloth bag and put that in there and sewed it up and had taken it to running water and made three wishes and threw it overboard. She went away from dere."[6]

The magical act consisted of carefully taking just the correct amount of dirt from the precise place—"her left track," placing the dirt in a pouch, and manipulating it according to specific instructions. When the victim then left the place, the client made the magical assumption that the ritual actions were mysteriously connected with her departure. That, on Middleton's definition and as we commonly use the term, is magic.

What Does Magic Do?

Magic continues to exist and flourish even in a modern world dominated by technological solutions and scientific reassurances. Is it a stubborn fossil of ancient beliefs, or does magic act in response to needs that are not met by technology? These are the hardest questions one can ask about magic. Answers have come from several intellectual traditons. Four answers stand out.

The pioneers of modern anthropology, Edward B. Tylor and James G. Frazer, claimed that magic does—or tries to do—what science does, but not so well. Magic is a primitive practical science that includes technology, medicine, and the rest. It is an attempt to tame nature for human advantage.

Later social scientists criticized their predecessors for taking the question too literally. They rephrased the question "What does magic do?" in a variety of ways, such as "What is the function of magic?" Magic does not *do* anything, but it serves various social and psychological functions: It is a way of organizing labor, solving social and legal disputes, or preserving authoritative knowledge.

More recently, the question has again been rephrased by those who favor symbolical interpretation: "What does magic mean?" is now the question that dominates cultural anthropology and other disciplines that are more sympathetic to the ideas of other peoples. This question leads us to look at the symbolic communication being expressed in the rituals of magic.

Finally, there is the naive insider's—the occultist—view.[7] Magic does what it claims to do: stop or start the rain, cure diseases, make a stranger love you. It does this by controlling powers that are not directly accessible to everyone, powers that are predictable and useful nonetheless. No serious social scientist would be caught taking this claim at its face value. In the West, such claims are left to the occultists and to followers of New Age ideas.

WHY DO PEOPLE BELIEVE IN MAGIC IN THE FACE OF EXPERIENCE?

A man returns to his village from a difficult hunting trip carrying a dead animal on his back. It is evening, and the sun has begun to set. If it sets before he returns to the safety of his village, the hunter's life will be in danger. So he pauses to perform a magical rite that includes putting a stone in the branches of a tree. This is done to slow down, or temporarily stop, the descent of the sun. But the sun goes down as usual, regardless of how often or how well the rite is performed. Why does he do it, then? His senses surely do not deceive him about the sun, it goes down as always. The same paradox exists for rain magic, efforts to heal certain illness, and other magical rituals. Why do people continue with magic when their senses tell them it does not work?

E. E. Evans-Pritchard, who recorded the case of retarding the sunset, cited more than twenty reasons for continuing with magic in the face of failure.[8] He called these "secondary rationalizations." One can always claim that a given ritual failed, for example, because an enemy worked better magic against it, thus enabling one's belief in magic to remain intact. But a researcher can also assume that magic is just a symbolic language that expresses the wish to have more time to get home. In that case, the ritual does not really fail; it was never meant to actually affect the sun. Similarly, another researcher may claim that magical rites serve only psychological or social functions and that magic is judged as a success or failure by such wider standards. For instance, rain magic always succeeds if it unifies social groups into cohesive economic behavior at appropriate times, regardless of actual precipitation.[9] These last two approaches, semiotics and functionalism, have no problems with the "failure" of magic. The earlier generations of scholars, Tylor and Frazer for example, argued that magic was meant to work. "Savages," therefore simply had to deny the evidence of their senses in favor of the authority of long-standing superstition. The contradiction between their senses and their beliefs could be rationalized in any one of the many ways Evans-Pritchard described. Belief prevailed over observation, and superstition governed the practice of magic. Most people outside the specialized fields of anthropology and history of religion still understand magic as such superstitious beliefs.

After living in Banaras and making several trips to tribal areas in Uttar Pradesh, Rajasthan, and Orissa, I discovered a surprising fact: Magic is rarely a simple matter of belief. Belief implies a set of intellectual assumptions and conclusions that is bridged by uncertain means. This process plays no key role in healing, cursing, or the other forms of magic I have observed. Few magicians and clients in Banaras ever ask themselves why their magic works or what it means. It works as a matter of nature. A man who inserts a key in the ignition of his Honda and turns it does not *believe* that the engine will start as a result of some causal chain. The act of turning the key and the firing of the engine are one event. Belief rarely figures in this type of action. But this is just a metaphor, and it should not convey the message that magic is based on an ignorance of mechanics, or on taking mechanics for granted. The point is different. Claude Levi-Strauss once noted that magic has a kind of necessity that resembles natural forces.[10] Magical acts are performed because they are connected to certain natural phenomena, and this connection is sensual and intuitive rather than intellectual. The magical act and the natural fact "register" in the awareness of the practitioner by means of the senses. Act and result are perceived as parts of one pattern, like the repeating forms in the apparent chaos of fractals or the blended figures in Escher's art. No mental speculation—belief—forms a part of the perceived connections in the complex event.

Without belief, the supernatural aspect of magic becomes moot. Middleton and Webster defined the connection between magical act and result as "supernatural." This is a common interpretation of magical beliefs, that is, that supernatural causal forces are at work. But not only is belief absent in most cases of magic I have witnessed; the explicit notion of supernatural—as opposed to natural—forces is meaningless. Is a ghost supernatural? Maybe it is by Western standards, where the known laws of nature rule out the possibility of such an entity. But in a culture where ghosts belong on a continuum of embodied existence ranging from gross body to pure soul, there is nothing supernatural about such a being. For many Indians, ghosts represent the same type of relation as a genetic link does for a Westerner. If a boy can have his father's nose for no visible reason (genes are hard to see), then a girl in India can have the spirit of her deceased aunt possessing her body. Just because it is strange, the experience of possession does not belong in a category that is contrasted to nature.

Attributing supernatural beliefs to other cultures is a very risky business because the concept of the supernatural is so slippery. A century ago European explorers might have detected supernatural beliefs behind every strange behavior they could not understand. Four generations of scholars later, ethnobotanists are going back to the same places, financed by government grants or backed by pharmaceutical companies, in search of medicines known only to the old herbalists and shamans.[11]

This book reviews some of the major theories that have explained—or explained away—magic over the last century. While every major theory, even those later debunked, teaches us something valuable about the phenomenon of magic, the very urge to explain magic, to reduce it to another level, leaves out something critical. The heart of *The End of Magic* is a description of the feature of magic that has always been left out of theoretical analysis. Magic is based on a unique type of consciousness: the awareness of the interrelatedness of all things in the world by means of simple but refined sense perception. This awareness can be called "magical consciousness" or, less ambiguously, the "magical experience." It is described in detail in Chaper 8, where symbolic interpretations and functional explanations of magic give way to a different perspective. Magical actions are no longer interpreted only as symbols. They constitute a direct, ritual way of restoring the experience of relatedness in cases where that experience has been broken by disease, drought, war, or any of a number of other events. Magic does not seek to "fix" an objective world; it addresses an awareness of a bond that is neither subjective nor objective. It straddles the line between the perceiver and the world because the two are part of a unified system, a mental ecology. I call this bond *empathy* in the final chapter of this book. But the magical experience is not a mystical or metaphysical concept. It is a natural phenomenon, the product of our evolution as a human species and an acquired ability for adapting to various ecological and social environments. Although I take the occult claims of Banaras magicians seriously, the description of their experiences is naturalistic, as Chapter 8 shows.

This book pitches some difficult and controversial ideas. Several chapters in the second section of the book, after the major theories of magic have been discussed, explore the theory of the "magical experience." This new theory is unfailingly phenomenological; the level of reality it describes is experience itself, not its underlying "causes."[12] An illustration should make this point clear.

When a man offers his love to a beautiful woman he has pursued for years, what is he doing? An evolutionary biologist, geneticist, or ethologist might claim that, pressured by inexorable biological drives, he is merely trying to maximize the chances for the survival of his genes. A psychoanalyst might claim that the lover is acting out a neurotic obsession with his mother and is completely enslaved to infantile predispositions. A sociologist, perhaps feminist, might claim that this infatuation is really about social control of a woman or gaining the social status associated with such a "prize." But the lover would surely protest—and show his love letters to prove—that his love is really a pure cherishing of one of God's most beautiful creations. No ulterior motives taint his perfect love, and he will care for her children also as divine beings. A theory of love can reduce the man's emotions to another level of analysis, one he neither recognizes nor feels. But how does the man experience his love? What is the connection between genetic survival and the conscious terrain of his feelings toward and perceptions of that woman? Commonsense and introspection show that the two levels are not identical. Chapter 9 discusses the relation between material causality (for instance, genes) and mental experience. The point here is that *both* are true. To deny the lover's experience is as foolish as to reduce humans to behavioristic impulses.

In the case of magic, no serious theory has ever taken into account, in a detailed and explicit way, the contours of the magical experience, the awareness of magicians and their clients as they perceive the effects of their rituals. This is precisely what *The End of Magic* does for magic in general and in Banaras specifically. This approach does not deny the validity of earlier theories, but it tries to restore some of the "magic" lost in magic after it had been reduced to other things. The final chapter of the book describes magical phenomena in Banaras as the expression of magical consciousness in action. The extraordinary occult claims and experiences are the subject not of causal analysis (except for Chapter 13), but of relational description. The reputation of some sorcerers as mind readers, for instance, does not require a PSI-style laboratory for testing. In Banaras the reading of minds depends on subtle forms of nonverbal communication that skilled or intuitive practitioners can read like an open book. "Mind" is not an internal organ but a wide-ranging system of signals that extends far beyong the individual. It is relational. The magician is the man or woman who creates the context in which minds enter a relationship, and this is often experienced as an "occult" event. And although the experience is in fact extraordinary, it is completely natural.

NOTES

1. Lee Siegel told me about Omji and added vivid, if overly explicit, instructions for finding the apartment. Professor Siegel had written *Net of Magic: Wonder and Deceptions in India* (Chicago: University of Chicago Press, 1991). He is a fine amateur conjurer.

2. Numerous additional terms describe the many aspects of what we commonly call magic, spell, curse, witch, talisman, and so forth. they will be given in context.

3. All cases recorded from Banaras are based on firsthand observation and the usual methods of storing such information. Secondhand and other sources will be noted.

4. *Baba* is an honorific term used for respected teachers or elders, but also for foreigners being panhandled.

5. *The Encyclopedia of Religion,* ed. M. Eliade, vol. 9 (New York: Macmillan, 1987), p. 82.

6. Harry Middleton Hyatt, *Hoodoo—Conjuration—Witchcraft—Rootwork: Beliefs accepted by many negroes and white persons, these being orally recorded among blacks and whites* (Hannibal, Mo.: Western Publishers. Memoirs of Alma Hyatt Foundation, 1939), p. 572.

7. *Occult* derives from the sixteenth-century Oxford Dictionary usage referring to something that is not apprehensible to the mind or subject of ordinary understanding. The term was applied to practices presumably based on hidden powers—not necessarily supernatural, but inaccessible to scientific measurement. This usage is still pervasive today, but it is hardly a universal feature of magic everywhere. See Mircea Eliade, *Occultism, Witchcraft, and Cultural Fashions: Essays in Comparative Religions* (Chicago: University of Chicago Press, 1976).

8. E. E. Evans-Pritchard, *Witchcraft, Oracles and Magic Among the Azande* (Oxford: Clarendon Press, 1937), pp. 475–78. His discussion of slowing down the sunset is at p. 469.

9. Gregory Bateson actually ridiculed those who believe that rain rituals are meant to cause rain—that they are "magical." His words are quoted in Chapter 8.

10. Claude Levi-Strauss, *The Savage Mind* (Chicago: University of Chicago Press, 1966), p. 221.

11. The ethnobotanical search for traditional drugs has become trendy and occasionally lucrative in recent years. See Mark J. Plotkin, *Tales of a Shaman's Apprentice: An Ethnobotanist Searches for New Medicines in the Amazon Rain Forest* (New York: Viking, 1994). See also a critical review of this work by J. Worth Estes in *Natural History,* March 1994, p. 62. Another recent widely read article is by Paul Alan Cox and Michael J. Balick, "The Ethnobotanical Approach to Drug Discovery," *Scientific American* (June 1994), with bibliography.

12. Phenomenology is a difficult philosophical doctrine usually associated with Edmund Husserl, Moritz Geiger, Max Scheler, Martin Heidegger, among others. The principles of philosophical phenomenology have been applied to religious material by scholars like Gerardus Van der Leeuw, W. Brede Kristensen, and Mircea Eliade—but not always with precision.

PART ONE

Theories of Magic

ONE

Magic Explained Away

Westerners who arrive in Banaras to conduct research, study music, or just live among Indians waste no time in shedding the outer signs of their Western identity in favor of kurtas and pajamas. Successfully blending into the street scene is essential to their well-being and effectiveness. Some bring portable computers and tape recorders, but very little else. Just fifty-five years earlier, at the final glow of the setting Raj, the Vienna-born Christoph von Fürer-Haimendorf arrived in Bombay armed with formidable introductions to the British aristocracy and then hauled truckloads of equipment to the Deccan hills;[1] he needed, among other things, a tent with beds, a table and several chairs, cooking equipment and eating utensils, vast amounts of food, medicine, clothing (impeccably khaki), several pairs of shoes, books and notebooks, lamps, and a floor covering. Sitting high in his folding chair, calk helmet at his side, he would interview the naked tribals crouching in front of him. In such a way he produced some of the best ethnographic work anywhere. But Fürer-Haimendorf never failed to maintain a sense of cultural superiority, an unstinting admiration for the white man's rule, that stretched the distance between himself and the people who shared their knowledge with him. Like the Raj, this brand of fieldwork has now passed away. This is a good thing for those who wish to understand magic in India, or anywhere else. Being such an elusive experience, seemingly suspended between subjective feeling and objective knowledge, magic would undoubtedly escape the grasp of a superior and detached observer.

Magic claims to be unusual: It is seldom about commonplace events. In its light, humans and animals appear to interact across boundaries

17

of language and nature; under its spell, the human mind seems to control matter and affect natural elements over vast stretches of space and time. But appearances can deceive. During the past century the phenomenon of magic, which is dispersed more widely than even religion, has been attacked from various quarters. On the one side have been the detractors who deny the very experience that practitioners claim to undergo. On the other side are the sympathizers who accept some magical claims but have found scientific reasons to make magic unexceptional. Consider the possible responses to the following case.

ᘓ   ᘓ   ᘓ

Case 1.1

Lowering Fever in Ancient India

A person who suffers from severe or persistent fever calls on the service of a healer, who ties a striped frog to the foot of the bed by means of blue and red strings that are fixed under the armpits of the frog. As he sprinkles the patient with water the healer recites:"May the fever that returns tomorrow, that returns on two successive days, the impious one, pass into this frog."[2]

There are numerous ways that detractors can deny that the healer does anything extraordinary here. They could say that the frog "symbolizes" the quality of coolness and that the rite merely expresses the desire for health, or that primitive people mistakenly think that cold animals are capable of drawing the heat from fevered people in the way a valley "draws" the water from the mountain. Or they could say that healing is a social phenomenon and that the ritual follows certain codes that only careful sociological analysis can unravel. These are some of the possible arguments on the side of the detractors—those who deny that anything out of the ordinary ("occult" or "magical") actually takes place.

Opposing the matter-of-course skeptics are the sympathizers—modern-day occultists, New Age scientists, and many lay observers like Lorilai. Ironically, those who sympathize with magicians and their clients can also be effective at turning the magical event into ordinary, commmonsense, and mundane science. A deferential acceptance of occult claims can result in "new scientific" models. Thus, in answer to the question How does a magical rite work? one could claim that a placebo effect is triggered by an elaborate manipulation of the patient's emotions and attitudes; the patient heals simply through the power of his mind—his faith—to accelerate the natural healing process. Magic on this account is not truly extraordinary, either; it only reveals the enormous inventiveness we possess for curing and healing, some of which is yet to be explained by modern medical models. We look at this argument in greater detail in Chapter 7. Imagine, however, that the patient is not human but an animal. Could one speak of a placebo effect in such a case? A related and more sophisticated interpretation of how such healing of animals is possible will be described shortly. But in the process magic must also be explained away by those who are guided by a sympathy for magicians and their claims.

🔊 🔊 🔊

Case 1.2

Healing a Calf

Larry Dossey tells this fascinating story from his childhood days in Texas. One day his father summoned a *curandera*—folk healer—named Maria to save one of his calves. The animal had cut itself somehow, and the wound became worm-infested. It was common for such relatively minor mishaps to result in the death of the animal in those days before antibiotics, because the squirming mass of maggots would eventually eat away at the host until it died. When all other forms of therapy failed, a folk healer like Maria no longer seemed like a silly option. Dossey recalls his father's hushed conversation with the Mexican woman, who then went alone to the sick animal.

"Disappointed, I viewed Maria from a considerable distance. I saw her dark figure kneel before the calf, which was on its side. It seemed curiously unafraid of her. She made several passes with her hands over the animal, and then, after she remained still for many minutes, her lips began to move." Maria never discussed her method with the boy, but Dossey recalls the following words that his father said to him: "Maria knows why the calf is sick. She says it has a strong will and is always misbehaving. It got the cut on its flank from barbed wire when it tried to escape the pasture and the rest of the cows. She says the infection is the price it has paid, but that it is a very smart calf and has learned its lesson. She made a bargain with the worms. She told them they have succeeded in teaching the calf a valuable lesson. But if they stay, the calf will die and they will eventually die with it. It would be better for everyone if they leave now and spare the calf."[3]

And so, the worms and the calf accepted the *curandera*'s mediation, and the calf healed. Dossey, in pursuit of bigger game, neglects to explain how human words can mean anything to both the calf and the worms. Of course, there is nothing extraordinary, let alone "supernatural," about communicating with animals. Pet owners do it all the time. But worms are a different matter, and, besides, Dossey makes a strikingly broader point. He claims that disease—even among animals—occurs in a specific ideological and emotional context, and healing is more effective when the entire context figures in the cure. This may explain the fact that during physician strikes in several countries during the past few decades, mortality rates actually went down for the duration of the strike. But Dossey's point is outstanding because it encompasses animals and humans alike. Although we never discover the *curandera*'s key for communicating with worms, Dossey can undoubtedly imagine a future scientific paradigm that explains the psychological basis of all sentient life.

This type of scientific reasoning, shared by many popular writers on the New Science lecture circuit, has the potential eventually to annihilate the claims of magicians. Imagine, for instance, that with the increasing sophistication of medicine and the move away from a crude, mechanical view of the body, every case of magical healing will be explainable by means of the new medical idioms. What, in such an unlikely event, will remain of healing magic as a unique event? Nothing, of course. The phenomena we now call magical will be relegated to such areas as ethnomedicine, or they will be honored as "old ways wisdom," or they will become enshrined in some other manner. Physicians will learn to apply the old practices in new clinical settings, and the extraordinary claims magicians often make will become commonplace, until they disappear into mere prognostication and a lofty bedside manner. This is a pipe dream, of course. The same magician who treats jaundice with occasional success also performs rituals to make or stop rain, travels to astral regions, or claims he can make a man explode into flames just by looking at him. No placebo effect there. So while New Scientists may embrace certain forms of traditional healing, their theories do not help us understand magic in general.

Return for a moment to Dossey's healer, who could communicate moral instruction to two species of animals. Assume that it is not the content of her words, their meaning, but some other quality that heals. Now compare this with the story I was told by a *sādhū*—an Indian holy man.

অ অ অ

Case 1.3

The Swamiji's Buffalo

Once, before he became a renouncer, Swamiji had a buffalo. It was a big female that gave a lot of milk. One day he wanted to make a milk offering to the spirit of the Peepal tree, so he went to milk the cow. But a ghost entered her, and she would not give milk. He begged the cow and beat her with a stick, to no avail. Finally his father said to him: "the milk of the cow is like a mother's milk or like your urine. It must come from the heart. You must reach her heart. [So he tried different ways to do this] then he chanted the Gāyatrī Mantra: "We meditate on that excellent light of the divine Sun; may he illuminate our minds." Finally he sprinkled the cow with water, and the ghost left. Then she gave plenty of milk.[4]

I have since seen the Swamiji treat many people with his mantras, old people and infants, a few animals as well. No one knows the words of the mantras he mumbles today, and few would ever claim that the buffalo understood the words of the sacred Gāyatrī Mantra. They would say, instead, that the words are powerful *regardless* of whether you understand them or even hear them. They are often only whispered, then blown on the patient.

We can recover magic by means of this insight. If sound can heal, even across the boundary of species, it acts independent of meaning. It is a matter not of reasoning with worms but communicating by vibration. This does not tell us what magic is, but where we might look for it. If the power of magical words is not in their meaning, what they point to, then we should not be surprised that the same healer who impresses us with his psychosomatic genius also tries to control the clouds. For him there is no distinction between the sentience of a human patient and the behavior of a cloud. His magic does not rely on verbal communication or objective classifications. It is not about meaning, or ideology.

This is a risky claim, to which this entire book is devoted. I argue that magic is a unique and subjective state of mind that often defies accurate description because it transcends meaning, the very stuff of our thought. The experience of magical events rests first and foremost on the sensory perception that all elements in the world are interrelated, not in a mystical union, but in a tapestry of natural interactions. The essence of magic, as we see in Chapter 8, is this engagement of the senses in a pattern of relations. To be magical, this engagement must be sensual and empathetic in a special sense. When it is elevated into an ideology, for instance the trendy "New Ecology" (Lovelock's Gaia Theory is an outstanding example), it loses its immediate experiential force.[5] Ideologies and philosophies are never magical, regardless of their content. Just as the buffalo responded to the quality of the mantra's sound, not to the meaning of its words (which have nothing to do with giving milk), just so the magical state of mind must be experienced in its intrinsically subjective and sensory quality.

Unfortunately, its subjective nature makes magic excruciatingly slippery: Too often one culture's science is another's magic, and vice versa. I am reminded of the following wry entry in Verrier Elwin's diary from February 12, 1935. Three years after the English anthropologist joined the tribal Gonds of Karanjia, India, he noted: "Vaccinator comes, and dispensary filled with weeping children. Some roll on ground roaring with fear. Many parents also forcibly brought in. Mrs. Panda Baba done, but immediately goes home and rubs off serum with the sacred cow-dung, thus avoiding any ill effects."[6]

If magic is a matter of perception and is intrinsically subjective, it is probably most accurate to avoid using it as a noun. There is no such thing as magic, only a magical attitude, and following it a magical rite or belief. The noun implies the existence of an objective thing, like medicine or meteorology, and we have seen how easily such things can be made to disappear. The subjective attitude is the only valid way of considering magic; I call it the "magical experience," or "consciousness." You can find it in the operating room of Mt. Sinai Hospital in New York just as much as in the bushland of South Africa. At the same time you may develop an ideology of planetary interrelationship that resembles Navajo cosmology but still miss the mark on magical experience. Think of magic as the nonverbal power of sound or as the eloquence of touch, and you will be on the right track.

NOTES

1. Christof von Fürer-Haimendorf, *Life Among Indian Tribes: The Autobiography of an Anthropologist* (New Delhi: Oxford University Press, 1991).

2. The Kauśika Sūtra of the Athrava-Veda. ed. Maurice Bloomfield. (Delhi: Motilal Banarsidass, 1972).

3. Larry Dossey, *Meaning and Medicine: Lessons from a Doctor's Tales of Breakthrough and Healing* (New York: Bantam Books, 1991), pp. 1–3.

4. This story was narrated by the Kajjal Baba, a charismatic renouncer who healed villagers and city residents long before he became a holyman.

5. James E. Lovelock, *Gaia: A New Look at Life on Earth* (Oxford: Oxford University Press, 1991); see also Edward O. Wilson, *Biophilia.* (Cambridge, Mass.: Harvard University Press, 1984). There are numerous works in this category, but few as influential as these.

6. Verrier Elwin, *Leaves from the Jungle: Life in a Gond Village* (New Delhi: Oxford University Press, 1992), p. 141.

◪ TWO ◪

The Strange Case of Alfred Wallace

I arrived in Banaras at the municipal airport, eighteen kilometers down a lush country road from the city. But that is unusual. Most people—pilgrims—arrive by train or bus, squeezed into packed cars with their belongings wrapped in cloth and tied by means of rope. They are usually villagers or residents of small towns in Bihar or Uttar Pradesh, who rarely have the chance to ride the rail system that links the holy city to the rest of India. They arrive at the busy station dazed by the contrast between the city's sacred reputation and the chaos of the station: hundreds of people rushing to board the train even as the pilgrims are trying to disembark, scrawny red-shirted porters carrying huge packages on their heads yelling at them and shoving them out of the way, beggars, hawkers, and the dreaded pickpockets jostling around them competing for what little money they brought.

But suddenly, relief. A distinguished-looking man, large and confident, dressed like a pundit, approaches the pilgrims and addresses them in a quiet voice. "Welcome to Banaras, my friends!" he says. The pilgrims nod bashfully and ask in a strange Hindi, "Is there a bus to the center of the city?" As soon as they speak, the stranger has them pegged. Vastly experienced, he not only knows their caste, profession, state, and district but can practically identify the village they left. "You have come a long way from ———," he says, naming their place of origin to their complete astonishment. "I know much about you because I am an *ojhā*—an exorcist. I have been waiting for you. There is bad news at home." He lowers his voice dramatically as they come closer, worried. He tells them that a young sister or daughter has become possessed with a horrible ghost since they left home. She will soon be lying ill, suffering miserably. The villagers are stunned, but the *ojhā* has earned their trust. He takes them now to a small temple on the banks of a pond. The place is renowned for its effectiveness as a place of exorcism. An elaborate and expensive ritual will now be performed for the sake of the poor girl. The *ojhā* will remove the ghost into a ball of rice flour, and it will be cast into the pond. The pilgrims will give away most of their pilgrimage funds, but they will return home to find the girl healthy.[1]

🐚 🐚 🐚

Case 2.1

Wallace Goes to a Séance

In 1886, while visiting Boston on a speaking tour, Alfred Wallace was taken by William James to a séance where several apparitions were expected to materialize. In Wallace's own words, "eight or nine different figures came, including a tall Indian chief in war-paint and feathers, a little girl who talked and played with Miss Brackett, and a very pretty and perfectly developed girl, 'Bertha,' Mr. Brackett's niece, who has appeared to him with various mediums for two years, and is as well known to him as any near relative in earth-life. She speaks distinctly, which these figures rarely do, and Mr. Brackett has often seen her develop gradually from a cloudy mass, and almost instantly vanish away. . . .

The other figure was an old gentleman with white hair and beard, and in evening-dress. He took my hand, bowed, and looked pleased, as one meeting an old friend. Considering who was likely to come, I thought of my father and of Darwin, but there was not enough likeness to either. Then at length I recognized the likeness to a photograph I had of my cousin Algernon Wilson, whom I had not seen since we were children, but had long corresponded with, as he was an enthusiastic entomologist, living in Adelaide, where he had died not long before."[2]

Wallace was not the only famous individual in England who was attracted by the lure of ghosts. The list of converts to spiritualism included also the renowned physicist Sir William Crookes, the Oxford philosopher Henry Sidgwick, and other notables such as Fredrick Myers and Sir Arthur Conan Doyle. Still, Wallace's passionate embrace of spiritualism may have been the strangest, when we consider his career as a naturalist.

Alfred Russel Wallace was a self-taught man, trained as a land surveyor, a socialist whom conservatives today would regard as a bleeding heart. Though lacking Charles Darwin's wealth, he managed to finance his own world travels and spent years in the tropics. By the time he reached twenty-one years of age, he was known to Darwin as an excellent collector of beetles, butterflies, and birdskins. One day in 1858, about twenty years after Darwin's *Beagle* journey, when Darwin's evolutionary theory was nearly complete, Wallace sent a letter to him. To Darwin's amazement and shock, the twenty-page letter contained what Darwin himself acknowledged to be a near perfect abstract of his own natural selection theory. The young man had intuited the same solution to the question of the emergence of new species that Darwin had painstakingly constructed during years of research. Though he could not scientifically prove it, Wallace had discovered the correct mechanism of evolutionary change, and Darwin would always acknowledge the young man's feat of intuition.[3]

The idea of evolution itself was not, of course, an original Darwin or Wallace invention. In a variety of forms, evolution dominated the thinking of late-eighteenth and early-nineteenth-century geology, paleontology, and biology.[4] In fact, the simple concept of evolution—the idea of unfolding or developing—did not entirely contradict the pervasive and dominant Christian worldview. Theories of the "chain of being" were consistent with the theological "argument from design" and with close-ended views of change. The argument from design held that the complexity and the order of nature demonstrate the will or design of a Creator; because nature does not contain its own intelligence, a Higher Being must be responsible for the ability of natural phenomena to reach such heights of design. The close-ended, or teleological, view simply regarded evolution as a fixed process leading toward a goal, which is "man."[5]

Even the new classification system of Carolus Linnaeus, which was based on empirical observation of minute physical detail, demonstrated to many the will and the rationality of a Creator. Closer yet to the time of Darwin were the theories of Georges Buffon, Paul D'Holbach, Jean Lamarck, and Darwin's grandfather, Erasmus Darwin. Although they shared the post-Cartesian materialism of later naturalists, they still could not find the conceptual key to explain the obvious empirical facts of species. What they lacked was the nature and cause of the minute incremental changes that added up, over time, to speciation. One must note that Lamarck's explanation, the inheritance of acquired characteristics, enjoyed a brief supremacy even in the twentieth century. The problem, as the great Darwinian biologist Ernst Mayr recently remarked, was not an empirical failure to recognize the facts of speciation or to acknowledge the diversity of the zoological record.[6] It was a conceptual problem made more complicated by the fact that nineteenth-century England had not freed itself from the teleological thinking of mainstream Christianity. The influence of ideology on the conceptual aspect of scientific thinking is a well-recognized fact today. In fact, the solution that Darwin finally proposed—natural selection, or "survival of the fittest," in Herbert Spencer's terms—could be regarded as the naturalist's equivalent of Malthusian economics, which had a strong influence on the upper middle class of English society, including Darwin.

Even with the publication of Darwin's *On the Origin of Species* in 1859 and the gradual ascent of natural selection, most naturalists could still not bring themselves to abandon teleology altogether. Alfred Wallace, ostensibly one of Darwin's closest allies, joined the larger group of researchers, which included Sir Charles Lyell, the American botanist Asa Gray, Richard Owens, and others who stood against Darwin, Thomas H. Huxley, and Sir Joseph Hooker, the unflagging materialists. The teleologists held that the biological mechanism of selection, even if accepted, did not disprove the existence of a guiding principle above and beyond nature.[7]

The issue was starkest in connection with the evolution of the human species and mind. Darwin, at great personal cost to his social standing, refused to place humans outside the evolutionary scheme:

> "[T]he difference in mind between man and the higher animals, great as it is, certainly is one of degree and not of kind. We have seen that the senses and intuitions, the various emotions and faculties, such as love, memory, attention, curiosity, imitation, reason, etc., of which man boasts, may be found in an incipient, or even sometimes in a well-developed condition, in the lower animals . . . the ennobling belief in God is not universal with man; and the belief in spiritual agencies naturally follows from other mental powers." [8]

Although morality is accompanied by higher powers of reasoning, it is ultimately based on "social instincts," which humans share with other animals, especially those that run in packs. Darwin's closest ally, Thomas Huxley went further, boldly arguing that "thoughts are the expression of molecular changes in the matter of life, which is the source of our other vital phenomena."[9]

Wallace was horrified by these ideas and tirelessly sought to undermine them.[10] Consciousness, he felt, remained a mystery unilluminated by Darwin's gross error in *The Descent of Man* (1891). One wonders how much of Wallace's passion derived from intellectual conviction and exactly how much it owed to what Huxley called "lunacy." But mad or not, Wallace was heavily armed with arguments. He claimed as his major objection that if natural selection and adaptation equipped creatures with only the minimal tools for survival in a particular environment, then the overly developed brain of even the most primitive savage would be an evolutionary waste—an impossibilty. The brain with its magnificent mental capacities, he concluded, could never be explained in strictly evolutionary—or even naturalistic—terms.[11] Another power, a Spiritual Being, had to account for the human mind. "Whereas life *may* conceivably be regarded as the result of 'chemical transformations and molecular motions, ocurring under certain conditions and in a certain order'," no combination of merely material elements, no matter how complex, could ever produce the "slightest tendency to originate consciousness in such molecules or groups of molecules."[12] Consciousness is radically different in principle from matter, he believed, and its existence in the bodies of material creatures can never be explained by the same laws that govern the body. In fact, Wallace maintained, consciousness is consistent with the existence of spirits independent of bodies. This was an outrageous position for a renowned naturalist to take. But Wallace told a contemptuous Huxley that convincing proof was available "anthropologically," in the context of seances conducted by spiritualists.

SPIRITUALISM

The spiritualist movement that captivated Alfred Wallace in 1865 was still young and vigorous. Spiritualism had taken off following the reported events that befell the Fox family in Hydesville, New York, early in 1848.[13] According to the testimony of John D. Fox and his wife, they woke up one night in their newly acquired house, awakened by raps, knocks, and the sound of moving furniture. A few nights later Mrs. Fox began to communicate with the source of the noises. She quizzed the intelligence behind the sounds, and it rapped correct answers to her questions. Finally, the source identified itself as the spirit of a Mr. Duesler who had been murdered in that house years earlier. News of the discovery spread quickly, and the Foxes became celebrities. Over the course of the following years, the three Fox daughters assumed the role of mediums, communicators with the spirits of other dead people. Propelled by the increasing fame of the Fox sisters, the spiritualist movement gained an immense following and great notoriety in the United States and England. Among its leading luminaries were W. Stainton Moses and Daniel Douglas Home, who enjoyed the support of numerous intellectuals. Even the repeated exposure of fraud among mediums and the occasional confessions of wayward practitioners, including the Fox sisters, could not destroy the movement altogether.

The claims of spiritualism were few and simple:

- The spirit of a deceased individual survives death in a nonembodied state but with the same personality.
- A few unique persons are capable of contacting these spirits and passing information between them and their survivors.

The phenomena of spiritualism are related to the spirits' efforts to draw attention and to communicate and to the methods of the mediums for receiving information. They include raps and other noises, apports and the manipulation of objects, automatic writing, psychic photography, touching, appearances, and clairvoyance or clairaudience. The earlier forms of spiritualism tended to include mostly rapping and table levitation or other simple physical phenomena. These, of course, were the easiest to fake, so, with the improvement of detection methods such as infrared photography and video technology, spiritualist phenomena became increasingly mental. This meant that the mediums reported to their sitters information obtained from the spirit about its life, including both past and future events.

Alfred Wallace began his experiences with spiritualism as it was ascending in popularity in England. But this is not to say that he was risking nothing by lending his name in support of its practitioners and phenomena. Carl Jung noted years later that Wallace, along with Myers, Crookes, and Sidgwick, was worthy of admiration for "having thrown the whole of [his] authority on the side of non-material facts, regardless of . . . the cheap derision of [his] contemporaries." Though motivated by deeply felt private drives, Wallace used spiritualism as an empirical support for his position on the evolution of the mind.[14]

Darwin, who was something of a mentor to the younger Wallace, felt that his scientific materialism was being outflanked by two forces: the prevailing Cambridge and Oxford Anglican orthodoxy led by the likes of Richard Owens, who refused to submit the Creator's greatest creature to naturalistic reductions, and the continuing belief in the occult. Even such a close ally as Wallace accepted the existence of a mental, not to say supernatural, realm that lies entirely ouside the domain of biological science. In short, Christianity and the occult shared an aversion to Darwinism and its reduction of all existence to some form of matter.

Wallace's fascination with the occult was probably a result of an aversion he shared with Darwin toward the dominant forms of Christianity. In this respect, Wallace, the great evolutionary biologist, makes a splendid godfather to New Age spirituality. He was unmoved by the ascending Victorian naturalism while being bitterly disenchanted with orthodox religion. His inherent sense of justice and his appreciation of the uniquely human potential of mind and spirit led him away from evolution and Christian ethics alike and toward the third path of spiritual evolution as described by the spiritualist movement. But perhaps Wallace's touching ennoblement of humanity reflects back on his own nature, which Frederick Myers, a sympathetic observer, described in the following terms: "[Wallace's] worst credulity as to the good faith of cheating mediums belongs to a separate compartment of his mind—or rather forms a part of his innocent generosity of nature, an unwillingness to believe that anyone will do anything wrong." [15]

Should this pathetic epitaph hang around the neck of anyone who believes in magical or occult phenomena in this day and age? It seems that a slightly schizophrenic mind, reinforced by a childlike trust, is the only explanation for the toleration of occult claims among modern scientists such as David Bohm. At the same time, we know more today about magical practices around the world than Wallace could ever have imagined, despite all his travels. This irrevocable divorcing of magical practices from occult claims was the product of the scholars of Alfred Wallace's era, and especially the pioneering work of Edward B. Tylor.

NOTES

1. I have watched this operation and own one of the pamphlets the *ojhās* give the pilgrims. The participants and the site of exorcism shall remain nameless for obvious reasons. Other practitioners, patients, and locations will be named wherever permission has been given.

2. Alfred Russel Wallace, *My Life: A Record of Events and Opinions,* vol. 2 (New York: Dodd, Mead, 1906), p. 356.

3. Adrian Desmond and James Moore, *Darwin* (London: Penguin Books, 1992), pp. 468–69

4. Arthur O. Lovejoy, *The Great Chain of Being* (Cambridge, Mass.: Harvard University Press, 1936); Robert J. Richards, *The Meaning of Evolution* (Chicago: University of Chicago Press, 1992); Murray J. Leaf, *Man, Mind and Science: A History of Anthropology* (New York: Columbia University Press, 1979).

5. The pre-Darwinian naturalistic theories, best embodied in William Paley's *Natural Theology,* make perfect sense—if Darwin is wrong. For more on this, see Richard Dawkins, *The Blind Watchmaker* (New York: Norton, 1987), pp. 3–5.

6. *Scientific American* 272 (August 1994): 24–25.

7. On the savage comments by Bishop Samuel Wilberforce against Huxley at the Oxford debate of 1860 and on Huxley's rejoinder, see Desmond and Moore, *Darwin,* pp. 492–99.

8. Charles Darwin, *The Descent of Man and Selection in Relation to Sex,* 2 vols. (London: Murray, 1971), p. 143.

9. Quoted in Alfred Russel Wallace, *Natural Selection* (London: Macmillan, 1875), p. 207; see also Thomas H. Huxley, *Man's Place in Nature and Other Anthropological Essays* (New York: Appleton, 1902), pp. 146–56.

10. On Wallace, see Martin Fichman, *Alfred Russel Wallace* (Boston: Twayne, 1981).

11. Wallace, *Natural Selection,* p. 193.

12. Fichman, *Wallace,* p. 118.

13. On spiritualism and the Fox sisters, see Early Wesley Fornell, *The Unhappy Medium: Spiritualism and the Life of Margaret Fox* (Austin: University of Texas Press, 1964), and Slater Brown, *The Heyday of Spiritualism.* (New York: Hawthorn, 1970).

14. Fichman, *Wallace,* p. 130.

15. Ibid., pp. 129–30.

ꇙ THREE ꇙ

The Association of Ideas
Bringing People Together

The rise of modern anthropology in England coincided, paradoxically, both with the new theory of evolution and with the popularity of spiritualism. Edward B. Tylor could not have been anything but shocked by the "duping" of such renowned figures as Wallace or Crookes.[1] His anthropology, particularly his explanation of magic, had to take account of both evolution and the popularity of the occult in England. Working in a culture that was reaffirming an ancient passion for spiritual possibilities, Tylor had to take magic seriously enough to reject it as bad thinking.

On the truth of spiritualism Tylor declined to pass judgment; this he left to trained detectives. But he placed the entire occult craze in historical perspective along with witchcraft and other "survivals" from the distant past, before the physical sciences had yet learned to disengage spirits from nature or to think in terms of causality. In other words, the popular fashion sweeping through the salons of Europe and America was nothing more than a type of animism, which Tylor regarded as the earliest form of religion. It continued to exist as a cultural survival, like some unnecessary limb, ignored by physical evolution, that suddenly finds unexpected use. In the present case its use was the psychological consolation of a melancholy celebrity who might be uplifted by the thought that his soul had been sent to America for some "rough fixing." [2]

Meanwhile, Tylor argued, throughout the course of human history, all other forms of primitive religion have evolved from their crude early forms to their present higher forms, just as biological creatures have evolved. The primitive form of sacrifice, for example, had been based on the idea of an exchange of gifts, but it evolved through successive forms to its present ascetic conception in the higher religions as giving or sacrificing for no material reward whatsoever. Unfortunately, while Darwin painstakingly constructed a mechanism by which physical evolution takes place, Tylor found no equivalent mechanism for his evolving cultural forms.

Magic was an exception to the evolutionary pattern seen in the religious and practical aspects of culture. Its survival in Victorian England testified to the persistence of primitive ways of thinking, which Tylor called the "association of ideas." Instead of recognizing true causality in natural events, primitive peoples—including some Englishmen—were misled by the resemblance or the proximity of objects into thinking that they were related.[3] Though hardly a traveler himself, Tylor insisted that magical thinking usually pervaded primitive cultures in remote parts of the world, where evolution had overlooked a portion of humanity. Unlikely as it may have seemed, however, the same kind of thinking became popular in the salons of London, in the form of spiritualism and other occult fads. Since evolution could not possible have bypassed members of Darwin's own race, the only explanation for the popularity of magic in England had to be psychological.

Tylor has been criticized both for his social Darwinism and for psychologizing magic and ignoring its social, ritual, and symbolic aspects. But he was forced by historical circumstances to regard magic as he did. The optimism of positive science had yet to overcome the teleology of Christian cosmology or to shake off the pesky popularity of occult practices. Occult claims had to be taken seriously—literally rather than figuratively—if only to be debunked. Tylor's achievement in this area was still considerable. By regarding magic as a form of prescientific thinking—the "association of ideas" as opposed to proper causality—and by rigorously placing modern spiritualism in historical perspective as the fulfillment of certain psychological needs, Tylor took the occult out of magic.

James Frazer, by far the most famous expositor of magic, later elaborated Tylor's notion of the association of ideas and beefed it up with a monumental collection of esoterica in *The Golden Bough*.[4] Like Tylor, he was a Darwinist and a scientific positivist, a forward-looking intellectual who, had he reflected on the strange case of Wallace, would have been shocked by the scientist's backsliding into "ignorance." One need hardly speculate how Frazer would have applied the "association of ideas" to erotic magic.

🐚 🐚 🐚

Case 3.1

Love Magic

One day, as I was sitting with Girja Prasad at his stall behind Hariścandra Ghāṭ, two women approached but stood quietly off to the side. They were wearing inexpensive saris, and the younger of the two held a heavy basket of fresh produce from the nearby market. They silently watched the Tantric sorcerer talk about this and that and waited for him to acknowledge their existence. Finally Prasad stood up and wordlessly walked around to the back of his shop. The two women followed him there. They spoke in muted tones that were completely drowned by the noise of the chaotic alley. After some time Prasad came around to the front and crawled into his tiny shop. He shuffled bottles containing powders of various colors, moved stacks of cloth and leaves, unwrapped nylon and opened bags till he found one tiny jar with a rusted lid. This he took to the rear of the shop. A few minutes later I saw the women retreat down the alley without turning back. Prasad calmly returned to his seat and began to survey the street like a bored man.

In a city where privacy sticks out like the skimpy dress of a European tourist, the secretive behavior of the two women was too much for me. I asked Prasad why they came to him. He answered immediately, showing neither reluctance nor enthusiasm, that the younger of the two—the daughter of the elder—felt that she had lost the love of her husband. She came for a love remedy.

"So what did you give her out of that rusty old jar?"

Prasad took out the jar and unscrewed the lid. "These are the seeds of the Mohini plant." He showed me two dry seeds of *Erodium maximum*.[5] "When you put them next to each other, they curl together like two lovers. When the lady will put the two seeds in her husband's food, with the correct mantra I have given her, and she adds much salt, her husband will love her." When I asked Prasad for the words of the mantra, he changed the subject.

Love in India, love magic specifically, is spectacularly elusive. A rich and evocative history of erotic art, literature, and magic, has been displaced by a puritanical silence. Unlike any other form of magic and sorcery, no one wants to talk about love and sex. If love potions and recipes are ever used—as Prasad insisted—the topic was tightly sealed off to me. The most I could get was a vague warning from a kindly hotel owner who said, half jestingly, when I moved to an apartment, that if I should find a ring under my mattress (left there by the cleaning woman), I should dispose of it as quickly as possible. That brought to mind an entry from Elwin's diary, which I had been reading:

> December 29. Adri's husband mixes in her supper a Love-Philtre (*Tila Dilruba*. Regd. Use it once and your most proud and indifferent darling shall be enslaved for ever. A packet of six times. Price Rs. 2 only). But Adri spots it in time and gives it to her little brother on whom it has no apparent effect.[6]

This slim "material" has to disappoint the collector of magical formulas and recipes. I could not help wondering whether I had witnessed a miraculously rare transaction behind Prasad's booth at Hariścandra Ghāṭ. Perhaps only a desperate woman would put her sense of dignity on the line and risk exposure and ridicule in order to procure a magical potion from a street vendor. Perhaps most wives would be equally satisfied to coexist with an indifferent mate. If the newspaper matrimonial ads are any indication of the true state of affairs today, then romantic attachment has no place in the perfect match:

> Highly educated cultured, well-placed professional N. India Brahmin parents of 26 yrs., very fair, slim, extremely beautiful, affectionate daughter, gold medalist and post graduate topper in a reputed American university holding a good job in Bombay, invite alliance from highly educated, smart, handsome, broadminded boy from a respectable Hindu family well settled in own profitable business or profession with growth prospects . . . (*The Times of India*, January 9, 1994)

American credentials have become extremely desirable in today's matrimonial market, whether in the form of education, a greencard, or corporate connections. These have undoubtedly displaced the British connection and also reflect with some accuracy the increasing liberalization of the Indian economy.

This lackluster state of love strikes a classicist as paradoxical in light of India's magnificent erotic literature in which magic, as expected, plays a prominent role. The *Atharvaveda* and the *Kauśika Sūtra* were far richer resources for unhappy lovers who lived more than two millenia ago. A respectable portion of the texts' encyclopedic range was reserved for romantic affairs that required magical attention. For instance, a woman who found herself in competition with another for a husband(!) could mix the Bāṇāparṇī plant (*Lypea hernandifolia*) with diluted curds from a red goat and sprinkle this around the bed of her rival. As she did this, she would recite a mantra: "I dig up this plant, the most powerful among herbs, to overcome rival women and obtain a husband." With additional mantras that praised the power of the plant and its leaves, the woman would tie a leaf to the foot of the bed and throw other leaves over the bed.[7] The same procedure could be used to maintain the love of a husband who had been overpowered by love for another woman.

Vātsyāyana's *Kāmasūtra*, India's greatest contribution to the world's collectors of erotica, made full use of the powerful resources available in the *Atharvaveda*, a substantially older compendium. The *Kāmasūtra*, of course, is a testament to human confidence in the mastery of science over the affairs of the heart. A twist of the moustache and a raised eyebrow (across a crowded room), timed with the precision prescribed in the *Kāmasūtra*, will be devastating to an unsuspecting woman. But for the coy lover, or for one who rejects every advance, more esoteric methods must be summoned. When all else fails in the deployment of seductive charm, a bone of peacock or of a hyena covered with gold can be tied to the right hand. Similarly, one can tie onto the hand a bead made of jujube seed or of a conch shell, either one affixed with mantras taken from the *Atharvaveda* or from other magical sources.[8] The *Kāmasūtra* does not stop there, of course. With unwavering thoroughness, it covers a vast range of methods designed to gain love or even to go beyond love. If a man rubs a mixture of the powders from the white thorn apple, black pepper, and honey on his penis before making love to a woman, for example, he will subjugate her entirely to his will.[9]

India's erotic-magical literature is so extensive and explicit, in fact, that when James Frazer went fishing in his library for examples of homeopathic or imitative love magic, he turned first to Indian texts (in German and English translations).[10] He would certainly have enjoyed watching Prasad demonstrate the qualities of the Mohini seeds that made for an effective love remedy, where the curling and intertwining of two seeds resembles the passionate embrace of two lovers. Resemblance or analogy is "mistaken" for causality in Prasad's mind or those of his clients, so Frazer would argue with relish. The bad thinking and the pseudocausality, in a phrase, "the association of ideas," bring his clients together. This way of thinking can also drive them apart, of course, and cause them to rely on other senses such as touch. Isn't that, after all, the reason that so many villagers around Banaras roll their shorn hair into a tight ball, mixed with the hair of others, and stuff it into the crevices of the mud huts?[11]

Frazer's joy has spilled over into our smug feeling of superiority over this manifest superstition, not to say stupidity. But the fact that magical practices look like the association of ideas does not necessarily imply an inability to think properly. Such a judgment reflects a profound ignorance of the social and symbolic goals of magical behavior. Of course, Frazer initially had no access to the theories of Emile Durkheim and Bronislaw Malinowski, not to mention Levi-Strauss. However, the later editions of *The Golden Bough* appeared after sociological and anthropological theories had moved beyond the simplicities of homeopathy. The fact that our own popular conception of magic has not followed suit is a testament not to the endurance of Tylor's and Frazer's ideas but to the tenacity of simple prejudice.

NOTES

1. Edward Burnett Tylor, *The Origins of Culture* (New York: Harper Torchbooks, 1958); see also Brian Morris, *Anthropological Studies of Religion* (New York: Cambridge University Press, 1984), and Stanley Jeyaraja Tambiah, *Magic, Science, Religion, and the Scope of Rationality* (Cambridge: Cambridge University Press, 1991).

2. Tylor, *The Origins of Culture*, p. 143.

3. Tylor was not the first to see this obvious feature of magical thought. Two and a half centuries earlier Francis Bacon called the association of ideas "sympathies and antipathies"—an idle and slothful form of conjecture. *The New Organon and Related Writings* (New York: Liberal Arts Press, 1960), p. 83.

4. James G. Frazer, *The Golden Bough: A Study in Magic and Religion* (New York: Macmillan, 1935). Frazer has generated a vast industry of secondary literature, in recent decades mostly unfavorable. For two fairly recent appraisals of his work, see Jonathan Z. Smith, *Map Is Not Territory: Studies in the History of Religions* (Leiden: E. J. Brill, 1978), and Mary Douglas, *Purity*

and Danger: An Analysis of the Concepts of Pollution and Taboo (London: Routledge & Kegan Paul, 1979). See especially Douglas's concluding excoriation of Frazer at p. 28.

5. "Mohinī" means enchantress, a charm of seductive feminine powers. Prasad did not know the botanical name of the plant from which the seeds came.

6. *Leaves from the Jungle: Life in a Gond Village* (Delhi: Oxford University Press, 1992), pp. 135–36.

7. Kauśika Sūtra 36.19–21; *Atharvaveda* 3.18.

8. *Kāmasūtra* 7.1.10–11.

9. Ibid. 7.1.24.

10. Frazer, *The Golden Bough*, 1.77.

11. This is a common practice in Nagwa, and in other hamlets around Banaras, for avoiding the danger of magical manipulation of the hair.

⩘ FOUR ⩙

From Magic to Social Function

⩘ ⩘ ⩘

Case 4.1

The swamiji and the cow

A man once had a cow on whose milk he relied for his food and livelihood. One day the cow stopped giving milk, and the man knew that a witch had cast a spell on it, either by means of some mantra or with his evil eye. So he went to a Tantric guru and asked for help. The guru said, "I can help you with your problem, but you must answer this: What do you want more, to catch and punish the witch or to make the cow give milk again?"

The cow owner considered his words carefully because he knew he had to be truthful.

"Both, Swamiji. I want the milk, and I also want to punish the witch."

The guru was unhappy with this answer and insisted that only one choice was possible, so the man chose milk.

The Tantric guru gave him some herbs over which he had cast a mantra and told him to burn these under the cow's nose. Then he added, "The cow will give you milk, but the first milking will produce yellowish and poisonous milk, so throw it in the river." The man did as he was told and got his milk back.

One day when the man was sitting with Swamiji, a neighbor came in and complained about severe pains. Swamiji examined him thoroughly and finally said:

"You have been coveting the property of your neighbors instead of being satisfied with what you have. Go home and avoid even looking at your neighbor's things, and your trouble will disappear." The man nodded gratefully and left.

"You see?" said Swamiji to the milkman. "There was no need for revenge. His own actions took revenge on him." [1]

My informant marveled at the discrete but perfect power of the swami to demonstrate justice and produce a healing with one simple gesture. The sociologist in me sees the swami as a clever and resourceful opportunist who awaits the right moment to announce his magic. That moment is entirely conditioned by social expectations; the magician must only wait for all the pieces to fall into place; remove these social and psychological conditions and magic itself collapses.

The beginning of professional sociology signaled the end of theories that explained magic as a mental phenomenon of the individual. The crude and often provincial evolutionism to which Frazer subscribed gave way to a genuine science of society. Sociology showed no tolerance for armchair speculations on such things as "bad science" or "errors of reasoning." Because magic clearly served social functions, a new generation of professional sociologists set out to define and explain it in some collective manner.

EMILE DURKHEIM AND COMMUNAL EXPERIENCE

Emile Durkheim was a French rabbinic student who grew up and matured during the Third Republic. Like Frazer and Tylor, he was influenced by Herbert Spencer, but unlike them he rejected the intellectualist idea that magic was an illusion or bad science. By the time he wrote his great work, *The Elementary Forms of the Religious Life,* and as a professor of sociology in Paris, Durkheim was taking Frazer's typology of magic for granted, while filtering out the armchair speculations of the older scholar.[2] Durkheim was the first to replace Frazer's mentalistic interpretation of magic with a comprehensive and coherent sociological theory. In Durkheim's work individual errors of thinking were replaced with social modes of association, a collective force worthy of serious academic study.

〽 〽 〽

Case 4.2

The *Unchalka* Grub

The actors of this rite decorate themselves with designs representing the unchalka bush upon which this grub lives at the beginning of its existence. Then they cover a buckler with concentric circles of down, representing another kind of bush upon which the insect lays its eggs when it has become adult. When all these preparations are finished, they all sit down on the ground in a semicircle facing the principal officient. He alternately bends his body double by leaning towards the ground and then rises on his knees; at the same time, he shakes his stretched-out arms, which is a way of representing the wings of the insect. From time to time, he leans over the buckler, imitating the way in which the butterfly flies over the trees where it lays its eggs.[3]

This ritual could easily have been used by Frazer to illustrate magical thinking. By imitating the insect, he might have said, the actors think they control its behavior for their own gain. Here is a primitive magical precursor to religion, a low rung on the ladder of human evolution.

Durkheim turned this over on its head. Sympathetic magical behavior is impossible to deny here, but it hardly dominates the rite. The ritual is essentially a communal event, and it owes its sacred force to that basic fact. Its effectiveness—its sanctity—springs from the collective consciousness it exhibits, not from its imitative (sympathetic) logic. But Durkheim insisted that even the magical forms of reasoning could never have originated without the collective, essentially religious, quality of a communal imagination. The principles on which such reasoning is based, analogy and contiguity, would never have occurred to the mind of the individual because "nothing in experience could either suggest or verify them."[4] The "external experience" of any individual, the sensory perception of the world, can reveal only proximity in space and time. Individual experience, Durkheim claimed, can never disclose the causal relation among objects in the world. Causality, conceived in its primitive form as force, is the product of an "internal" experience, an experience shaped by the communal characteristics of collective processes. It is the moral and ideological primacy of communities—the "collective consciousness"—that shapes the form of inferences on which laws governing natural phenomena are based. In other words, the logic of the world and the logic of social relations correspond by means of "homologies."

In the case just described, Frazer would be wrong to claim that the imitative nature of the performance is meant to produce an abundance of grub. The ritual is a communal-solidarity practice. Its participants believe themselves to be the animals they imitate, their totem, which they mark upon their bodies. By acting together as members of a "species," they show themselves to be members of an organic community. The goal of the rite can only be success in reproduction, which will guarantee the longevity of the totemic group. The specific gestures and the bodily articulations express the wish for this goal; they imitate the behavior of animals for totemic reasons, not for the purpose of controlling the course of natural events.

Durkheim managed to eviscerate Frazerian theories by extending the necessity of natural phenomena to primitive thought. He de-"rationalized" the process that is implicit in magical events in favor of collective forces. The effectiveness of a rite, according to Durkheim, is measured by a strict social determinism, while "nature"—the insect—is a meaningful category only when it has become humanized by means of social symbols. The result, incidentally, is that magic, as we commonly understand the term, is marginalized out of the mainstream of religious beliefs and practices.

BRONISLAW MALINOWSKI AND THE CONTEXTUAL VIEW

Bronislaw Malinowski was a Polish-born citizen of Austria who immigrated to England and became fascinated by Frazer's *The Golden Bough*.[5] Malinowski was in Australia when World War I broke out, and, as technically an enemy alien, he had to be interned. Thanks to the help of influential friends, the internment confined him to several New Guinean islands, including the Trobriands. There Malinowski invented modern anthropological fieldwork and built a reputation on which to feed his ego for decades.

Malinowski was not the first to describe magical rites in great detail. Others had visited remote tribal societies and brought back a wealth of descriptive material. But Malinowski was the first to place his enormously detailed accounts in a complete context: the physical ecology of the Trobriands, the economic activities and the technological accomplishments of its inhabitants, their social, intellectual and religious life. Viewing such a broad range of topics, Malinowski was able to demonstrate that magic derives its meaning from the way it functions within the social and economic systems of the Trobriands. The following case was described in typical detail in his magnum opus, *Coral Gardens and Their Magic.*[6] Only brief excerpts can be quoted here.

🐚 🐚 🐚

Case 4.3

Inaugural Garden Magic

All the men bring their axes to the magician, who lays them on a mat spread upon the bunk along the side opposite to the fireplace. To each axe a piece of dried banana leaf, about six inches by four, has been tied. The main part of the leaf lies flat against the blade while the other part is left free. After the spell has been uttered the free flap will be folded over; but first some of the magical mixture must be inserted between the leaf and the cutting edge of the axe, and mixture and blade be left open, so that the voice of the *towosi* and the magical virtue which it carries can penetrate into the blade and the herbs. After the axes have been placed on the mat, the magician takes some cooked fish and puts it down on one of the three hearthstones in his house with the following words:—

FORMULA I

"Here, this is our oblation, O old men, our ancestral spirits! I am laying down for you, behold!

"Here, this is our joint oblation, O Yowana, my father, behold!

"To-morrow, we shall enter our gardens, take heed! . . ."

This act as well as the exhortation recited during it is described as "the shredding of the spirit's oblation." The word "to shred" refers here to the tearing off of small bits of fish and placing them on the hearthstone. The words of this incantation are spoken in a slow, solemn, persuasive voice. It is not regarded as a *yopa* (spell), and it is not uttered in the usual singsong of the magical formulae. . . .

The blessing of the spirits being thus invoked, and their presence in a vague, mystical way established, the magician now proceeds to the charming of the axes. He places a second mat over the axes, only leaving a sufficient aperture for the breath carrying his words to penetrate between the two mats, and then he utters in the clear, melodious singsong characteristic of magical incantations, what is perhaps the most important formula in the whole system of Omarkana garden magic, the *vatuvi* spell:

FORMULA 2

I. "Show the way, show the way,
Show the way, show the way,
Show the way groundward, into the deep ground,
Show the way, show the way,
Show the way, show the way,
Show the way firmly, show the way to the firm moorings.

*   *   *

"The belly of my garden leavens,
The belly of my garden rises,
The belly of my garden reclines,
The belly of my garden grows to the size of a bush-hen's nest,
The belly of my garden grows like an ant-hill;
The belly of my garden rises and is bowed down,
The belly of my garden rises like the iron-weed palm,
The belly of my garden lies sown,
The belly of my garden swells,
The belly of my garden swells as with a child.
I sweep away.

II. "I sweep, I sweep, I sweep away. The grubs I sweep, I sweep away; the blight I sweep, I sweep away; insects I sweep, I sweep away; the beetle with the sharp tooth, I sweep, I sweep away. . . .
"I blow, I blow, I blow away. The grubs I blow, I blow away; the blight I blow, I blow away. . . .
"I drive thee, I drive thee off, begone! The grubs I drive, I drive off, begone! The blight I drive. . . .

Thus in the hearing of all the ancestral spirits, the magician recites the long sacred spell over the axes.[7]

Malinowski followed this vivid and detailed description by reminding his readers that he had not reproduced all the repetitions of the spell, especially those used by the magician to deal with other pests. Consequently, the full effect of its interminably long duration and its mesmerizing repetitions has been watered down. The drawn-out, elaborate chant accompanies a relatively simple physical procedure, namely, folding a banana leaf over the axe.

For Malinowski, any attempt to analyze a magic ritual without considering what takes place before and after the rite is useless. Magic is always performed along with some other activity, which is technical in nature and reflects the Trobrianders' efforts to control their world. The rite just described is one of many that punctuate the various phases of agricultural work. Other rites accompany seeding, harvesting, storing and distribution of crops. Different types of magic rituals are performed with the distinct phases of boat building and launching, as well as with other elements in the economic and technological areas of Trobriand life. But, one may ask if the Trobrianders have mastered the science of gardening, and can successfully produce enough food, why do they need magical rites? According to Malinowski, the Trobriander occasionally reaches a "gap" in the success of his activity. A hunter fails to catch his prey; a gardener fails because of drought. The mastery over practical activities does not eliminate the anxiety that stalks actions in which chance plays a role. More precisely, these are activities that may be influenced by other forces over which technical skill can never extend: "Thus magic supplies primitive man with a number of ready-made ritual acts and beliefs, with a definite mental and practical technique which serves to bridge over the dangerous gaps in every important pursuit or critical situation." [8] The magical act does not bridge these gaps in practical terms, but it pacifies the anxiety that chance produces.

Still, Malinowski suggested, magic is not just an emotional crutch (it is this position that has attracted for Malinowski the greatest amount of criticism). Magic is also an "organizing influence" in the communal life of the Torbriands. By punctuating the progress of economic activities at regular intervals, magic mobilizes the community to act in unison. It synchronizes the efforts of the participants along the schedule imposed by taboo days, by focusing on certain garden plots at given times and by coordinating labor.[9]

But how does the magic rite accomplish this goal? How do the specific details of each particular rite serve its emotional and social ends? In order to understand the precise relations between each aspect of the rite and each aspect of its social and psychological function, we need to look at the social status and the ritual condition of the magician and his assistants, the temporal and spatial taboos associated with the rite, the origin and preparation of the materials used, and other factors. For lack of space, I will focus on three ritual elements that Malinowski regarded as essential to magic—sympathetic objects, emotionally charged imitative behavior, and the spell. By means of these elements the magic rite exerts its greatest force.

Malinowski argued that certain objects are selected for use in the magic because they resemble the things on which they are expected to have an effect: "Generally these [foods] are sympathetically connected with the substances which he uses in his ritual or with the aims of his magic." [10] "Sympathy" brings to mind Frazers' two principles of magical thinking, similarity and contact. Because of similarity, certain substances, foods, objects, or persons are avoided during part of the rite and at other times are exceptionally powerful and necessary. Malinowski did not say why a banana leaf is used to secure the spell around the blade of the axe, nor did he indicate which herbs are placed between the leaf and the blade. If his general observations apply, we would expect these to be related, in a sympathetic fashion, to the crop that will be planted.

The principle of sympathy is seen in what Malinowski called the "mimetic" manner of manipulating the objects used in the rite. He cited another example from sorcery, in which a bone, a stick, or the spine of an animal is thrown in a symbolic way in the direction of any enemy one wished to injure. The emotional setting, the gestures, and expressions of the practitioner are of utmost importance here: "For the sorcerer has, as an essential part of the ritual performance, not merely to point the bone dart at his victim, but with an intense expression of fury and hatred he has to thrust it in the air, turn and twist it as if to bore it in the wound, then pull it back with a sudden jerk. Thus not only is the act of violence or stabbing reproduced, but the passion of violence has to be enacted." [11] Like Freud, Malinowski emphasized that the emotional expression of the ritual act connects it to its end because the rite itself does not fully enact the death of the victim. Magic rituals play out the emotions of revenge and produce a cathartic experience, but no more; their effectiveness remains subjective. Unfortunately, Malinowski gave too little information in the case of gardening magic to judge its mimetic emotional effect.

The central element in the case I have described, and according to Malinowski the most important feature of Trobriand magic, is the spell.[12] The spell holds, then unleashes, the recoiled power of the magical rite. It does this in three distinct ways. First is the phonetic character of spoken and chanted words, their sound and rhythms. The spell imitates natural sounds, such as those of the wind and thunder or the sounds of various animals and even of other humans. By reproducing the voices of nature, the rite "symbolizes" natural phenomena and influences them through similarity. Frazer's "ghost," as Stanley Tambiah put it, is still roaming these grounds, but Malinowski's emphasis on the word and its power of symbolization would eventually lead to more sophisticated analyses of magical sound (see Chapter 15).

The second factor in the ritual power of the spell is the explicit statement of the desired ends: "The belly of my garden leavens. . . ." By stating the desired state of affairs with a specific emotional intonation, the participants add an emotional depth to the rite as a whole. While the phonetic-imitative quality of the words is magically effective in producing the desired ends, the semantic force (the meaning) of the words is said to be strictly emotional. The words of the spell do not force natural events to obey; words evoke certain feelings that color the magical ritual as a whole. This observation indicates that Malinowski had indeed taken a huge qualitative leap form the literalist magical interpretation of Frazer. He was far more subtle in his explanation of the psychological functions of magic in specific contexts.

Finally, the spell acts by mythological allusions to spirits, ancestors, or other cultural figures. Malinowski surprisingly regarded this third feature of the spell as the most important. I say "surprisingly" because Malinowski's own collection of spells does not exhibit this feature in every case. Allusions are usually limited to implicit and obscure references. Still, the mythical allusions of the spell link it directly with the belief in the authority of magic and explain the need for performing it in a precisely regulated way. In other words, magic gains its cultural prestige by means of these references as well as its ideological context, its meaning. For this reason, spells are important to a researcher of Malinowski's type of anthropology, as opposed to that of Radcliffe-Brown or Durkheim: The symbolic language of the spell contains the manifesto of the cultural-anthropological approach to magic.

Malinowski's contributions were seminal. He redirected attention away from the relation between the agricultural rite and fertility and toward the proper framework in which to evaluate the effectiveness of magic, its social and cultural spheres of influence. The very notion of efficacy was redefined in a way that made symbolic modes of analysis more appropriate for judging the goal and effects of the rite. In Malinowski's pioneering work the boundary between magic and religion began to dissolve, and Frazer's shadow started to dissipate.

NOTES

1. This episode was narrated by O. P. Sharma, who added that he knew all the parties involved. Curing domestic and farm animals by smoke inhalation is a commonn practice throughout India, though the plants used vary from region to region.

2. Emile Durkheim, *The Elementary Forms of the Religious Life.* (New York: Free Press, 1965); on the life of Durkheim see Steven Lukes, *Emile Durkheim, His Life and Work: A Historical and Critical Study* (New York: Harper & Row, 1972).

3. Durkheim, *The Elementary Forms,* p. 394.

4. Ibid., p. 405.

5. On Malinowksi's life and work see Raymond Firth, ed., *Man and Culture: An Evaluation of Malinowski* (London: Routledge & Kegan Paul, 1957), and Bronislaw Malinowski, *A Diary in the Strict Sense of the Term* (Palo Alto, Calif.: Stanford University Press, 1989).

6. *Coral Gardens and Their Magic* (New York: Dover, 1978). Malinowski also dealt with magic in *Magic, Science, and Religion and Other Essays* (New York: Doubleday Anchor Books, 1954) and in *Sex, Culture, and Myth* (New York: Harcourt, Brace & World, 1962). Only compelling reasons of brevity justify my omission of the important works on magic by Evans-Pritchard, Levy-Bruhl, Levi-Strauss, Edmond Leach, and a few others. Some of this ground is covered in Stanley Jeyaraja Tambiah's *Magic, Science, Religion, and the Scope of Rationality* (Cambridge: Cambridge University Press, 1991).

7. Malinowski, *Coral Gardens,* pp. 95–99.

8. Malinowski, *Magic, Science,* p. 90.

9. Malinowski, *Coral Gardens,* p. 67.

10. Ibid., p. 66.

11. Malinowski, *Magic, Science,* p. 71.

12. Ibid., p. 73.

FIVE

Psychological and Symbolical Theories of Magic

The life of the Indian woman—like a sari she wraps around her body in public—extends in tightly woven threads and shows no seams. The sari curls around her body, over and over, limiting her stride to measured steps, and hides the individual contours of her person. It also covers her hair, which is not really hers because it too is pulled back into a tight braid, until no single strand can rebel. To the untrained eye she seems to glide effortlessly from childhood to old age over a tapestry of roles and locations in which no joints are visible; every passage is closely choreographed by ritual and guarded by custom.

But now and then a crack appears in this picture, at first as fine as that single strand of hair. If left unattended, which is often the case, the crack breaks open with demonic energy and shatters the facade of a woman's roles and expectations. Disturbed and even frightened as the family members may then become, they are seldom taken altogether by surprise. They simply declare her possessed by a ghost (*bhūt-pret*). By doing so they define the problem clearly and draw the battle lines: They can then take the possessed woman to a place where she stands a chance against the ghost. One such place is the tomb of Baba Bahadur Sayyid, near the cantonment area of Banaras.

The four whitewashed walls enclose a small world that mirrors the underside of the ordered universe outside. One Thursday late in January, two hundred women, and no more than twenty men, were crammed into an area barely larger than a tennis court. All were sitting facing the tomb of the Muslim saint, from which direction one enters the compound. The effect on the visitor is immediate and emotionally shattering; I saw sad and dazed faces, tormented bodies, and a tumult of crazed gestures. Few of the women were entirely lost in the power of the ghost who took over their bodies and souls. But here and there a clearing was made for a woman whose ghost was "playing" with her body. She would rock and sway from side to side, eyes closed and loose hair flailing wildly. Another woman was just then standing on hands and knees, gyrating the front of her body one way, her bottom the other, as if around a mechanical axis that was about to break. Others around the compound were flinging their heads at the ground, hands clasped behind their backs. This gesture of reverence—prostration with hands locked together behind the back—is taken to macabre extremes, either in desperate beseechment or a demonic mockery of supplication. Only the care of an attending family member prevented serious harm. I saw an old woman pulling out clumps of white hair as if angry at the final relic of her womanhood. Another was rolling on the ground and wrestling with an invisible opponent who was making horrid gutteral sounds. Just behind her a woman was vomiting white foam and laughing loudly. Many were babbling while relatives were straining to decipher their words; others were crying or sobbing. All these women had loosened their braids and, with their disheveled hair and passionate, haunted eyes, possessed an erotic, fiery beauty that made the men there look away.

All this I saw almost instantly, or perhaps I should say "felt," because the experience was overwhelmingly auditory, and even tactile. The courtyard was pulsating with unleashed energy, with burning hot female energy. Everyone swayed to the rhythm of a drummer who was hidden from view but kept on drumming as if his instrument were the communal heart. I found a narrow space and sat there. It was next to a young man in Western clothes who was intently watching the woman rocking beside him. She swayed back and forth rhythmically and sobbed loudly. Every now and then she wailed out the baba's name and then prostrated herself until her head touched the ground. Her name, he said, was Lalmani Devi, she was his wife. They were both around twenty years old and had been married four years earlier. They had been living happily together, and Lalmani got along with her mother-in-law, in whose house she lived. But after four years of marriage they still had no children. Lalmani rarely mentioned her failure to conceive; she was still very young. But one day Lalmani went to visit her mother. It was during her period, when she was polluted and unapproachable to her husband. As she was walking on the road to her parent's village she was suddenly assaulted by a ghost who tore into her side—she felt a sharp blow—and changed her entire life. After she returned home she began experiencing headaches and became extremely moody. With no reason or warning she would suddenly break into tears or rage and start shaking uncontrollably. She refused to sleep with her husband and cursed his mother. Their small household shattered into chaos. After a few weeks of this, her husband brought her to Baba Sayyid's tomb and continued treatment there every Thursday until her condition gradually began to improve.

PSYCHOLOGY AND MAGIC

Illness is a cultural concept that travels poorly across boundaries.[1] Even simple notions such as moodiness and depression, not to mention complex ideas like schizophrenia or paranoia, are bonded to our Western views on the self and the person, on material causality, and on the nature of scientific explanation. My bare presentation of Lalmani's problem is so foreign to her worldview that she would probably not recognize herself in it. So how can one explain her possession? The mere translation of her symptoms into modern terms already creates serious distortions from her point of view. The next stage of theorizing about the meaning of possession removes us one huge step further. But maybe a careful straddling of the boundary between the two perspectives can minimize the problem. Sudhir Kakar, an eminent Indian psychoanalyst, describes these possessions and exorcisms as a traditional Indian idiom for psychological events.[2] The time when these women are most vulnerable to possession—difficult periods of transition such as puberty and marriage—is equally dangerous in the thinking of Western psychology. The fact that most of the patients are women, the place of possession, and the identity of the ghost—usually a fairly close and recently departed female relative—reveal to Kakar the "true" psychological nature of such events: "We saw above that the single largest category of patients, comprised mostly of young women who come to Balaji [a Hanuman temple and a Hindu equivalent of Baba Bahadur in Bharatpur] in search of healing, are suffering from a hysterical disorder; or, if one prefers to use the traditional idiom, they are possessed by the ghosts of forbidden sexual and aggressive wishes. Though the individual variations in all these cases are of great interest from the clinical angle, the wide prevalence of hysterical personality among Indian women and their use of this particular myth of passivity [possession] are also reflections of certain social conditions prevailing in the society. . . . I am struck by their accumulated and repressed rage, the helpless anger of young women at the lack of their social emancipation being the canvas on which the individual picture of hysterical illness is painted." [3]

Kakar's very Freudian way of looking at such possessions rings true despite the fact that clinical and social concepts such as hysteria and emancipation are entirely ethnocentric. His psychoanalytical tools may be very successful in predicting the occurrence of possession among certain women, and even in treating it. But he has not brought us very close to explaining magic in psychological terms. Even if Lalmani suffers from a hysterical disorder, repressed rage or sexuality or whatever, she came to Baba Bahadur for a magical cure, not for psychoanalysis. The event of possession perhaps is not magical—this can be debated—but the exorcism is entirely magical. The curing that takes place at Baba Bahadur does not owe its effectiveness simply to the cathartic power of confession. That is Kakar's reading of the healing process, and here he is off the mark.[4] Patients and their families claim steadfastly that the effective healing force is the water given to the patient to drink. The water had been injected with "power" by contact with the tomb of the saint Baba Bahadur Sayyid and is the essential part of the magical treatment. A possessed patient may even forgo the visit to the sacred place, and the water can be brought to her at home. But she will not heal without the water. In objective "scientific" terms there may be a strong mental component of self-healing here, but the event of magical healing is certainly not reduceable to the emotional release experienced in the courtyard.

To understand what happens in psychological terms, it is necessary to repeat that our notion of self and person is culturally defined and that magical events may rely on entirely different conceptions (for more on this point see Chapter 14). This is exactly how Carl Jung interpreted instances of possession. In one clinical case he worked with a profoundly learned and intelligent man who somehow had managed to convince himself that he was suffering from cancer. The reassurance of his physicians and the arguments of his analyst failed to quiet his morbid fear of the rapidly spreading disease created by his imagination. He could not accept the fact that he had authored his own imaginings, and this was the crux of his mental illness. Jung argued that normal adults do not feel responsible for an illness that invades their body, but they own up to whatever occurs in their conscious psyche. This attitude—

"prejudice," as Jung called it—is a very recent development in Western cultures: "Not so very long ago even highly civilized people believed that psychic agencies could influence our minds and feelings. There were ghosts, wizards, and witches, daemons and angels, and even gods, who could produce certain psychological changes in human beings." [5] A fleeting rage or thought of passion would then be attributed to an external agency that had "invaded" the mind or soul. This kind of thinking resulted not only, or even mainly, from a primitive philosophy but from a porous sense of self lacking rigid external boundaries.

But possession and exorcism lend themselves too easily to psychological interpretation. Most other cases of magic, as a matter of fact, are far more elusive and demand that the psychologist reduce the entire range of magical phenomena to some universal category. Sigmund Freud had a different kind of magical rite in mind when he reduced magic to infantile neurosis.

Freud on Magic

Freud did not think of magic in social terms. The forms of magical thinking or behavior evident in primitive societies, he felt, were caused by cognitive developmental factors, rather than by communal needs and symbols. Although Freud read many of the required texts on magic, his thinking represents a fallback to the ideas of James Frazer, fortified perhaps by astute clinical observations of neurotic patients. This may be due to the fact that his understanding of magic merely served the larger task of psychologizing culture and tracing its origin to a single event of patricide. A monumental ambition left him with no resources for thinking originally about magic. Even the cases on which he based his explanation of magic were taken straight out of Frazer.

🔊 🔊 🔊

Case 5.1

Fertility Rites

In some parts of Java, at the season when the bloom will soon be on the rice, the husbandman and his wife visit their fields by night and there engage in sexual intercourse to encourage the fertility of the rice by their example. There is a dread, however, that prohibited, incestuous sexual relations may cause a failure of the crops and make the earth sterile.[6]

Freud quoted a few other examples out of *The Golden Bough* and concluded that they clearly demonstrated Frazer's principle of the similarity between the act and the desired effect. Additional cases illustrate the second principle of Frazer's typology, contiguity. Both, according to Freud, must be reduced to the one basic folly of all magical thinking, namely, the dominance of the association of ideas.[7] As both Tylor and Frazer had put it, magicians and their clients confuse ideal connections with real ones; they project their own mental states onto the objective world. Freud went one step beyond this mentalist analysis to a more rigorous psychological explanation.

Freud's theory of magic was developmental, rather than static. He argued that primitive people possessed an immense belief in the power of their own wishes. These wishes were accompanied by bodily action intended, at first, to "give a representation of the satisfying situation in such a way that it becomes possible to experience the satisfaction by what might be described as motor hallucinations."[8] Magic is the psychological behavior that anticipates the satisfied wish before the practical procedure for actually satisfying it is undertaken. Sex, for instance, is related to fertility by this emotional fulfillment of desire. The ritual orgy evokes a state of satiation that anticipates agricultural plenty. Gradually the emphasis of magic shifts from the motive for the act to its "measures," that is, to the ritualized form of the magical ritual. Carefully ritualized intercourse in the field—every sensual act choreographed—now becomes a practical method for attaining the desired goal. The final result of this psychological process is an overvaluation, or even omnipotence of thought, a symptom that may also be found in the obsessional acts of neurotics. And like the neurotic patient, primitive people can experience the projection of their own "thought" with a vivid ferocity.

Freud's deceptively pale theory comes alive when one looks at specific instances. Allan Strang, the young patient in the play "Equus," felt an overwhelming attachment to a beautiful black horse. The power of his bond certainly matched the intensity of the mystical identification reported between shamans and their animal helpers, yet the boy was seriously ill. He loved his mother and she loved him, incestuously; he worshiped Christ, whose torments on the cross became Allan's own physical self-abnegation and emotional repression; his father, though caring, was far too distant. The boy's fear, lust, and self-loathing combined in his young psyche to become a potent neurosis that he projected onto the stunningly sensual animal. The result was not only tragic but magically bizarre: The boy blinded the horse for witnessing, even causing, his impotence while making love to a girl. Freud would argue that the same clinical insights that an analyst would use to fathom Allan's tormented identification with the horse can be brought to any other magical context.[9] And once the neurotic heals, his personal magic dissolves. Similarly, as cultures move from infancy to intellectual maturity, magical practices lose their power and appeal. The phenomenon itself—magic—is empty.

Jung on Magic

🐎 🐎 🐎

Case 5.2

Pulling Through a Hole

When a baby has an enlarged navel, wedge open a white oak tree and pull him through. . . . On putting the child through a tree, first observe that it must be early in the spring before the grass begins to vegetate; secondly, that it must be split as near east and west as it can. Thirdly, it must be done as the sun is rising. Fourthly, the child must be stripped quite naked; Fifthly, it must be put through the tree feet foremost; sixthly, it must be turned around with the sun, and observe that it must be put through the tree three times. . . .[10]

Pulling through holes is a common cure for a variety of ailments around the world, even today. The practice described here was recorded in North Carolina in this century. What would Jung have made of it had he seen this ritual with its elaborate stipulations? Jung was in fact aware of healing rites that involved pulling patients through holes in the head of their sick-beds. His complex interpretation of these rites makes one surprising fact clear: As he tried to understand magical events, Jung refused to explain them away. He accepted their occult claims. Other theorists, certainly Freud, explained magic by reducing it to more basic phenomena: Magic *is* infantile neurosis, it *is* a ritual pacifying of fear, and so forth. Such theories enjoy an elegant simplicity, and they can never be disproved by the claims of magicians. Their answer to the occultist question Is there such a thing as magic? is resoundingly negative.

Jung, in contrast, took the claims of magicians at their face value. As a card-carrying phenomenologist by his own description, Jung relied on experiences as the facts of his research. If a neurotic patient makes outrageous claims, these cannot be disregarded in therapy. So it is with the facts of magic, and religion in general, which must be accepted as true by virtue of the fact that they are experienced. This attitude has made Jung the intellectual godfather of the New Age, watered down unfortunately by intermediaries like Joseph Campbell. But one must not underestimate the complexity and the subtlety of Jung's interpretation of magic and religion. He may lack the clarity and incisiveness of Freud or Frazer, but his mistakes are far less grand, too.

At its simplest level, the ritual of pulling a sick boy through a hole is magical because it tries to enslave to human will forces that are normally thought to be beyond its control. This is the first condition of the magical rite. And there is far more: Magical techniques are "psychic" in a special sense, and they are usually directed at the sacred, at something Jung called *numinosum*. Magic differs from religion precisely because it brings the psychic into relation with the sacred in a manipulative manner. But magic and religion go hand in hand: All religions contain magical devices in the form of invocations, incantations, sacrifice, meditation, and yoga, as well as self-inflicted tortures of various descriptions.[11]

In claiming that magic brings together the psyche and sacred realities (*numinosum*), Jung did not refer to supernatural revelation in a theological sense. The sacred, he argued, consists of the forms of the collective unconscious with its psychic archetypes. It reveals itself through the surfacing of psychic forces, either in a religious way (revelation) or magically. The theater for these profound events is the individual self and the imagination. Jung claimed that God is one such archetype of the collective unconscious, and so are Christ and Buddha. As archetypes that surfaced in human history, they have become symbols for the integration of the self with the sacred. Their path is open to all individuals who can assimilate the psychic power of symbols in their conscious lives. Magical traditions, such as alchemy, according to Jung, facilitate the process of integrating the symbols of the sacred within one's personal life.

Alchemy is a psychic technique that responds to a deep rift in the Christian view of the sacred. Throughout its history, Christianity consistently and dogmatically separated good and evil and made the relation of good and evil an absolute antinomy—an irreconcilable opposition. Evil was expelled from the realm of individual nature into the dark realms of witchcraft, demonology, and Satanism. As no one could live up to the unnatural standards of purity, Christians became either torn or repressed and sought consolation in the persecution of demonized persons and peoples. Alchemy, in contrast, developed techniques that were expressed in mythical terms for reintegrating the self by a reconciliation of opposites. The magical healing of the boy by pulling through a hole is one such case of alchemy. It is a symbolic reintegration of a self, a rebirth. The careful correspondences with the sun and with vegetation makes this clear. The rite magically produces its effects by controlling the psychic symbols by means of which the boy is reborn.

But magic is not just a symbolic event, it works. According to Jung, what makes a ritual such as incantation or a tradition such as alchemy effective is the relationship it creates between psychic facts and corresponding external events. Jung called this acausal relationship *synchronicity* and defined it as "a coincidence in time of two or more causally unrelated events which have the same or a similar meaning." [12] Examples are surprisingly commonplace, and Jung's has the ring of familiarity: On a given day his tram ticket bears the same number as his theater ticket, which he buys shortly after buying the train ticket. That same evening he receives a phone call during which the number comes up again as someone's phone number. Many people today would advise him to rush out and buy a lottery ticket.

Jung did not claim that these events were related in some unknown causal way. Causality implies a continuity in space and time that is always discoverable in principle. Synchronistic events, in contrast, are not just events whose causes are as yet undiscovered. By their very nature these events are linked only in their meaning, in the way a psychic archetype makes itself manifest in relation to certain corresponding external events. Space, time, motion, and energy—the elements of causal relations—have no bearing on synchronistic events. This abstract idea can be demonstrated, according to Jung, in psychical research on extra sensory perception (ESP). Jung extensively cited the work of J. B. Rhine of Duke University and accepted his experimental results as accurate in order to make a very interesting point about psychic phenomena. In one experiement Rhine used a pack of twenty-five cards, each five of which showed the same symbol: a star, a square, a circle, wavy lines, and a cross. These have since become the standard tools of ESP research. The subject must guess the identity of each card as it is being turned over in an adjacent room. Most of the subjects failed to score higher than chance probability (five hits), but some scored far higher. One "gifted" man averaged ten hits and once guessed all twenty-five cards correctly. Gradually the distance between the subject and experimenter was increased, until they were across the ocean from each other. This had no impact on the results of the test. Even more striking, positive results could be obtained when the subject was asked to guess the identity of cards that would be turned over only at some future time. These subjects were able to anticipate events that had not yet taken place, beating a probability of 1:400,000. What can one make of such results, and especially their independence from space and time? In the case of ESP, Jung concluded that no "transmission" of information takes place at all! The ability demonstrated by gifted ESP subjects is not a perception that goes beyond the senses, because perception implies a transfer of energy or some such form of causality. Instead, there is a falling together, or a simultaneity of two events, one psychic and the other objective: "The subject's answer is not the result of his observing the physical cards, it is a product of pure imagination, of 'chance' ideas which reveal the structure of that which produces them, namely the unconscious." [13] This is the collective force that consists of archetypes and can become manifest in a variety of ways. The extraordinary results of Rhine's experiments, in Jung's view, demonstrate the rare success in allowing the "affects" of archetypes to surface simultaneously with controlled external events.

Synchronistic events have traditionally been considered magical because they defy commonsense perception in space and time. Rhine's gifted subject may have been a diviner in another age and put his talents to medical use. He might have employed certain ritual techniques to get himself in the "mood" or state of mind. The surfacing of archetypal "affects" and coincidence of external physical processes have taken place throughout human history and have been subject to willful control in magical contexts. Jung quoted Albertus Magnus who in turn was citing the great Muslim theologian Ibn Sina (Avicenna) when he wrote: "[A] certain power to alter things indwells in the human soul and subordinates the other things to her, particularly when she is swept into a great excess of love or hate or the like. . . . It can be proved by experiment that it [the excess] binds things [magically] and alters them in the way it wants." [14] Magic, in sum, consists of a willful control of unconscious archetypes—passion in Ibn Sina's quote—to manifest the sacred or to defy common causality and achieve extraordinary affects in which the psyche and the world correspond. The extraordinary claims of magicians are indeed extraordinary, and Jung was the only major thinker to think so.

Semiotics and Magic

Pscychoanalytical theories reduce magic to other levels of reality. Under the gaze of the analyst, magic simply vanishes into a neurosis. The sociological theories of Durkheim, A. R. Radcliffe-Brown, and the social anthropologists have the same effect, although without the couch. But in the tug and pull of competing intellectual traditons, symbolical interpretations of culture and magic have held their own. While the dominant sociological theories explained magic in causal terms taken from other levels of discourse, the newer symbolical "cultural anthropology" developed along monistic lines. It sought to interpret the meaning of magical expressions as a kind of language. This symbolical approach drew on a number of major conceptual innovations. In 1953, two years after his death, Ludwig Wittgenstein's *Philosophical Investigations* was published.[15] It elaborated the notion of a "language game" as a form of relative cultural communication and interaction. At about the same time Shannon and Weaver developed their information theory, which was followed closely by the development of cybernetics.[16] These ideas extended systems of information and communication to all levels and forms of human behavior. In analyzing behavior as communicative acts, questions of cause and effect—the stuff of the old positivism—gave way to notions of right and wrong or correct and incorrect. Analysis became criticism. During the 1950s and 1960s a large number of cultural theories were nurtured on these developments and on reinterpretations of Malinowski and Max Weber. Victor Turner, F. G. Bailey, Clifford Geertz, and others began to treat culture as a richly symbolical text; the "Whorf-Sapir hypothesis" claimed that language determines behavior, and hermeneutics as a self-consciously subjective discipline began to dominate the comparative study of cultures.[17] These developments, and others, were guided by the assumption that the student of cultural events does not have a privileged perspective from which to explain by reduction. Instead, scholars must interpret rituals, myths, games, and every other form of cultural performance by using the events' own communicative grammars and taking into full account their symbolical contexts. The most precise recent application of this approach to magic was carried out by Stanley Tambiah. Because his interpretation elaborated and refined the semiotic possibilities in the work of Evans-Pritchard and Malinowski, he also took his cases from them. The following two examples were recorded by Evans-Pritchard but are quoted here from Tambiah's version.

🐚 🐚 🐚

Case 5.3

The *Araka* Creeper

At a certain time of their growth the stems of the creeper *araka* lose their leaves. These are replaced by a double row of bands joined to the stalks, which little by little dry, split, and fall in small pieces just as the extremities of the hands and feet disappear in "la lepre mutilante." This creeper is highly thought of as furnishing treatment for this kind of leprosy.[18]

Frazer's old principle of similarity—"like attracts like"—would fail to explain what is happening here because the analogy between the disease and the plant is not just positive (similar) but negative as well. In the case of the plant, the falling of the leaves is part of a natural cycle, whereas in the case of the disease it is degenerative and terminal. The plant is used to express a more abstract relationship that can be stated in the following way: "May the leprosy disappear and health appear, just as the shedding process in the creeper stimulates growth."[19] But how can the mere use of the creeper convey such an abstract desire? In order to answer this we need to follow Tambiah's argument.

Tambiah understands magical acts, consisting of both verbal formulas and object manipulation, as "performative acts by which a property is imperatively transferred to a recipient object or person on an analogical basis."[20] The term *analogy* extends Frazer's homeopathic principles to more sophisticated and precise linguistic grounds. It is used to answer this question: Considering that not all objects in a magical rite resemble the condition one wishes to avoid or obtain, why are certain objects used out of the entire range of available materials? It is necessary to shift attention away from the "inherent" powers of the objects to their symbolic qualities. Convention assigns values to such symbols, and practitioners transfer them to the goal of the rite by means of positive and negative analogy. An elaborate symbolic language emerges for ritual occasions based on complex systems of analogy. Incidentally, the transfer of analogous qualities in magical rites differs from scientific analogies in that the practitioner does not *predict* the features of the analogous phenomenon on the basis of the manipulated objects. Instead, he transfers their qualities in an act of persuasion, rationalization, or evocation.

Analogies do not apply directly between the ritual objects and the goal of the ritual. They apply separately to the internal relation among the objects and to the goal of the rite. In Tambiah's scheme this is called a "vertical" relation: "The rite consists in persuasively transferring the properties of the desired and desirable vertical relation to the other which is in an undesirable condition."[21] The ability to express abstract purposes by means of concrete objects results from emphasizing the relationship *within* properties belonging to manipulated objects (vertical relations), rather than the direct similarity between this object and its corresponding goal. Another case illustrates this process further.

🔊 🔊 🔊

Case 5.4

Fowl Excrement

Ringworm in children is called *imandruruakondo* (*ima* = sickness, *nduruakond* = fowl house). It is so called because the scabby patches of the disease resemble fowl's excrement: hence they appear to consider the disease due to the afflicted child having eaten food grown on a dung heap in the vicinity of a fowl house: hence also they consider the remedy to consist in fowl's excrement dried and reduced to ashes and mixed into a paste with a little palm-oil and applied to the ringworm.[22]

Again, Tambiah contradicts Frazer's brand of homeopathy, because the resemblance between excrement and scabs on the skin is a false one. Instead, Tambiah argues, "the relation of fowl to excrement is one of elimination of (unwanted) waste product, while that of scabby skin on child is one of (unwanted) adherence to body." The analogy is not between objects or states but between relations, in this case elimination. The point of the ritual emerges from the relations between each pair of objects, rather than the objects themselves. But just as important, the two pairs (fowl/excrement; skin/scabs) are not brought into the analogy because one has the direct power to affect the other. The nature of the vertical (internal) relations indicates that the analogy is persuasive: It is meant to express the desire for a particular state.

And this precisely makes magical acts unique. They are "illocutionary"—a term coined by John Austin—or performative. The spells spoken in the rite, as well as the manipulation of objects, do more than convey information (locutionary acts) or produce results among the participants (perlocutionary acts). Words and rituals, Tambiah emphasizes, are performative actions that express a command, wish, promise, apology, or other optative state. They can be judged not by standards of true/false but rather by those of valid/invalid, correct/defective, or felicitious/infelicitous. The magical rite, then, is unique because of its "performative or "illocutionary"quality, which is based on analogical reasoning.

With this theory Tambiah has now left behind all traces of the Frazerian literalism that plagued many earlier theorists. But Tambiah also acknowledges the Frazerian *form* of magical thinking, namely, its reliance on similarity. His theory allows Tambiah to criticize Evans-Pritchard for judging magical rites by the standards of Western causality. Evans-Pritchard asked how the practitioners of magic deal with its failure to produce results. On Tambiah's theory the question becomes irrelevant, because the magical performance is not subject to this type of practical consideration. But Tambiah's expressive theory raises a different question: The Azande have, in fact, devised elaborate and explicit systems of secondary rationalization to accompany their magic. Why would they develop these intellectualizations if they did not consider magic an activity that should be evaluated on the basis of its effectiveness? Perhaps the need to explain the failure of magic arises simply out of recognition that one is expressing a wish. Even failed expectations sometimes demand an excuse.

Notes

1. For the difference between illness and disease, the latter a biological concept, see Ann McElroy and Patricia K. Townsend, *Medical Anthropology in Ecological Perspective* (Boulder: Westview Press, 1989), p. 49.

2. Sudhir Kakar, *Shamans, Mystics and Doctors: A Psychological Inquiry ino India and Its Healing Traditions* (New York: Knopf, 1982); Kakar's work contrasts sharply with efforts to define psychological events in traditional Indian terms. See, for instance, Deborah Bhattacharya, *Pagalami: Ethnopsychiatric Knowledge in Bengal* (Syracuse: Maxwell School of Citizenship, 1986).

3. Kakar, *Shamans*, p. 76.

4. Diane Marjorie Coccari also commented on the healing at Baba Bahadur Sayyid in her dissertation, "The Bir Babas of Banaras: An Analysis of a Folk Deity in North India." (Ph.D. dissertation, University of Wisconsin, 1986). But she was convinced that most of these women were staging their histrionics as a cultural performance. All meaningful action is performative, of course, but I think Coccari failed to convey the sense of distress that drove the visitors to such convulsions.

5. Carl G. Jung, *Basic Writings* (Pinceton, N.J.: Princeton University Press, 1990), p. 495.

6. Sigmund Freud, *Totem and Taboo* (New York: Norton, 1989), p. 100.

7. Ibid., pp. 103–4.

8. Ibid., p. 105.

9. Another horse that is magically animated by the obsession of a neurotic boy is D. H. Lawrence's "The Rocking-Horse Winner."

10. Wayland Hand, *Magical Medicine* (Berkeley: University of California Press, 1980), p. 2; Hand's is by far the most detailed comparative study of magical healing based on folkloristic sources in the West.

11. Jung, *Basic Writings*, p. 489.

12. *The Structure and Dynamics of the Psyche* (Princeton, N.J.: Princeton University Press, 1975), p. 441.

13. Ibid., p. 436.

14. Ibid., p. 448.

15. G. E. M. Anscombe, Ruch Rhees, and G. H. von Wright, eds., *Philosophical Investigations* (Oxford: Oxford University Press, 1953).

16. C. E. Shannon and W. Weaver, *The Mathematical Theory of Communication* (Urbana: University of Illinois Press, 1949); N. Wiener, *Cybernatics* (Cambridge, Mass.: Technology Press, 1948).

17. There is no single exhaustive summary of twentieth-century theories of magic. In addition to Tambiah's brief book, mentioned earlier, there is also Robin Horton, "Tradition and Modernity Revisited," in *Rationality and Relativism*, ed. M. Hollis and S. Lukes (Cambridge, Mass.: MIT Press, 1982).

18. Stanley Tambiah, "The Form and Meaning of Magical Acts: A Point of View," in *Reader in Comparative Religion: An Anthroplogical Approach,*

eds. William A. Lessa and Evon Z. Vogt (New York: Harper & Row, 1979), p. 357.

   19. Ibid.
   20. Ibid., p. 353.
   21. Ibid., p. 356.
   22. Ibid., p. 358.

SIX

New Science, Old Magic

Sociological and symbolical interpreters of magic singlemindedly ignore the occult questions that magic raises. The social sciences simply have no methods for inspecting extraordinary causal claims, which they regard as superfluous to the real purpose of magic. Any effort to verify or falsify occult claims would simply sidetrack the researcher from the proper manner of understanding magical phenomena. Hard scientists, who like to tinker with ideas, are more likely to take the boasts of magicians literally, if only for the sake of exposing their fakery. No academic scholars take occult boasts more seriously than the editors of *Skeptical Inquirer*, who have yet to find a "genuine" case of magic.

Recently, however, a new trend in medical and physical research has begun to regard magic both literally and sympathetically, as an area worthy of serious study. This chapter looks at a few representative ideas and asks whether such new-science projects explain magic, or explain it away.

ADAPTATION

Adapting to a city like Banaras is not as difficult today as it was a short generation ago. Electricity, running water, motorized transportation are like those in any other city. Still, a southern Oregonian used to his surrounding forest of ponderosa pines and madrones will invariably experience some form of stress as he makes the adjustment. For me, sleep was the hardest of all, as the following diary item shows.

> Last night I did not sleep too well. Every time I fell asleep the *chowki-dar* arrived, preceded by the thumping beat of his stick on the pave-

ment, anouncing his arrival with a shrill whistle blow. By 3 A.M. I had calculated that his patrol circuit took thirty-five minutes, give or take a few for relieving his bladder or for some other urgent task. The *chowkidar*—or night watchman—is a universal fixture of middle-class Indian neighborhoods. A solitary figure of advancing years, he is armed with a long stick and a whistle and wraps himself in a blanket that obliterates his peripheral vision. Ours was a puzzle: He showed up only every four or five days, and after a night or two he disappeared again. I assumed, or hoped, that he was spread very thin over several neighborhoods. But his irregular visits prevented me from adapting to his noise, though my landlord was not similarly affected. "We sleep very well with the *chowkidar* or without him," he told me in the morning when I complained.

"But why do you even need him? Your gate is locked. Your house is locked. And it is always full of people."

"You see, we live on the edge of this poor neighborhood." He pointed down the street at the mud shacks that only a generous stretch of the language could embrace as a neighborhood. "There are many thieves living there, and some are quite cunning."

"Fine, I see the point. But why does he need to whistle?"

"It lets us know that he is out there doing his duty, and we can sleep more soundly."

"Oh."

He added: "And he beats the stick on the ground to let the thieves know he is coming around and they had better scamper off."

"Now wait," I objected. "It also tells them when to hide, and then when he leaves they can continue their work."

"That is no problem." My landlord waived his hand in a gesture of bemused dismissal. "In India everyone has the right to earn his living. The *chowkidar* lives by his whistle; the thief lives by his wits."

With that he burst out laughing. I just sighed and went back upstairs, hoping tonight would be the thief's turn.

Mind and Health

Noise that causes sleepless nights in Banaras is only one form of environmental hazard, of course. Others are the heat, dust, and smoke, crowding in the streets, the bacteria in food and water. None of these are life threatening, but they force the new arrival to adapt. Sounds must be tuned out; activity is curtailed at certain hours, the body fatigues quickly; water is boiled and drunk frequently to fight dehydration. Stress accompanies many of these conditions.

Stress has been defined as "a relationship between the person and the environment that is appraised by the person as taxing or exceeding his or her resources and endangering his or her well-being."[1] Throughout history humans have had to adjust to stress, and usually they have been successful. Evolution has endowed us with this capacity on the genotypic level: This is the reason Inuit tend to have short limbs and equator dwellers have dark skin.[2] Culture supplements the genetic changes selected for adaptation to a particular environment and allows quicker changes. The stress I experienced in my first few weeks in Banaras is the first phase of adaptation to a new environment. It was accompanied by immediate bodily reactions such as raised blood pressure, general fatigue, decreased respiration, and increased ventilation, as well as by mental symptoms such as irritability and depression. Like the football player who must play in Denver at high altitude over the weekend, I knew that these symptoms would disappear immediately on my departure. Between such immediate stress responses and the genotypic changes of entire populations, which are transmitted to offspring, are the somatic and permanent changes that individuals undergo to lessen the symptoms of stress. Loss of hearing may be one such change, or the adaptation of the intestinal system to new bacteria after a period of discomfort.

The relatively new field of medical anthropology, and more specifically medical ecology, studies the dynamics of human adaptation to the environment. This area of research is bidirectional or systemic and therefore avoids the distortions of anthropocentrism. Disease is analyzed as the disruption of an equilibrium in a system that contains both the human organism and its environment. Pathogens are not an arbitrary invasive force of nature but often result from human intervention in and disruption of ecological systems. Malaria, for instance, developed from the relatively recent use in Africa of the agricultural technique of slash-and-burn, which created environmental conditions conducive to the breeding of malarial mosquitoes. Enough time has now elapsed to select for a population with sickle cells as a genotypic adaptation in those areas. But if such a population rises above a certain point, mortality rates from sickle cell anemia also rise sharply.[3]

Often stress itself—a pervasive condition for modern humans—has a devastating effect on health. As people have had to adjust to more rapidly changing environments, and to the demands of contemporary economic pressures, they have also become more vulnerable to a variety of noninfectious diseases including coronary heart disease, cancer, gallstones, varicose veins, obesity, appendicitis, dental cavities, and asthma. Many of the cases being treated by Banaras magicians may be related to such causes. One young woman who came to see the Kajjal Baba healer, for instance, told him she had previously consulted several allopathic physicians for her breathing difficulties and her upper chest pains. The healer explored her medical and personal history before determining that she was fit for treatment. He found out, among other facts, that she had recently become betrothed to a man she did not even know. The baba treated her in his usual manner (see Chapter 7) for three consecutive weeks, at the end of which she claimed that she could breathe more easily.

To what extent is magic a folk-medical approach to healing such stress-induced illness? Will the expansion of medical thinking in the direction of mind/body interaction eventually explain away all cases of magical healing? How would such explanations proceed? The language of psychosomatic illness, negotiated cures, and placebo-effect healing has frequently been used to describe the effect of folk healing. The placebo effect, for instance, is is a well-documented dramatic phenomenon. Patrick D. Wall, a renowned pain specialist from University College of London, cites a remarkable example of the placebo effect:

> The second example I wish to quote is the work of Hashish et al. (1988) who examined the effect of ultrasound on the pain and trismus and swelling which follow wisdom tooth extraction. Wishing to determine the effective dose they found that the ultrasound machine was equally effective whether the machine was turned on or not, provided that the patient and therapist believed it was emitting sound. The interest and surprise of this paper is not that elaborate placebo was highly effective in reducing pain, but that it was also extremely active in reducing the swelling."[4]

The state of the art in mind/body medicine has progressed rapidly in recent years. One fairly recent medical theory may go a long way toward explaining some mental types of healing; it is known as psychoneuroimmunology (PNI) and, though still far from mainstream, it is gaining adherents in the medical community.

Psychoneuroimmunology is a mouthful name given to a growing research program in behavioral medicine that studies the effect of mental factors on health and disease. The term implies that the mind (*psycho*) can influence the immune system via the brain and the nervous system (*neuro*). Martin Seligman, for instance, has shown that mice exposed to unpredictable and uncontrollable stressors were far more susceptible to disease than those exposed to similar but controllable or predictable conditions.[5] PNI is predominantly an experimental discipline that began with a modest program.

While scientists tend to be cautious in extending such observations to humans, experiments and observations have increasingly pointed to a connection between stress and emotions and the immune system. Although the physiological basis of this connection has not been fully uncovered, it is clear that cells of the immune system respond to the signals of the biochemical messengers from the central nervous system. The stimulation or inhibition of neuropeptide production is clearly affected by emotional or psychological states. Stressors such as noise at night, examination pressures, and travel are real factors in the weakening of the immune system, resulting in vulnerability to a variety of pathogenic or nonpathogenic diseases. The recent death of a spouse reduces the body's production of lymphocytes and increases the likelihood of early death for the surviving spouse, especially men. Researchers have even found that, from an epidemiological point of view, the mental and emotional stability of a community plays a more determinative role in health than exposure to environmental toxicity, smoking, drinking, and other causal factors.

These are daring hypotheses because they claim that disease can, to some extent at least, be controlled or reversed by "mental" treatment such as relaxation, imagery, hypnosis, biofeedback, meditation, and even placebo. PNI has thus led to a proliferation of holistic medical writings on the more popular level. Best-selling works such as Joan Borysenko's *Minding the Body, Mending the Mind,* Deepak Chopra's *Quantum Healing,* Larry Dossey's *Meaning and Medicine,* and Herbert Benson's *The Mind/Body Effect* are leading patients to view health in the wider context of lifestyle choices.[6] And because many of the authors in this area have explored alternative—often mystical—worldviews, readers are becoming increasingly familiar with traditional Asian practices associated with meditation, breath control, and even shamanism and folk healing.

Where does magic fit in all of this? It would certainly be interesting to analyze some magical rites in terms that are derived from new medical models. Even infectious diseases among children and animals such as cattle, which are often related to immunological weakness, can be "treated" by buttressing the emotional context in which the patient lives. The ritual healing practiced by a traditional healer may be addressing the emotional aspects of illness in its cultural language. Of course, it would be naive, even quixotic, to assume that the magical rite *heals* pathogenic illness in the strict medical sense. Most people and animals heal naturally; evolution has seen to that. Still, the conditions for healing can be enhanced, and the rate of recovery can be speeded up, by using methods that operate on the mind as well as the body.

ﺍﻟﺸ ﺍﻟﺸ ﺍﻟﺸ

Case 6.1

Healing Warts in Ashland, Oregon

A respected Ashland physician prescribed the following remedy to a ten-year-old girl who had warts on her hands:

1. Find an object that you like such as a feather (the girl selected a potato).
2. For three consecutive mornings take that object outside and wet it with morning dew.
3. Place the object on the wart for three minutes.
4. The following weekend take the object to a lake or river and throw it in so that it will not be found. It can also be buried in dirt.

The girl followed these instructions, and the warts disappeared a few days later.[7]

Some may be tempted to explain healing magic as an implicit mental approach to illness. The principle that seems to guide healing is precisely the need to manipulate the mind of patients in order to facilitate self-healing. But there is a catch here: As we shall see in Chapter 7, magic applies to an ever widening clientele, including patients who do not know they are being treated, even natural "patients" such as fields, trees, and rain clouds. New Medicine may help explain the healing of some patients, but it does not allow us to extend that explanation to the full range of magical action. The magical healing of an infertile field and an asthmatic teenager are simply too dissimilar. We need, in short, a more basic and general principle than the one provided by the New Medicine.

CHANGING WORLDVIEWS—FROM ORGANIC TO MECHANISTIC AND BACK

Great scientific revolutions begin not with a new way of looking at the world but with a new understanding of old perceptions. Only after the new paradigm becomes established does commonsense begin to change as well.[8] But this takes time. Thus, despite the fact that the hard sciences, from physics to biology, have begun to shift toward a more organic paradigm of the world, our commonsensical perception is still steeped in the Newtonian and Cartesian world machine metaphor that has prevailed for three hundred years. Ironically, the mechanistic worldview had itself displaced a stunningly successful model that finally shattered itself against emerging technology and the absurdities of witchcraft persecution.

🐉 🐉 🐉

Case 6.2

A Case of Witchcraft

In October 1601, several townspeople from Hardness in Devonshire went before the judge Sir Thomas Ridgeway to give legal deposition. They accused Michael Trevisard—a fisherman—and his wife, Alice, of witchcraft. Each of the accusers recounted the circumstances of his own misfortune at the hands of the witches: "Alice Trevisard, it appears [writes George Lyman Kittredge in his account] had fallen out with John Baddaford, Joan's husband, and had "said unto him that he should go to Pursever Wood and gather up his wits." The precise meaning of this railing escapes me, but I fancy it was equivalent to calling John a scatter-brained fool. . . .

"Within three weeks after [Joan alleged], the said John Baddaford made a voyage to Rochelle, in the Hope of Dittsham, and returned home again out of his wits, and so continued by the space of two years, tearing and renting his clothes, in such a sort as four or five men were hardly able to bind him and keep him in order."

Joan's accusations against Alice Trevisard continued to range over several other misfortunes she suffered in her pathetic lot. Due to her enmity toward Alice, she could conceive of no other agency for her troubles. Unfortunately the record does not show what Sir Thomas Ridgeway did with the testimony, or what became of Alice Trevisard. The depositions were recorded in duplicate, in the form consistent with evidence used at judicial proceedings.[9]

While women and men of occult knowledge were paying the price of nonconformity to social and ideological norms, thinkers such as Francis Bacon—himself a prosecutor—objectified nature over and against its observer. Bacon's ideas were the first indication of the emerging modern, scientific worldview, though he did not yet imagine the world as a large machine but saw it as still organic and feminine; now, as Bacon put it, it would become the task of science to "hound nature in her wanderings" and to "torture nature's secrets from her." [10] The archaic and organic folk perception of the world was not yet discarded because no competing secular view existed to replace it. [11] But following the conceptual and empirical discoveries of Copernicus, Kepler, Galileo, Descartes, and, finally, Newton, the basic metaphor for nature became thoroughly mechanized. [12] Even organic processes such as reproduction and growth were conceived mechanically. The new world—Newton's and Descartes's—consisted of the following essential features: Space and time are absolute, objective, and separate contexts in which the world exists; material particles act on each other in space and time according to mechanical and deterministic laws created by God, a distant Primal Mover. [13]

To complement this worldview, Descartes divided all matter into two exclusive types—spatial matter (res extensa) and thinking matter (res cogitans), or body and mind. Because the distinction is absolute, the new rules of nature articulated by Newton could not possibly affect mind as they move matter. In other words, body and mind remain forever separate.

NEW SCIENCE

The certainty of scientific enlightenment, or rather its unambiguous conception of causality, began to dissolve in the nineteenth century. James Clerk Maxwell, who calculated the speed of light, was the first to show physicists the limitations of Newtonian mechanics by explaining the behavior of electromagnetic waves and fields. [14] At the same time, geologists and natural scientists began to refine a variety of evolutionary theories. Darwin's great achievement was not the idea of evolution per se but the empirical discovery of a causal mechanism—natural selection—by means of which species emerge or disappear. Gradually, this too would introduce a new notion of causality, one that is not mechanical at all but organic, that is, ecological and systemic.

The creeping changes in the scientific imagination became a full-fledged revolution with Albert Einstein's special and general theories of relativity.[15] Einstein showed that an observer's frame of reference—an apparently absolute spatial concept—can contract or shrink in relation to another frame of reference at extremely high speeds. The loss of absolute space and time as objective contexts in which all actions take place shook the certainty in an absolute universe, and particularly the place of humans in it. It also changed the notion of causality and the linear narrative according to which all of life had been conceptualized up to that point in the modern imagination.

While Einstein's theory of relativity, later to include gravity as well, began to shape the popular conceptions of space and time, a more profound revolution in the scientific view of matter was taking shape. A number of scientists, including Niels Bohr, Werner Heisenberg, Max Planck, Einstein himself, and others, were closing in on the most fundamental problem in nineteenth century physics: how to reconcile Newton's and Maxwell's views of matter. Particles and waves had acquired the force of logical oppositions during the nineteenth century, and neither could be disproved. Quantum mechanics, as it was interpreted by the "Copenhagen school," was the theory—amply backed by repeated experimentation—that nature at its most minute level is both particulate and wave-like.[16] The most that could ever be said about an individual particle is limited to its role in an ensemble—a field or a wave. Or, in other words, fields of particulate relations are the basic datum of physical study, and the language that described position, direction, and speed of individual elements in space no longer made any sense. This change did not come from a failure to make accurate observation—it was not epistemological. It was the most plausible conceptual way of reconciling the paradoxical results of precise empirical observations. This is the essential philosophical upshot of the so-called Heisenberg uncertainty principle, which asserts that any effort to measure the location of an atomic particle disrupts its energy, while any effort to quantify its energy distorts its position. These distortions arise from its dualistic wave/particle nature and make all predictions about microphenomena merely probabilistic.

The complex mathematical theories of relativity and quantum mechanics have been translated too quickly into sensational justification of mystical and occult ideas.[17] Pupularizers who are not physicists and physicists who are philosophically naive have looked to physics for a New Age cosmology that would undoubtedly make room for extraordinary claims.

෧ ෧ ෧

Case 6.3

Dematerialization and Bilocation

In 1905 several of Iceland's leading scientists decided to investigate the paranormal and chose Indridason as one of their subjects. At the time, Indridason was just a country bumpkin with no previous experience with things psychic, but he quickly proved to be a spectacularly talented medium. He could go into trance quickly and produce dramatic displays of PK [psychokinesis]. But most bizarre of all, sometimes while he was deep in trance, different parts of his body would completely dematerialize. As the astonished scientists watched, an arm or a hand would fade out of existence, only to rematerialize before he awakened.
    . . . According to Haraldsson, Sai Baba does bilocation one better. Numerous witnesses have reported watching him snap his fingers and vanish, instantly reappearing a hundred or more yards away.[18]

This Icelandic report was published by the Society for Psychical Research in London, which is hardly a disinterested party. The astonishment of the scientists can be put into perspective in light of a common observation made by conjurers that the more sophisticated and intellectual the audience, the easier it is to dupe. As long as magic continues to be defined as a method of producing miraculous phenomena, some New Age scientist will rush to lend his great reputation to occult claims, quickly undermining his own standing in the university. Most recently this has happened to the Nobel Prize winner Brian D. Josephson. Josephson was a Cambridge University quantum physicist who became interested in telekinesis, poletergeist, and similar phenomena. His colleagues have written him off as having taken leave of his senses. David Bohm has also become the ideological godfather of several New Age cosmologies. He has tried to reconcile relativity with quantum theory by dividing the world into the "implicate" and the "explicate" orders of being.[19] The implicate order is a new way of conceptualizing the stucture or organization of the universe: "This order is not to be understood solely in terms of a regular arrangement of *objects* (e.g., in rows) or as a regular arrangement of *events* (e.g., in a series). Rather, a *total order* is contained, in some *implicit* sense, in each region of space and time."[20] The word "implicit," Bohm explains, means to fold inward or enfold. So each region of space and time enfolds within it in some sense, the entire universe.

In contrast, according to Bohm, an explicate order is one in which the relations among parts of the universe—causality—is external. Implicate relations are different in principle and can be illustrated by means of a hologram or, more simply yet, by means of a drop of ink in a laboratory container. When a drop of ink is placed in a viscous fluid such as treacle, which is held in the space between two jars, one inside the other, and the outside jar is slowly rotated, the drop stretches out and becomes a line, then subtly blends into the fluid. If the jar is rotated in the opposite direction, the ink eventually returns to its original state as a drop. If a few more drops are added the pattern becomes more complex but follows the same principle. At any given point in the rotation of one or more molecules of ink, the drop's position can be explained in mechanical or quantum terms. An observer who saw only this limited point and had no knowledge of the entire context might explain the behavior of the molecule in local terms relating to the adjacent molecules that appear to push it or interact with it in some fashion. This is how causality is usually conceived. An implicate explanation recognizes that the molecule of ink at any given point in time is defined only in terms of the number of revolutions of the outer jar. It does not owe its positon to the molecule next to it—this is merely an explicate phenomenon. Instead, both molecules are seen at any given moment as participating in an overall process (the turning of the jar), and when this process is reversed each molecule returns, via its own path, to its original drop of ink.

Of course this is only a metaphor or a model for Bohm's conception of the universal implicate order. But it can explain or account for the apparent dematerialization of a body part and its rematerialization elsewhere. The physical laws that govern this phenomenon are as yet unknown, but they will explain the strange behavior of quanta—or passengers on Starship *Enterprise* beamed up by Scotty—without resorting to probability or the effect of the observer's point of view.

THE NEW ECOLOGY

Other New Science projects open up opportunities for speculation on the mind's relation to the world, a central component of the magical experience. During the nineteenth century, systemic and cybernetic theories, which until then had been used in mathematical and mecahnical contexts only, began to be applied to biological areas such as animal physiology. The human body, for instance, which looks as if it should be extremely unstable in its upright posture, exemplifies a controlled (cybernetic) system that uses feedback signals to adjust to changing conditions in order to retain balance. The inner ear, the eyes, and the sensors in the muscles, tendons, and joints (proprioceptors) allow humans to make rapid unconsious responses that stabilize the body.

By the middle of the twentieth century, systemic theories had given birth to ideas like the ecological community, and the concept of the ecosystem emerged. This trend began with Stephen A. Forbes and R. L. Lindeman, who, like Forbes, was a limnologist. The ecosystem then became "the basic unit of structure and function for ecological analysis."[21] Systemic ecological theories take nature as a holistic system with self-regulating mechanisms that control changes and adjust to changing inputs.[22] The role of humans is usually disruptive and even destructive to ecological communities, but in the long run humans also succumb to natural control mechanisms, as we saw in the case of the sickle cell trait and malaria. The cybernetic model of nature has recently reached its logical limits in the controversial work of James Lovelock and of Gregory Bateson.[23]

Lovelock's "Gaia Hypothesis" takes the entire biosphere, the surface of the planet as a whole, as one adaptive organism, which he named Gaia after the Greek goddess of the Earth. The atmosphere and everything below it, from oceans and mountains to the smallest microorganism, constitute one complex system that has adapted over four aeons to stellar, geophysical, and local conditions, resulting in diverse forms of life. The biosphere, in short, is the largest living organism on this planet. Lovelock's biochemical analysis, which is far from accepted by mainstream biologists, finds its match in Gregory Bateson's psychological and philosophical speculations.[24] Bateson added little to the scientific discussion of the ecosystem, but with a characteristic lack of timidity he extended his notion of mind to the ecology. Since a mind is a system, he wrote, "of pathways along which transforms of difference can be transmitted, mind obviously does not stop with the skin. It is also all the pathways outside the skin relevant to the phenomenon you want to account for."[25] "Difference" is an extremely difficult concept relating to the basic unit of information that travels within the circuits of mental systems. In a phenomenological way, "information" extends our notion of circuit so that when a man chops down a tree, the characteristics of the tree, the behavior of the axe, and the man constitute one entire mental system. It is fairly easy to show how such ideas might be manipulated to describe, and perhaps even to explain, the behavior of magicians in traditional communities. The Gaia cosmology matches many magical and mystical worldviews. The ecological psychology of Bateson resembles the descriptions of the intimacy magicians feel toward their natural environment. With the physics of enfoldment, these might even be used to try and analyze the effectiveness of some magical rites. Unfortunately, any attempt to explain occult phenomena, which I take as the occasionally effective rites of magic, is premature if not misguided. David Bohm, alas, was one of the Israeli conjurer Uri Geller's biggest fans in the scientific community (see Chapter 13). At the very most, new scientific thinking provides some tools for analyzing the *mental* experience of interconnectedness that characterizes magical contexts and that are discussed in Chapter 8. But these tools can be used only in conjuction with anthropological and philosophical methods if we are to keep both feet firmly on the ground.

NOTES

1. Kenneth R. Pelletier, *Mind as Healer, Mind as Slayer* (New York: Delta/Seymour Lawrence, 1992), pp. xl–xli; Robert Ornstein and David Sabel, *The Healing Brain* (New York: Touchstone, 1988).

2. Roberto A. Frisancho, *Human Adaptation: A Functional Interpretation* (Ann Arbor: University of Michigan Press, 1981); Alexander Alland Jr., *Adaptation in Cultural Evolution: An Approach to Medical Anthropology* (New York: Columbia University Press, 1970)

3. Ann McElroy and Patricia K. Townsend, *Medical Anthropology in Ecological Perspective* (Boulder: Westview Press, 1989), pp. 83–92.

4. Patrick D. Wall, "The Placebo Effect: An Unpopular Topic," in *Pain* 51 (1992): 1.

5. Cited in Pelletier, *Mind as Healer,* pp. xxxiii–xxxiv.

6. Joan Borysenko, *Minding the Body, Mending the Mind* (New York: Bantam, 1987); Deepak Chopra, *Quantum Healing: Exploring the Frontiers of Mind/Body Medicine* (New York: Bantam Books, 1990); Herbert Benson, *The Mind/Body Effect: How Behavioral Medicine Can Show You the Way to Better Health* (New York: Simon and Schuster, 1979); Bernie Siegel, *Love, Medicine and Miracles* (New York: HarperCollins, 1986). Obviously, this is only a tiny sample from a rapidly growing library.

7. This case was reported by the physician, who wishes to remain anonymous, and by the girl herself. The warts are caused by infection due to a weakened immune system, which can be reinvigorated by psychological means.

8. Thomas S. Kuhn, *The Structure of Scientific Revolutions* (Chicago: University of Chicago Press, 1970).

9. George Lyman Kittredge, *Witchcraft in Old and New England* (New York: Russel & Russel, 1956), pp. 7–12. The modern reader who marvels at the remarkable coincidence of a man (John Baddaford) going mad three weeks after Alice's curse should consider the actual sequence of events: John goes crazy for some reason, and his distraught wife (Joan) suddenly remembers that weeks earlier her despised neighbor Alice had cursed the man. Her presentation at court is then tailored to match her emotional reaction.

10. Quoted in Carolyn Merchant, *The Death of Nature* (New York: Harper & Row, 1980). It is easy to overstate the sexist and violent imagery of Bacon as Carolyn Merchant does. Such "metaphormongering" tends to give the old writer's metaphor a life of its own apart from the intended meaning, in this case discovering difficult truths.

11. In fact, the same Francis Bacon attributed to nature an immanent spirit that animates "every inanimate body." *The New Organon and Related Writings* (New York: Liberal Arts Press, 1960), p. 208.

12. Klaus Maurice and Otto Mayr, *The Clockwork Universe: German Clocks and Automata 1550–1650* (New York: Neal Watson Academic Publications, 1980).

13. Rene Descartes, *A Discourse on Method* (New York: Dutton, 1951); Isaac Newton, *The Principia* (Amherst, N.Y.: Prometheus Books, 1995) and *Mathematical Principles, 1686.* (Berkeley: University of California Press, 1946).

14. James Clerk Maxwell, "A Dynamical Theory of the Electromagnetic Field," in *Scientific Papers*, vol. 2 (Cambridge: Cambridge University Press, 1890).

15. Albert Einstein, *Relativity: The Special and General Theory* (New York: Holt, 1920). Hundreds of readily available books on Einstein's theories range from the obtuse to the simplistic. For a brief and simple summary of relativity and its solution to the problems posed by Maxwell and other predecessors, see Alan J. Friedman and Carol C. Donley, *Einstein as Myth and Muse* (New York: Cambridge University Press, 1985).

16. Quantum has been a monumentally successful physical theory whose cosmological and commercial reverberations have now far outstripped the bounds of the purely technical. For an introduction, see Robert March, *Physics for Poets* (New York: McGraw-Hill, 1970); Fred Alan Woolf, *Taking the Quantum Leap* (San Francisco: Harper and Row, 1982); Heinz R. Pagels, *The Cosmic Code: Quantum Physics as the Language of Nature* (New York: Bantam, 1990).

17. Dozens of works can be cited as proof for this claim. Friedman and Donley quote none other than Niels Bohr as saying that "a profound truth could be recognized by the fact that its opposite was also a profound truth" (*Einstein*, p. 131).

18. Michael Talbot, *The Holographic Universe* (New York: Harper Perennial, 1991), pp. 160–1.

19. David Bohm, *Wholeness and the Implicate Order* (London: Routledge & Kegan Paul, 1980).

20. Bohm, *Wholeness*, p. 149.

21. S. A. Forbes, "The Lake as a Microcosm," in *Illinois Natural History Survey Bulletin* 15 (1925): 537–50; R. L. Lindeman, "The Trophic-Dynamic Aspect of Ecology," in *Ecology* 23 (1942): 399–418. The quote is from E. P. Odum, "The New Ecology," in *Bioscience* 14 (1964): 14–16.

22. For greater detail see Carol L. Crumley, ed., *Historical Ecology: Cultural Knowledge and Changing Landscapes* (Santa Fe: School of American Research Press, 1994).

23. James E. Lovelock, *Gaia: A New Look at Life on Earth* (Oxford: Oxford University Press, 1991); Gregory Bateson, *Steps to An Ecology of Mind: Collected Essays in Anthropology, Psychiatry, Evolution and Epistemology* (New York: Ballantine Books, 1972). Ecological thinking has also been encorporated into theology, feminism, and ethics. See, for instance, David Kinsley, *Ecology and Religion* (Englewood Cliffs, N.J.: Prentice-Hall, 1995), and T. C. McLuhan, *Way of the Earth* (New York: Simon and Schuster, 1995).

24. "Gaia is just a metaphor," says Stephen J. Gould. "I don't see anything *causal* in Gaia." *Scientific American* (August 1995): 41.

25. *Sacred Unity: Further Steps to an Ecology of Mind* (New York: Cornelia & Michael Bessie, 1991), p. 165.

PART TWO

The Nature of Magic

⚅ SEVEN ⚅

Concentric Rings of Healing

Here is where we stand today on the occult nature of magic: Like religion and baseball, magic is regarded as an essentially social phenomenon. It is ritualistic and symbolic, and it is used to gain certain goals best described in sociological terms. In short, there is nothing "magical" (occult) about magic, the claims of its practitioners to the contrary nothwithstanding. Of course, this is an implicit position—no scholar will actually test a magical claim in the way a physicist or medical researcher would test a scientific hypothesis. The mere suggestion sounds absurd because it implies that we need to take the claims of magicians literally, either accepting or rejecting them on empirical grounds. But with the demise of Frazer, the literalistic—occultist path has been sealed off, except to researchers in the area of paranormal phenomena.[1] Instead of taking the boasts of magicians literally ("I can heal your infertile field"), the sociology and the symbolism of magic have come to dominate academic interest. The only admissable hypotheses deal with social function or symbolic meaning.

But perhaps a different set of speculations could also be considered. Assume, as a working hypothesis, that the earliest form of magical practice was the healing of sick and injured people. This is a fairly tame proposition; commonsense accepts it with little struggle. Assume also that the healing of an injured hunter, for instance, was based on the best *direct* medicinal knowledge. In other words, the treatment was not a ritual occasion or a symbolic plea for health. A man's leg was broken while the man was chasing an ibex; the leg needed to be set, and the swelling had to be brought down. Bear in mind that we have no way of knowing of what the actual treatment consisted. But it would be far more speculative to claim that it was some ritual propitiation of spirits who caused the injury. Zoologists and ethnobotanists have recently found that even chimpanzees are capable of identifying curative plants for a variety of ailments.[2] It is not such a leap of the imagination, then, to assume that early hunters were familiar enough with their environment to recognize the properties of several plants, herbs, and roots and to apply these in a variety of situations. Clearly, a few of these pharmaceuticals and methods of application would prove more effective over the long run than others and would be retained.

Some of these or similar practices would eventually be applied by extension to an ever-widening range of patients and situations. If a feverish hunter with a broken bone or an infected bite could be healed, then perhaps so could an infant with fever, a third person who was away from the camp, a dog, a tree, the weather. We see in Chapter 8 what kind of an imagination might extend effects from the conscious adult subject all the way to distant natural beings and even objects such as rainclouds. As similar healing methods are applied to widening realms, they take on the *appearance* of symbolic thinking: They seem to leap by means of an intellectual analogy from the human patient outward. But to say that this extension is simple symbol making is already to assume that the two "patients" being compared (hunter/rain cloud) belong to two distinct orders of being: a conscious person versus an insentient and grossly material object. The gap between the two, commonsense protests, is too great: It can be bridged only by symbols, and therefore the "curing" of the cloud must be read symbolically. But if the hunter and the cloud are perceived as belonging to the same order of being, if they are somehow interrelated, then the leap from one to the other is not metaphorical; it is indexical and magical.[3] We next look at this outward extension as practiced in Banaras.

HEALING IN BANARAS

If quantity is a sign of need, no act of magic is more necessary than curing illness. In Banaras magical healing outstrips every other form of practice, including, most notably, astrological divinations. Hundreds of healers work in the city, treating everything from childhood diseases to age-related troubles and from humans to cattle to trees and, finally, boats and rickshaws. The magicians range from family members who may have been handed down one remedy and its form of application to temple priests who have assembled huge pharmacies and practice a full repertoire of applications. In the search for health, Banarsis ignore doctrinal, sectarian, and caste boundaries without a thought. One healer, for instance, exorcises Hindu ghosts on Tuesdays out of a small Durgā temple. On Thursdays he moves over to the other side of the veranda, and there he treats Muslim patients. But he never turns away a Muslim on Tuesday or a Hindu on Thursday. He simply moves. Eighty percent of the healers are men, most more than fifty years old. Few of the women healers are younger than sixty. Although only two or three among the healers I met were illiterate, books are seldom used by any magician, with the possible exception of temple priests. The traditions embodied in magical healing are very loose and open to improvisation. Magicians pass their knowledge to disciples who learn by observation, discussion, and memorization of verbal formulas and who finally become empowered by initiation. I saw no evidence that the dynamic healing scene was passing away or that it was being displaced by the speedy proliferation of modern medicine. The allopathic physicians tend to be described on the street as greedy technicians with quick needles, antibiotics, and painkillers for everything. The institution that produces them, Banaras Hindu University Medical School, is regarded more contemptuously than a political party.

If an observer were to apply occultist questions to the situation I am describing, they would be: "Does the vibrancy of the magical healing traditions indicate that it works? If so, what makes magical healing effective; is it faith?" When asked these questions, Banarsi magicians smile and shrug. To them, speculations about faith and mind healing body are entirely beside the point. The treatment would work regardless of faith; it is intrinsically powerful. The faith question is simply our own way of ruling out the occult by looking for mental factors. Faced with the unshakable confidence of magicians, the Western rationalist may fall back on another occultist question: "Can magic really heal a nonbeliever, or even an unaware subject?" To qualify for the designation of magical (by Lorilai's occultist standards), the power of healing must extend through the following concentric rings of influence:

conscious subject (adult)
↓
nonconscious subject (child; unaware adult)
↓
animal
↓
inanimate objects
↓
nature

The innermost ring—conscious subject—is further divided into mental and physical problems in a classification that is so arbitrary the reader must approach it with extreme caution. We have seen earlier that it is nearly impossible to make such a distinction in many cases: a rash may owe its origins to nonpathogenic causes, and so also heart disease, epilepsy, cancer, and other diseases. Some problems, a leg broken in a falling accident or a dog bite, are a little easier to classify. To some extent, this classification appears to concern those magical healers who question the patient not only about his life circumstances but also about his medical history and which physicians he has seen and with what results. Simple physical problems will be referred back to allopathic physicians.

At any rate, the widening spheres of magical influence serve as the organizing method for the cases described in this chapter, beginning with the innermost and moving out.

Conscious Subjects

Mental. A boy called Anu came with his parents to the Kajjal Baba. He was a slight eighth grader with dark, panic-stricken eyes. Something horrible had happened to him three days earlier, and he became partially amnesiac. He could not remember his own name or relate what had happened to him, though he seemed to recognize his parents. Anu was extremely disoriented and obviously had no idea where he was or why he was there. His father was directing his every movement: obeisance to Swamiji, sitting down, removing his cap. Swamiji took the facts of the case—not much really. He then told the father that the boy had been assaulted by a *jin,* a Muslim ghost. Then he began the procedure, first with a light sprinkling of water and mantras. Suddenly a young man approached Swamiji. He interrupted the boy's treatment, whispering for about ten minutes into Swamiji's ear—possibly concerning impotence. No one seemed to mind, but the boy became distracted and tried to leave so his father had to restrain him. Then the serious splashing began, and the father struggled to keep the boy down. The Kajjal Baba was throwing large handfuls of cold water from his urn onto the boy's face. Before Anu could gather himself, the spicy *kajjal* (lampblack) was applied to his eyes, and pandemonium ensued. The boy shrieked as his mother began to wail; he tried to run away and squirmed hysterically in his father's grasp. He was forcibly laid flat on his back so Swamiji could pour the water over his face, as he does to many other patients. The boy gagged and flailed his arms and legs, as if drowning in a mighty river. Finally, Anu's father loosened his grip, and the boy shot up and dashed out. His parents hurriedly followed as Swamiji called for them to bring him back in two hours. The treatment would continue until he improved.

Physical. When someone's back suddenly hurts, a vertebrae coming out of joint perhaps, the traditional Banaras way of dealing with the situation is to summon an *ultā janma*—a person who was born legs first. One can always be found somewhere in the city. According to reports, that person will kick the patient in the back (*"latmardana"*), and the problem will thus be fixed. This treatment is widely regarded as *totakā*—a form of magic, which is accepted as unfailingly effective. The term *totakā* is a specific name for magical practices that involve direct contact, as opposed to *tonā*, which operates at a distance. When a tumor or swelling appears on the body—say, the leg—for no apparent reason, a knife is passed over it and onto the ground three times in a symbolic fashion. It is "cut into the ground"—that is *totakā*. But if someone "passes over your tea"—that is, casts a shadow on it—before you have had a chance to drink it, drinking will surely cause illness. This is a case of *tonā,* much like the throwing of an evil eye (*najar*). For a cure you must "cut" another cup of tea in the fashion I have described and drink it.

卐 卐 卐

Case 7.1

The Amateur Chiropractor

One day I went to Omji to meet with the twenty-three-year-old man who had been an *ultā janma* baby: He was born feet first. Manoj was a political science student who was working on his M.A. in preparation for civil service examinations. His grandmother had told him about his special powers and once showed him all he needed to know.

Patients with sore backs come to the pleasant-looking, stocky boy, who instructs them to sit on the ground. He asks them which side is troubled, then places his hand on the opposite shoulder to brace himself. He runs his foot down the back on the painful side and touches the floor with his foot after each stroke. He does this either seven or eleven times, and the person "becomes well." The pressure Manoj applies with his foot is not very hard, and the sensation is pleasant—if you are well. It is not strong enough for spinal adjustment.

Manoj has never heard of chiropractors or healers who specialize in back adjustment. He confesses not to know why his *toṭakā* magic works and adds that the treatment should be done in the morning before any food is eaten. He also emphasizes that no money can change hands or the patient will not be cured.

Mental/physical borderline—epilepsy cure. Epileptics in Banaras are said to be recognized by their fits ("convulsions and fainting") and also by the fact that they are afraid of water and fire.[4] Few people are known as specialists in this illness, though a young member of the Dom family who does this work shared his procedures.

To begin the treatment, the healer forces the patient to take a bath, then stand for fifteen minutes in front of dead bodies about to be cremated, inhaling the smoke of the funeral fire. The healer brings the wheat flour he will need for the procedure, while the patient brings five packs of molasses. The healer prepares dough and puts it on the ashes of the funeral pyre. The dough bakes directly on the ashes, which are made white by means of a mantra, for twenty minutes. The patient is made to look at the bread for ten minutes while it is baking. During that entire duration, the healer repeats a mantra. Then the two sit facing each other. They put the bread on top of a broken funeral pot, which had been used for that same body. The healer tells his patient to eat the bread in front of him. He claims that the bread contains the power of the fire. Each of the five bites is eaten with a piece of molasses, but a portion of each must be left uneaten. When he finishes with one piece, the patient must go and get a drink from the Ganges. If the patient does not show dramatic improvement, the healer gives the five leftover molasses-bread mixtures to a dog after summoning the animal with a mantra. The dog—a notorious scavenger in Banaras—eats the mix directly from the healer's hand. After each piece, the patient must lick the hand of the healer from which the dog had eaten.

The entire procedure is repeated eleven times on Tuesdays and Sundays. If he still does not get better, the patient is told to come at night. He strips naked. The healer recites a mantra and tries to find out who threw this ghost—the cause of the illness—at him. Then he hits the patient five times to drive out the ghost. Sometimes the entire rite I have described is repeated at night, with a shivering and naked patient. The young Dom practitioner had been taught this procedure by Bhairav

Ram Baba, his guru. He had been instructed on the procedure down to its minutest detail and given the mantras. According to the healer, the mantras are the "real" source of the treatment's effectiveness.

Nonconscious Subjects

Long-distance sorcery (ṭonā). A prosperous-looking young man came to see the Naya Chowk Tantric one evening.[5] He was dressed in a brown suit made of a rich fabric. He left his patent leather brown shoes at the door and took his place in the back of the room. The baba looked at him and smiled. Later that evening he called the young man to move closer and anounced to the room that the man was undoubtedly having tax problems. And he was right! The young man was a businessman from Bangalore visiting Banaras on business. He told the magician that he had been summoned for a tax audit and that he was probably in serious trouble. He described his situation in great detail, then gave Babaji two hundred rupees—a vast sum of money. The Tantric took the money, then got up and left for the cremation grounds, where he would perform the magical rite. Two hours later he returned and reassured the Bangalore man that his affairs were settled.

Three days later the young businessman returned to the room where Babaji was working with a large group of patients. He took his place in the back and sat quietly. Babaji ignored him. When all the patients left and only the disciples remained, the Tantric baba spoke: "How is your problem today? Someone died in the tax office, no?" Everyone was stunned, but the businessman nodded and smiled sadly. "Yes," he said, "the deputy auditor died suddenly, and they canceled all the audits for the time being." Then he got up and approached the Tantric. He bowed and touched the baba's knee with his forehead. He reached into his pocket and pulled out a stack of bills and placed it under the mat on which the Tantric was sitting. "Please, sir," he begged, "do not kill anyone else for me. I fear the bad karma." Babaji laughed and said, "Don't worry, the karma is mine. I can deal with it."

Healing infants. A fortyish man with an older woman assistant works next to the telegraph office in Kammacha. His clinic is a simple storefront-apartment on a busy street. Two or three merchants sell trinkets for kids who are being brought there for treatment. No unusual airs, crowds, or excitement of any kind indicate the nature of the place. Dozens of practices like this one can be found throughout Banaras. People bring young children for healing on Tuesdays, which suggests they are mainly Hindu. The practitioner puts a *sūtra* around the child's neck. It is a simple string threaded inside a one-inch piece of green bamboo reed. The bamboo grows, according to the healer, in muddy places and must have seven joints in order to be effective. As he puts the *sūtra* over the child's head, the healer silently recites mantras. Then he touches a knife to the temple of a child and jerks it back, repeating this seven or eleven times. When the bamboo dries in a few days, the child will be healed. One may buy such a *sūtra* for an absent child too sick to come. The practitioner places it on his heart and recites mantras silently before handing it over to the parent.

People who bring a child give the healer a lemon as an offering. Older people bring bananas. The healer cuts the lemon and waves it around the child's head. Finally he removes the illness with the knife to the rhythm of the silent mantras. He tells the parents to offer the lemon in the fire at home and then circle it around the head of the baby. The Kammacha healer claims to treat a varied and wide-ranging scope of diseases but heals mostly children suffering from loss of weight, fever, sleeplessness, and psychological problems. The healer rarely offers a diagnosis; he usually attributes the problem to the evil eye (*najar*). He treats older people for ailments such as persistent headaches, stomachaches, sleeplessness, rashes, and other problems that appear stress-related.

Antagonistic Subject.

स्र स्र स्र

Case 7.2

Porcupine Quills for Your Enemies

One day, as I was sitting with Prasad the Tantric, a nervous-looking young man approached the booth. He introduced himself as an *ojhā* from one of the peripheral city neighborhoods and asked for two porcupine quills. Prasad brought out his jar of quills, and the man took his time making a careful selection. The jar contained quills from both male and female porcupines, and he needed one of each. Prasad asked him why he needed the items, and the man answered directly, with no regard for secrecy. He said that he had a client who owns a house that he had rented to a local family. After a while the renters stopped paying the rent and refused to leave. The landlord was in the process of suing them for the rent and trying to evict them, but the law was very strongly biased in favor of tenants. So he felt that the only way to get these people out of his house was to bring severe family problems on them. The quills, taken from the most quarrelsome of animals and hidden in the house, will undoubtedly visit such trouble on these deadbeats! Prasad then asked the *ojhā* if he knew the correct mantras, and the man nodded. He found his two quills, paid five rupees, and left.

I asked Prasad if he would have given the man the harmful mantras, and he caught the moral whiff of the question. He shook his head and said he had asked the *ojhā* only out of curiousity. I then asked whether the intended victims need to know about the sorcery in order to suffer the consequences. Prasad smiled and told me I was missing the point. He said: "As soon as they find the quills and remove them, their troubles will end. No, the objects must be hidden very well in order to continue working."

Animals

A milkman living at the edge of the city owns three cows and several buffaloes.[6] The cows live in the tiny courtyard surrounding his hut. When a calf is born, it moves freely between the yard and the one-room hut. One day, months before I met him, the milkman's largest and most fecund cow fell ill. She stopped giving millk—her udders dried up and shriveled—and she became very moody and irritable. Because all the other animals were fine, the milkman suspected that a ghost had entered the body of the cow, perhaps through the machinations of a rival. He took a spicy red chili in his right hand and waved it in circles above the cow's head. Then he placed the chili in a fire. He also put green sugar-cane leaves in the fire, which emitted thick smoke. The milkman pulled his cow into the smoke and forced her to inhale. Meanwhile, he recited a mantra his father had given him. In such a way, the milkman told me, he drove the illness out of the cow.

Inanimate Objects

Sitaram is a master boat builder who works for fishermen and tour-boat operators on the Ganges. He works slowly and methodically, using the same tools that three or four centuries of craftsmen have used.

Tourists stop to photograph the "quaint, primitive" worker with his rope drill and his axe-like hacksaw. But his boats are superbly constructed and extremely durable. The boat owner who hired him in November 1993—Bansilal—boasted that he had purchased the very best Himalayan wood at 450 rupees per foot. The boat would last, he asserted, as long as the tree had lived.

When a new boat is finished, its owner hires a pandit to perform a *pūjā* ceremony inaugurating it. The boat is struck on "the head" by the carpenter, using his hammer, in order to be "brought to life." Prior to the *pūjā* the boat is tarred with a mixture of cow dung, coal tar, and ashes, then painted. The owner stamps his handprint on the boat, using rice paste, and dots the boat with turmeric. There are five special nails located in the middle of the baseboard of the boat that are critical to the integrity of the boat as a whole. They are put in when the two halves of the boat are put together, and a special *pūjā* is celebrated for that event as well. These nails contain the spirit of the boat, and their exact location must be kept a secret. A rival who finds these nails can destroy the boat and its owner with simple magic.

Sitaram insisted that he had placed the nails in the boat I watched him build, doing so when I was away. According to Banarsis, especially of the Mallāh boat caste, these nails are extremely lucky to have in the house, but if they are broken then they bring bad luck. Because a large number of Banaras residents belong to the Mallāh castes of boat people, several magicians use these nails in their sorcery and divination.

Not only boats, which are still constructed in the traditional way, are susceptible to magical influences. The same applies to trucks and rickshaws, both of which can actually become possessed by evil ghosts or affected by evil eye. A "possessed" rickshaw will be brought to a healer for exorcism.

Nature

Banaras sits in the midst of a rich agricultural area. The district encompasses dozens of villages that have changed very little in recent decades. Although efficient irrigation is widely used, any delay in the arrival of the monsoon is devastating. According to Hansraj Yadav, the coming of the rains is anticipated in the villages with mounting anxiety but not passivity. Villagers gather and sit near a stove in which milk and rice are brought to a boil by a *bhakta* who is a divination specialist (of the Yadav caste). The *bhakta* walks around the stove until it boils and works himself into a trance, becoming possessed by the goddess Śitala.

He is naked but for a loincloth. Then he puts his hand in the hot mixture and takes out a handful without burning his hand. He begins to forecast the future and answer questions: What disease will come, who has a secret enemy? If someone has a problem with a ghost, the *bhakta* identifies him by pouring milk in his hand without being told. The *bhakta* pours the milk over himself, then predicts when the monsoon should arrive, using the voice of the goddess, who answers through him. The villagers believe that by pouring the milk over himself, the *bhakta* forces the rains to come. They sing Pacara songs for the goddess, who is present in his person. All join enthusiastically because they need the rain and because the *bhakta* is famous for detecting any skepticism or animosity in the crowd. When he does, he pours the hot milk on the skeptic's hand. If it burns, the *bhakta* is vindicated![7]

In Banaras proper, if the monsoon is delayed, people immerse Śiva Lingams in water from the Ganges in order to bring the rain. Some light fires and cast straw and mantras into the blaze in order to produce dense smoke to attract the clouds. This may be a pan-Indian practice:

> Babu talked about the monsoon. He said that three years earlier a big prayer ceremony was held in Trivandrum. It took place during the pre-monsoon dry perriod and, by tradition and decree, began with the lighting of a fire. . . . The procedure also ordained that the blaze should be doused by rain, and this aspect had aroused considerable interest abroad. Several Western scientists were present, including an observer from NASA. . . .
>
> He gave me a solemn look: "I was *there*," he said, "I saw everything they did. The fire had been lit in a large wooden pavilion and when special mantras were chanted which caused the flames to jump ten feet, the building itself began blazing. Forty fire engines were parked nearby because of fears that the whole of Trivandrum would burn. The priests began throwing certain things into the fire. It started giving off smoke, very thick and pungent, which grew into a stupendous column thousands of feet high. Then, out of the smoke, sailed many eagles. The sky grew dark and quite soon torrential rain began to fall. Within minutes it put the fire out and everyone went home."
>
> "I don't believe a word of that," I said.[8]

THE MAGIC OF HEALING

Innovative medical hypotheses, as we have seen, can be used to explain some cases of magical healing. Psychoneuroimmunology, for instance, provides one framework for understanding the effectiveness of treatments for asthmatic or allergic conditions. PNI reduces the events that take place in the healing rites, and the response of the patient, to another language. That language—medicine—paraphrases the events in a theoretical manner that belongs to a different level of causality; neuropeptides, enzymes, and nerve pulses become the actors who interact to cause the healing. This theoretical language is alien to the healers and their patients: It fails to describe their conscious experiences. But more important, it seems absurd to extend the language of biochemistry from the case of healing a conscious adult patient to every other case. Rickshaws are not "healed" in the same way as teenagers, and rains are different from both.

Is there anything, however abstract, shared by all cases of healing magic? On a very general level, all possess three basic features: a patient (this could be anything), a healer, and a problem that needs to be solved. Unfortunately, this level of analysis is far too general because it includes both brain surgeons and Mercedes mechanics. But what makes all these cases magical in the minds of the participants? To say that Banarsis believe that all are magical is redundant: It does not tell us what is magical about them and adds no new information to the basic fact that they are all being practiced.

It is also easy to be too specific about these cases and to err on the side of strictness. If we take James Frazer's "contagion" and "similarity" forms of magical reasoning, which can be seen in the case of epilepsy, we then have to exclude the work of the Kajjal Baba and his eye lotion. No single mode of reasoning pervades all these cases. Similarly, the use of mantras does not extend to every case, and, besides, mantras are just as likely to be voiced in nonmagical events. The belief in a particular agency or power that heals—a goddess, a saint, or a spirit (*yakṣiṇī*)—is also far from universal. Sometimes it is the rite itself that is perceived to be effective; at other times it is the power of the mantra or a *yantra*. In other cases, it is a combination of powers, such as the curative properties of a root joined to the compassion of the goddess, both of equal importance.

Residents of Banaras share a few basic beliefs about the world, regardless of their religion or caste. They believe in different forms of divine powers and in an embodied soul that can become a ghost or evil spirit. They believe in rebirth—Muslims share this belief—and in the power of mantras. But when Banarsis become ill, they set aside their intellectual beliefs and visit a magician who has a reputation for specializing in that particular trouble. The magician will question them about their health and about the life circumstances that may have led to their illness, but never about their beliefs or worldviews.

All cases of healing share this feature: The particular illnesses are set apart from the ideological and sectarian life of the participants; the healing event is personal and, for its duration, it is the only relationship that counts. This is true even when the patient is a foreigner, a Muslim or a Sikh, or lives in a distant country and knows nothing of the cure being effected. In such cases the healer requires a photograph or an object belonging to the patient and always touches it and uses it as an essential link to the distant patient.

The first two universal features of magical healing, then, are (1) its practical and nonideological nature and (2) its dependence on a direct relationship with the patient. This second feature sets magical healing apart from standard forms of medical practice. "Direct relationship" can be taken one step further: The magician and his client, even if the client is a cow or a boat, always enter a relationship based on immediate sensory interaction, even intimacy. Touch, sound, smell, and sight are the most important elements in bonding this relationship, which I discuss in Chapter 16 as empathy. This observation, and its magical implications, incidentally, may hold even if the healer is a Stanford University physician practicing in New York. A patient may at times wish only to be touched by her physician; in some sense this is magical healing. The magical moment—the point at which plain healing becomes magical healing—depends absolutely on a sensory bond.

None of the magicians I observed felt that their methods were completely foolproof. All have experienced failure and the frustration of unsatisfied patients. Their magic is not an awesome force that never fails. It is, rather, one component in a very complex web of forces and often requires several applications to turn things around for the patient. Also, the results of magic are seldom final because the forces that swirl around Banarsis hardly abate with one cure. This is a very practical and worldlywise attitude that is shared by all healers and many patients.

What does the healing rite try to achieve, then? If it is not instant and permanent health—if, in other words, no "magical causality" imposes the magician's will on nature—what else is there? The answer is explored in Chapter 8 on the magical experience. Magical healing operates by cultivating a magical consciousness among the participants, an awareness that one's body is located at a central intersection within a system of relations. Illness ruptures this pattern, and healing restores the perception of harmony. This is true even when the patient is a three-wheeled scooter. We have seen that rickshaw drivers are excellent mechanics and will never entrust the mechanical repair of their vehicles to an *ojhā* (exorcist). But if the rickshaw suffers repeated mechanical failure despite superb maintenance—it is a lemon—or if business suddenly drops and stays low, if too many little mishaps begin to cumulate in the mind of the owner into a major disruption, then he will regard the rickshaw as ill in a nonmechanical sense, perhaps possessed by a ghost. The bond between driver and machine is both mental and physical; the machine is the extension of the driver's self. The magical rite will mend the tear in the subtle system forged between man and machine and will ignore the distinction that we make between two such disparate orders of being. All magical healing tries to do this: It restores the wholeness— the systemic completeness—in the consciousness of the main participants. The specific desired goal of a given rite is then perceived as inherently contained in the actions of the rite because the rite produces this relational consciousness. This is its magic.

NOTES

1. There are a few scholars, such as Robin Horton, who, like Frazer, take the claims of magicians as a distinct form of rationality. During the early 1970s a brief flurry of anthropological studies of occult phenomena followed the publication of the Don Juan books by Carlos Castaneda.

2. No sophisticated mental skills are required in such cases, and recognition may be entirely visceral. During bouts of influenza people find iron-rich foods such as eggs and bacon nauseating. The excessive iron happens to provide superb nourishment for the invading pathogen their bodies are fighting. See Randolph M. Nesse and George C. Williams, *Why We Get Sick: The New Science of Darwinian Medicine* (New York: Times Books, 1994), pp. 29–31.

3. On the meaning of indexical relations, see Chapter 15.

4. Epilepsy is called *apasmar* in Hindi, which means "memory loss." The disease is discussed, along with treatments, in the classical medical texts of India. The Dom's practice on the banks of the Ganges does not resemble the ancient treatments.

5. This man's name and location have been concealed. He is a Tantric, but not from Naya Chowk (the "New Market").

6. For more on animals and magic, see Chapter 14.

7. This material is based on Hansraj Yadav's testimony and was confirmed by his brother on a separate occasion.

8. Alexander Frater, *Chasing the Monsoon* (Calcutta: Penguin Books, 1990), p. 50.

ꙮ EIGHT ꙮ

The Magical Experience

Imagine stepping into a twenty-first-century video arcade and strapping yourself to a seventh-generation virtual reality (VR) machine. You program it to a desired location, such as a rain forest, then program the sensory sensitivity level to 9 (out of 10). You can also program a variety of other features: the number of unpredictable events, a preference for certain senses, your speed and strength, the level of violence (or pleasure) you can tolerate, and perhaps some psychic functions as well. Suppose, for example, you recognize a certain mushroom and put it in your mouth (in simulation, of course); the machine will then produce the appropriate hallucination. Imagine one extra feature, "the magic circuit." You program it into your "ride" and push the start button. The machine is astonishingly refined and the visual and other sensory perceptions are perfectly simulated, so your experience of being in a rain forest—after a few moments for acclimation—is uncanny. Because you have chosen a high level of sensory input, you become aware of extremely subtle movements in the forest around you, and soon enough you feel as menaced by some sounds as you are attracted to others. The quicker you can forget your modern self and become submerged in this world, the closer you come to the world of a hunter-gatherer from the last Ice Age.

Then the magic circuit kicks in, and a major transformation takes place in your awareness. You still see the ripe berries everywhere, and you still hear the hyperactive chirping of birds and the predator that is quietly proceeding upwind from you. But suddenly everything you see and hear and touch becomes interrelated. The chirping of the birds becomes meaningful suddenly because it is connected with something else that you perceive, say, a sudden splash in a nearby pond. The rich and fast flow of images you enjoyed as a tourist—or an animal—just a few moments ago has now been replaced by a narrative, a simple but meaningful story line. Everything you sense has a place in this narrative, and the meaning of every element derives from its place in the grid. As this happens, you begin to have a sense of yourself as the nexus of the scene, the bond that holds it all together. Everything your senses pick up is related to you in some intuitive way. You notice that the hissing of a green lizard draws a large boa constrictor in the same direction. The machine has coordinated its signals in such a way that you could not fail to connect the two events. But this electronic-neurological event is transparent, happening beneath the threshold of your awareness. You know only that you now feel related to lizard and snake alike, and you reproduce the lizard's sound to draw the snake in your own direction. This will come in handy for hunting, or perhaps for saving a child someday, but before any utility is discovered there is just the magic of interrelatedness. That magic is the first emergence of the mind from the animalistic immersion in the present flow of sense perceptions onto a coherent scene.

The model of the virtual reality (VR) machine—and that is all it is, a model—has its limitations. The player does not engage in rituals usually associated with magic and does not think magically. Only a refined sensing of an extraordinary world and simple reactions prevail in the model. These oversights will be corrected shortly. The purpose of the model is to draw attention to the type of experience—of interconnectedness—that underlies all magical events, at least ideally. The model focuses on the two dimensions of magic: the mental experience (perceptions, emotions, attitudes) and the physical link, which consists of wiring that hooks up the player to an expensive computer. The model demonstrates that hardware can produce a magical experience. Electronic impulses to the correct brain center accompanied by a mild jolt to the skin can form the scaffolding of a mental event. But does the analogy hold in real life? Was a Cro Magnon hunter "hooked up" to his world in a way that would explain the type of experiences he underwent when he performed hunting magic? Where was the wiring linking him to the world?

THE REALITY—A CASE OF MAGIC

Participants in magical events report unusual experiences and seem to believe that simple rituals can have extraordinary effects. They ignore the boundary between their own minds and the "objective" physical properties of the world. The VR machine model suggested that magical experience results from the way the participants—not just primitive hunters—are "linked" to their world. If no direct wiring (physiological link) can be found, then magic must be purely mental: a language or belief. But if the participants are "hooked up" through a natural equivalent to the fiber-optic wiring of the VR machine, then magic is far more than a cultural artifact—perhaps a bridge between physiology and psychology.

᠀ ᠀ ᠀

Case 8.1

Nailing Asthma

Wayland Hand quotes Randolph's description of an asthma curing rite in the Ozarks: "To cure asthma, bore a hole in a black-oak tree, at the height of the patient's head. Drive a little wooden peg into the hole so as to hold the lock of hair. Cut the hair and peg off flush with the trunk, when the bark grows over the hole so that the peg is no longer visible, and the patient's hair grows out to replace the missing lock, the asthma will be gone forever."[1]

I have selected this relatively contemporary American case for a reason: It allows us to avoid the mid-century anthropological debates about animistic beliefs and primitive mentality. The participants in this case may even be driving to the oak tree in their '35 Fords. A modern case also illustrates the fact that magic can be practiced anywhere, at any time. Of course, in actual performance the asthma cure was far more involved than Randolph's account. One can imagine a procession of neighbors, including several women "experts" along with helpers, the patient and her family, all noisily trudging through a field toward the black oak tree. As they get there, they argue about which side is best for drilling a hole and how the patient should stand on the uneven ground to get her exact height against the tree. The hole cannot be made too deep, and the peg must not be too thick. One almost sees the patient recoiling when her hair is pulled too hard. Weeks later some members of the original group begin to visit the tree daily in order to scrutinize it. They take turns stroking the spot to feel how well it has healed. If the patient has already begun to feel well even though the tree bark has not yet crusted over, reasons will be given and debated.

How is the cure for asthma related to the VR machine? The patient is obviously "bonded" in some way to the black oak; her healing appears contingent on the oak's own healing. She is measured against the tree, touching it to her full length—back to back. A tuft of the patient's hair remains in the oak bark, staying there forever, or perhaps like Ariel in *The Tempest,* it will be freed by a future Prospero. Both the patient's bald spot and the oak bark grow back and meanwhile are constantly compared to monitor the ongoing asthma cure. Traditional anthropology and folklore studies were interested in the bad causal thinking in such cases. The tree, early theorists claimed, was meant to invigorate the patient because the two touched and became identified by a false analogy. Today scholars focus on the felicity of the symbolic behavior the rite expresses. But I am interested in the senses. The bond that the ritual establishes between the patient and the tree depends on the senses—sight and touch in particular. This is a nonlinguistic bond, primitive perhaps beyond all other forms of culture. It is also the very heart of the magical event. The metaphor of the VR machine is alive and well in this real-life aspect of magic: The wiring of the machine has simply been replaced with the senses of the participants. This is a simple fact, manifest in every case of magic. The senses of the participants bind them to the context and provide the basic channels of magical information. How this happens is discussed next.

THE SENSES (WIRING)

The human body, even in its underachieving twentieth-century version, is the product of an extremely long evolutionary process. Its size and shape, the effectiveness of the eyes and the ineffectiveness of the nose, its color and hair covering, all these represent millions of genetic deals struck with ever-changing environments. Culture has come along only very recently to buffer humans from nature and to redirect nature's impact on the physical person. Obviously, culture surrounds a Madison Avenue executive more snugly than a !Kung bushman or a Mongolian nomad. But all three are still animals in many important respects. Biology still shapes much of who they are, despite the effects of culture, as popular books on ethology by Konrad Lorenz and Desmond Morris and the more technical works of E. O. Wilson have demonstrated.[2] Even cultural psychologists and anthropologists like Jerome Bruner and Clifford Geertz acknowledge this fact.

Metaphorically speaking, humans are still "wired" to their physical environment in a variety of ways. One may speak of "hard wiring"— the physical dependence on an environment—and "soft wiring"—the perceptual orientation. "Wiring" in both cases is a crude way of speaking about a relation to the world that does not depend on symbolic representation—the stuff of language or thought. All humans, even the urban executive, exist in a physical environment that shapes their lives in profound ways. They acquire certain genes from their ancestors and are more likely to pass some than others to their offsprings. If their culture favors blue eyes, blond hair, and great height, for instance, then social success—the type that opens doors at Newport yacht clubs—will tend to be associated (through "successful" marriages) with that physical type. In the harsher realities of the northern tundra, other genes are likely to be transferred through the favoring of certain behavioral qualities that make other matches seem attractive. Humans are also linked to their physical environment through diet, climate, altitude, pollution, or geographical isolation. Modern culture minimizes the effects of some factors, such as isolation or climate, but intensifies physical exposure to others, such as pollution.

"Soft wiring" refers to the relationship with an environment that humans enter into by means of the senses. Here, too, evolution has equipped us for survival even in New York. Vision is rarely used these days to gauge the distance and the speed of a charging bull rhinoceros in relation to the distance from a stout tree. Instead, one must often gauge the distance and speed of a delivery truck in relation to the width of the street. Both calculations have to be performed quickly, and our existence as a species testifies that we have become good at doing this. But what is the relation between seeing and calculating? Does one see "passively" like a camera and then (very quickly) perform mental calculations using the raw images "in the head"? Or is calculation somehow intrinsic to the act of seeing and based on movement and exploration in the environment? These questions and the discussion they generate bear on magic directly. The view that magic is essentially a cultural fact—and I claim that it is not—aligns itself with a view of the senses as instruments of higher-level calculations. Thoughts, expectations, and cultural norms aim the senses toward a desired target and snap the shutter, as it were. But if magic truly straddles the boundary between culture and nature—my hypothesis—then the senses that are essential in magical rites are no passive instruments of the mind. Although mind has an important role to play in the system of perception and response, it is not the captain of a ship, sitting at the controls and running the show. It is just another feedback loop, or several perhaps, but not the boss.

One side of the debate goes by the name "computationalism," or the top-down theory of perception. It supports the cultural-cognitive interpretation of senses in magical rites. The second position, called ecological or bottom-up theory, lends itself to the more adventuresome position espoused here: that the biological function of the senses determines the nature of magic to a large extent.

Computationalism

David Marr was a brilliant young researcher at the MIT artificial intelligence lab when he died in his thirties. His computational theory of vision has been a rare triumph in an age of professional skepticism and reflexive rivalry.[3] Ironically, that astonishingly successful theory of vision traces back to the nineteenth century and Helmholtz's Kantian idea that the mind processes raw sensations into meaningful scenes. Marr described a threefold process of increasing abstraction or "representation," from the first chaotic scene to the final perception. The first phase, the "primal sketch," sorts out varying illuminations, reflections of surfaces, transparencies, and other light qualities into basic visual features such as edges, lines, and blobs or light and shade blocks. The primal sketch then becomes the raw material for the second computational step, the "2 1/2-D sketch," which is a further abstraction from raw sensation. Geometrical figures now emerge out of the information given in the primal sketch so that a cube is represented before one can recognize a house. The final stage, the "3-D sketch," is the most elaborately computational and resembles Helmholtz's "unconscious conclusion." Now a recognizable object emerges in the perceiver's field of vision.[4] The entire process is nearly instantaneous and takes place below the threshold of awareness. But the computational mind calls the shots by manipulating increasingly abstract symbols. Not only does mind process momentary sensations, "primitives" as Marr called them, available up to this point, but it also relies on a *frame of reference* that is more permanent and cognitive. As R. L. Gregory once remarked, we not only know what we see but see what we know.[5]

Ecology—"Naive Realism"

Like the cognitive scientists he vigorously opposed, James J. Gibson regarded his own theory of vision as a processing of information. But he believed that the sense receptors could directly obtain "stimulus invariants" that correspond to the permanent properties of the environment.[6] Constant perception, a biological necessity for all creatures relative to their subsistence environment, depends on their ability to detect these invariants by means of exploration, body movement, eye motion, and other actions. In fact, the constant movement of the perceiver in its environment, which increases the quantity and the intensity of sensations, actually helps isolate the invariants present "out there." Consequently, "instead of looking to the brain alone for an explanation of constant perception, it should be sought in the neural loops of an active perceptual system that includes the adjustments of the perceptual organs."[7] The brain is not a computer that sorts raw information. It is a biological organ that directs the body as a whole to create a complete system of input and output that will resonate to the external information. The brain controls the organs of sense and causes them to interact with the environment in such a way that perception (input) and response (output) maximize survival in a given ecology.

If, for example, an ape finds a rock it must use as a tool in order to break open a skull, on the view of Gibson that rock simply possesses properties of "grabability" and "throwability" that are directly perceived. Gibson calls these qualities "affordances": a ripe fruit, one with the right color and solidity, has the affordance of "eatability," directly perceived by an animal whose senses have evolved to pick up these invariant qualities in objects. The computationalists claim that Gibson's is an untenable position and that the ape "perceives" the stone as a tool in a representational process that relies on higher brain functions such as learning and memory. Ecologists counter that for an animal to recognize an object as something else—tool, food, enemy, obstacle—it must have an *idea* in its mind to which it compares the present object. Such "mentalism" does not belong in the natural sciences, whether one is considering the behavior of kingfishers or humans.[8]

The senses have earlier been called "soft wires." They link the perceiver to an environment, either intensely, in the case of the forest dweller, or anxiously, for the New York executive. If we accept the ecological theory of perception, the sensory scenes are formed through ongoing exploration of "real" environments. On the computational theories the external world is only light patterns or other physical-chemical sources of stimuli. The mind is essential for making sense out of whatever the senses register. Of course, unlike Kantian idealism and radical empiricism, the two positions need not be mutually exclusive in every way. Computation, for instance, can be enhanced by the movement of the perceiver in the environment. The mind can then direct the body to readjust its movements in order to see a different angle or smell from downwind. For considering magical experience as a natural event it is essential that no central cognitive mechanism create the subjective world out of sheer chaos. There is no "mind," no self that reads raw sensory input (sensations) and then forms a mental life. This is a critical point: The senses involve humans—as well as animals—in a perceptual interaction with the world *with no privileged position for the observer.* The viewer is part of the scene, not a patron up in the balcony. The certainty we feel about being separate is a cultural artifact; it does not reflect the true physiological and functional relation between humans and their environment.

THE SELF IS NO COMMANDER-IN-CHIEF

Ecological theorists like Gibson have been accused of practicing a crude behaviorism, of leaving out the mind in their descriptions of the way animals and humans interact with their environments on the perceptual level. Simple introspection shows that consciousness, emotions, intentions, and attitudes deeply shape the way we see things. But introspection and commonsense can deceive. The ecologist claims that it is too easy to exaggerate the role of consciousness in the way humans go about their business. For instance, a substantial amount of sensory information is processed without one's having any awareness at all. Peripheral vision records events that may drastically effect mood and behavior without any knowledge of the "reasons" for such changes. Subliminal sounds and sights can have similar effects, as many advertisers know. It is even possible to drive a car dozens of miles with virtually no conscious awareness.

Folk psychology, the commonsensical view of the self as the agent of our actions, insists that consciousness or some form of self-awareness—the self as a whole—be in charge. The absent-minded driver, one protests, is a self who is simply otherwise engaged, perhaps in conversation, and can perform parallel tasks "mechanically." Unfortunately, neither "commonsense" nor "folk psychology" are simple or obvious. The two terms are generally used to describe two complex psychological conceptions of the self.[9] The first, commonsense, is the subjective or naive self we encounter on introspection. It is the subject of our feelings and moods, the maker of decisions, the sufferer of consequences. It is even the proprietor of the theater screen that shows whatever the senses have recorded. The second view of the self, folk psychology, is completely different: This is the social self developed through interaction with other social selves and defined by the attributes assigned from the outside and by one's projections onto others.

The two conceptions are not only distinct; they sometimes conflict. The self-concept often develops in relation to social expectations—ask any teenager—which run counter to the perceptions and drives of the subjective self. William James called these two distinct selves the "I" and the "me." Only the first is subject to personal experience, while only the second submits to sociological analysis. Of course the distinction can be blurred in fact. People may gauge their very own internal states on the basis of external cues taken from the reaction of others. Cultural psychologists such as Jerome Bruner and David Olson claim that the basic nature of experience is shaped, in early childhood, through interaction with others.[10] Children acquire certain behaviors, including language and coherent perceptions, by interacting socially with their primary caretakers. Even later in life a child may discover she enjoyed a movie only after observing her mother's reaction to it. Other researchers, including Jean Piaget, assign a greater role to biology alongside the social factors, but at any rate, the distinction between the subjective-naive view of the self and the social self is an accepted fact. The self is the product of both subjective experience and social fabrication. Taken together, the two conceptions reveal a very complex picture of the self, which psychological analysts have broken down into the experience of agency, self-reflectivity, differentiation from others, and unity.

THE NARRATOR VERSUS THE DIFFUSE SELF

Adults in our society experience themselves as narrators of their own life story. They possess a unity of consciousness, which according to psychologists begins to emerge around the age of three and which is often described (by men) as a "little man in the head" (a homunculus) who organizes the flow of events into a coherent chronology and places himself at the spatial center of these events. In the technical debates on the nature of consciousness, some neurophysiologists claim that this narrator is the essential feature of consciousness itself:

Personally, I would say that the only aspects of our mental life that deserve singling out as peculiarly conscious are those associated with the narrator, with *self-conscious* and *subconscious* and *stream of consciousness;* the others are important in their own right, likely essential foundations, but not to be confused with "the real thing." [11]

As already noted, however, this narrator or homunculus is a tangle of social and subjective facts. It is not a universal human phenomenon, a simple biological fact. Members of other societies, such as traditional India or Japan, neither define nor experience themselves as individual and separate selves. In fact, even in this country, as F. Scott Fiztgerald once pointed out, the rich are "different" from the rest of us. In India the "person" is an open and diffuse experience possessing no rigid boundaries that separate inside from outside and no single plot line (see Chapter 14 for more on this point). The unitary self—the person—in sum, is above all a cultural fact celebrated in New England but absent in India. Neurologists find it inconceivable that the brain possesses a single center, a command post, that reads everything else that goes on. Neurological explanation denies the existence of one neural "map" that reads all the other "maps," coordinates signals between them, and issues responses to other parts of the body.

According to both William Calvin and Gerald Edelman, coherent experience and the sense of plot must be based on a selectional neurological process rather than on a "reading" or "learning" of sensory input by a "little man in the head"—a self. Calvin calls this process the "Darwin Machine" and Edelman, "neural Darwinism." [12] This selectional process is a product of evolutionary pressures, and it is essential for planning ahead and creating meaningful scenes, or scenarios, that form the elementary mental tools for survival in primitive ecologies.

In fact, however, a careful phenomenological (experiential) inspection of the apparently coherent narrative stream reveals that it is not so coherent after all. It is complex and flexible, to say the least. Daniel Dennett, the philosopher of the mind, proposes a "multiple draft" picture of the mind to replace the old "Cartesian theatre," as he calls it. As a multitude of external effects travel through the senses and the nervous system to the brain, there is no one place in there, a pool or storeroom, where they are deposited and sorted into a coherent story. Instead, a

multitrack process occurs over hundreds of milliseconds, during which time various additions incorporations, emendations, and overwritings of content can occur, in various orders. These yield, over the course of time, something rather like a narrative stream or sequence, which can be thought of as subject to continual editing by many processes distributed around in the brain, and continuing indefinitely into the future. Contents arise, get revised, contribute to the interpretation of other contents or to the modulation of behavior (verbal and otherwise), and in the process leave their traces in memory, which then eventually decay or get incorporated into or overwritten by later contents, wholly or in part.[13]

There is no single narrative line inscribed once and for all, but endlessly revised editions that owe their ever-changing qualities to memory, language, culture, and, of course, biology. The unitary plot is a cultivated illusion in which culture often conspires with neurological factors. Even the raw experience of sequence, of time and causality, on close examination is flexible and reversible. Time is elastic; it varies speed and direction in often unpredictable sequences. Take away clocks, including natural ones, and the arrow of time collapses immediately.

We do not perceive or remember the mental narrative directly in its full complexity. Instead, we learn to impose a structure on a complex experience. The result of such learning is the conception of a unitary self. In other words, social and cultural views of the self deeply constrain a variety of ways by which internal and external events could be experienced. Learning and socialization galvanize a diffuse experience into a coherent tale. They do this by selecting certain aspects of the complex stream of consciousness and inhibiting others. But such inhibitions can easily be weakened in a variety of chemical and ritual ways: Drugs and alchohol may deeply alter the way the self is experienced, especially in its relation to the "external world." Mental illness, trauma to the head, or even grief may also shatter the socially constructed self. In his grief King Lear became a stranger to his surroundings and lost his own self:

> Me thinks I should know you, and know this man;
> Yet I am doubtful; for I am mainly ignorant
> What place this is; and all the skill I have
> Remembers not these garments.

Even lesser causes, such as ritual chanting, drumming, and dancing, produce similar effects, as we can seen in this inimitable account from Huxley:

> In one of its innumerable forms music is a powerful drug, partly stimulant and partly narcotic, but wholly alterative. No man, however

highly civilized, can listen for very long to African drumming, or Indian chanting, or Welsh hymn-singing, and retain intact his critical and self-conscious personality. It would be interesting to take a group of the most eminent philosophers from the best universities, shut them up in a hot room with Moroccan dervishes or Haitian voodooists, and measure, with a stop watch, the strength of their psychological resistance to the effects of rhythmic sound. Would the Logical Positivists be able to hold out longer than the Subjective Idealists? Would the Marxists prove tougher than the Thomists or the Vedantists? What a fascinating, what a fruitful field for experiment! Meanwhile all we can safely predict is that, if exposed long enough to the tom-toms and the singing, every one of our philosophers would end by capering and howling with the savages.[14]

It is no coincidence that magical rituals make so much use of chanting, singing, drumming, and dancing. These are meant not to produce ecstatic states or mystical visions but to weaken the intellectual and cultural constraints on the spontaneous experience of events. They dissolve the self.[15] And though many of the cultures in which magic is practiced—certainly India—do not emphasize a unitary individual self, other inhibitions still exist. For instance, the daily routine of assigned tasks and roles in village India limits experience as rigidly as our ideology of the individual self. Unbending prohibitions against free social interaction, reinforced by rules of pollution and purification, constrain the freedom of perception in India. The magician and his clients must therefore operate in a separate zone—a liminal space—in which psychic and social inhibitions dissolve. The ritual singing of devotional songs, accompanied by drumming, mesmerizes the patients out of their social identity.

MAGICAL THINKING

The removal of social and conceptual inhibitions—the diffusion of the self—is essential for the magical experience.[16] But it is not enough. Magic is also a matter of thinking, and generations of scholars since James Frazer have agreed, to a remarkable extent, that magical thinking differs from rational or scientific thought. But some exceptions apply.

There are two general ways of describing the nature of human thought in relation to the world: engaged and disengaged. Neurologists and cognitive psychologists speak of implicit and explicit learning, which correspond, from a neurological point of view, to engaged and disengaged thinking, respectively.[17] *Implicit* learning is associative and conditioned. It calls for repetition and does not require consciousness or an aware self. This is how a rat learns to cross a maze and humans learn to drive. *Explicit* learning is based on memory, language, and conscious awareness. It requires a self. Cultural knowledge—geography, morality, parlor games—is based on explicit learning, which begins to accelerate in the third and the fourth years of the child's life. Jean Piaget argued repeatedly that reasoning, which is essential for explicit learning, develops as the child learns to disassociate herself from her world, including even her own body. Awareness of a separate self and causal thinking emerge in tandem, he claimed.[18] Western ideology applauds individuation and separateness and crowns the mind that attains objective logic. Our culture insists that the mind not passively observe the world but look for objective relations and apply the logic of cause and effect to define "true" relations. Physical events are never related unless they are either cause or effect or, at the very least, correlated as two effects of a more basic—and as yet undiscovered—cause. These are cultural values perpetuated by explicit learning, not "objective" facts. For example, a man observes a bird alight off a tree, followed immediately—so it seems—by the blast of a gun. As a reasonable observer, he assumes, almost spontaneously, that the gunshot was the cause of the bird's flight. The information of the senses, that the bird actually took off first, is discarded in favor of a hypothesis generated by what the observer knows: The sound takes time to travel, and the bird heard the gun more quickly than the observer. Of course, if the second event was not a gun blast but a dog bark, or better yet the whispering of a spell, the relationship would become more problematic. For the Western observer it would cease to exist altogether as a relationship and be reduced to a coincidence: two unrelated events happening at approximately the same time and place. The reasoning of the aloof observer seeks to describe the objective "God's-eye-view" of the world as he removes himself from the scene.[19]

In contrast to the disengaged observer of an objective world stands the observer-participant. This relationship has frequently been assigned to the "primitive mentality." Lucien Levy-Bruhl has called it "participation," a quasi-mystical immersion in the flow of events.[20] Georges Batailles has also romantically characterized this as the origin of the religious experience.[21] In fact, however the engaged observer is a natural product of evolution and not as far-removed from the modern person as many assume. This observer sees the bird take off, then hears the blast. (His senses are keener than ours because he does not spend as much time in libraries and in cars.) He does not now think, as Frazer and Tylor told us, that the bird caused the blast because the two events were proximate in time. In fact he does not think about the two events at all, unless they are important enough for his survival to engage his interest. When that happens the bird and the loud sound become related as parts of a larger scene in which he too is a participant. It is a *meaningful* scene, not the causal relation among discrete events, that engages the observer who will use magic on occasion.

Surprisingly, the gap between the disengaged observer and the participant-observer, or between the primitive and the modern observer, is not vast. Recent studies in cognitive linguistics and philosophy have demonstrated that our language—and therefore our thinking—still retain many elements of participation. These are called "schemas" or "experiential schemas," among similar names. Terms of relationship such as "falling *in* love" and "getting *out* of a marriage," for instance, are based on metaphors of space and containment. Such metaphors, and many others like them, originate in a direct and preconceptual relation to physical environments but serve as the basic cognitive tools for highly abstract ideas.

George Lakoff observes that "the studies of basic-level categorization suggest that our experience is preconceptually structured at that level. We have general capacities for dealing with part-whole structure in real world objects via gestalt perception, motor movement, and the formation of rich mental images. These impose a preconceptual structure on our experience." [22] In other words, the world that we experience, as reflected in our language, is not a direct photographing of an objective reality that is then spliced into objective or "classical" linguistic categories. Instead, the world is largely fashioned by subjective elements—our sensory interactions with environments. Lakoff's thesis—applied to English, which is hardly a primitive language—is dramatic: The assumption that thought is truly objective is a great exaggeration. The basic tools of thought and language, the semantics and the syntax of categories, remain grounded in the "primitive" interaction patterns with a physical world. Lakoff calls the basic experiential patterns "kinesthetic image schemas," and with Mark Johnson he has listed some of the major ones, such as the container schema, the part-whole schema, the link, the source-path-goal, and others that are connected with simple experiences in space. [23] The most abstract and complex ideas can be traced to embodied experience by means of these schemas.

A central and profoundly ambiguous idea that dominates the way we think of relations is causality. By means of causality, thinking agents give themselves a sufficient mental distance from the world to create the illusion of a God's-eye view. Causality rests on these basic assumptions:

1. There is an agent that does something.
2. There is a "patient" (not necessarily human) that undergoes change to a new state.
3. These two properties form a single event: They overlap in time and space, or the agent and the patient come into contact.
4. The action of the agent preceeds the change in the patient.
5. The agent transfers energy to the patient.

Lakoff lists other properties of causality, all originating in embodied experience rather than belonging to the intrinsic structure of the world or a built-in mental syntax.[24]

Here is the main point of this entire discussion: The perceiver who is directly involved with the perceived relationships (as actor in a scene) is more likely to conceptualize them in terms of *relations* (link schemas) and *meaning* (interaction or participation with context) than as examples of objective or theoretical causality. According to cognitive semantics, relational thinking and meaning, the kind that typifies magical minds, is not different *in principle* from causal thinking, but the thinker-perceiver has simply not stepped back from the context. The essential distinction is not the ability or failure to reason. It is a psychological and ecological attitude toward events.

Several outstanding scholars have described magical thinking, from Tylor and Frazer to Levy-Bruhl, Levi-Strauss, and Tambiah. "Similarity" and "contact" have undoubtedly been the cornerstones of their theories of magical thought. A neighbor's tuft of hair or some dirt from her tracks in the mud relate magically (through contact) to the person herself. Cognitive semantics suggests that this type of thinking does not necessarily reveal a failure to reason scientifically but suggests perhaps more of a refusal. Magic in modern times has not persisted or disappeared in response to scientific rationality, although there seems to be an indirect relation between modernization—a product of scientific progress—and the decline of magic. In his epic study of magic in England, Keith Thomas has demonstrated that magic did not retreat in the face of advancing technology, medicine, or other material improvements in life.[25] He claimed that a basic shift in worldview accounted for the demise of magic. Current evidence amply bears this out. A recent book review in the *Times Literary Supplement* by Penelope Shuttle and Peter Redgrave states: "It has been estimated that during Lammas (August

Eve), within the confines of London alone, more than 80,000 people are engaged in the witchcraft or ritual magic celebrating Lammas." [26] It is patently absurd to think that such a vast number of participants have never heard of Newton or antibiotics. The changing worldview associated with the decline of magic, as we shall shortly see, is the product of psychological and ecological developments, not the emergence of scientific rationality.

THE FOUR CONDITIONS OF MAGIC

A magical event, including both experience and ritual performance, can exist anywhere and anytime, as long as the following four conditions are met:

1. Perception is heightened and relatively unconstrained by other factors. It is a perception of relationships, not merely of discrete objects.
2. The self or single-track narrator is relatively weak. A diffuse self is correlated with the strength of perception, especially of relations.
3. Thinking is explicitly embodied or relational on the single scale that includes both scientific rationality and magical thought. The thinker is not separated from the perceived relations in the environment.
4. A "program" or ritual must exist: Because the reason for magic is a break or a disharmony in the web of relations, prescribed methods for repair are followed, though not as rigidly as many scholars have believed.

These are the four basic conditions of magic—the components of the magical experience. Everything else is incidental, including ideas of supernatural causality, visions of sacred realities, superstitions, and beliefs in general. A magical event can be experienced, and ritually repeated, even in a major university hospital if the four conditions converge—though this is not likely.

The absence of these basic conditions explains the gradual disappearance of magical practice in the modern world. As noted earlier, the main factors associated with modernization and scientific rationality, which are responsible for the demise of magic, are not intellectual at all. They include urbanization and the distancing from a natural ecology, where the senses still serve a direct functional role. Tools of technology, such as television and radio, which tragically curtail the role of the senses as means of interacting with the world, are far more powerful than "reason." The prepackaged information of television, the two-dimensional electronic coding of images, even those beautiful landscapes on "discovery" shows, gradually dull the senses as instruments of exploration. And the near-exclusive emphasis on verbal information has all but eliminated our ability to read the world symbolically, to recognize the meaning of natural events as participants. Other modern obstacles to the magical experience include the glorification of the egocentric worldview—the rewarding of individualism over interaction and relationality. Magic depends on a free flow of information across loosely bounded spaces and among participants in larger scenes. A hunter will feel related to a prey whose meat he eats and skin he wears if he does not feel himself set apart within his social universe either (for more on this point see Chapter 12).

These and similar ecological factors affect the persistence of magic far more profoundly than Newton's mechanics or Pasteur's microbiology. Recall that the Trobrianders, who build and launch excellent, "scientifically designed" boats, still inaugurate them with a magical rite. Ecological and psychological factors have a direct bearing on the magical experience, of which thinking is only one component. Magic continues to be practiced where the senses are still refined, still a part of a human-ecological system. It is practiced, also, where the interactional self exists more in relation to others than as an autonomous agent set off against everyone else. In cultures that have not cultivated a derision for rituals as abject shells of meaningless repetition, magic thrives as the ritual restoration of the participant's place in a web of relations. In fact, ritual—the fourth condition of the magical mind—is the most easily overlooked.

Magical events usually contain a strong ritual dimension. Unfortunately, the concept of ritual is as complex and as ambiguous as magic itself. Understood in a strict manner, ritual consists of carefully staged repetitions of symbolic actions, which consciously point to some end. In the case of religious rituals, for instance, such symbols aim at transcendent, divine, or sacred realities. Rituals are emotionally powerful, even transforming, because participants submerge their entire persons in the flow of ritual events.

Magical rituals also use patterns of bodily gestures and manipulations, which are deeply moving. But magic is not identical with the ritual process itself, any more than science is identical with the game of obtaining grants. Consequently, while both religion and magic share certain ritual features, the similarity is only formal. For instance, the body in religious rituals is a public body: Participants enter states of embodiment that are meaningful in a communal sense above and beyond the simple sensory event. The bride becomes a wife by means of a religious ritual. Magical rituals, in contrast, are more likely to be private and intimate. Their power derives not from the social definition of a gesture but from the sensations and perceptions it evokes. For this reason, magicians, at least in Banaras, countenance variation and freedom, at least up to a point. While the religious ritual expresses public truths by means of the body, the magical procedure is the grammar of sense experience. It is repeated, but only in the service of experiential events of a practical nature.

Unfortunately, this is an elusive distinction, because magical rituals are not subject to complete freedom. The magical ritual skirts the fine line between personal experience (and need) and public symbols. The player in the VR machine may have been nearly overwhelmed by the concreteness of immediate events. He seemed to have discarded his sense of self, memory, and culture. But this lasted only for a short while. After that initial "immersion," his concern for the child at risk or his interest in an animal perceived as "prey" betrayed the cultural bias that framed his outlook. Cultural psychologists claim he could not have coherent experiences and memories of any kind without the "framing" and "affect regulation" imposed by the cultural context in which he operates.[27] The magical perception of stunningly concrete and interrelated events is thus only one moment in a complex experience that contains both natural and cultural elements. It would be a mistake, however, to differentiate the cultural and the natural as two mutually irreconcilable principles. The ritual of magic, the programming of the magical event according to symbolic actions, serves both ends of this experiential spectrum. With music and rhythm, the magical rite mesmerizes the participant into a natural way of perceiving events. At the same time, by using the logic of analogy and contact and by prescribing areas of magical concern—the parameters of magical behavior—the ritual also situates experience in relation to culture. The ritual ensures that magic does not become nature's way of usurping culture but acts as a natural affirmation of existing cultural values.

This dual role of the magical rite shows up in its language. The language of magic is twofold because it moves the participants along the spectrum of natural and cultural action: It is affective and moving on the one hand and a symbolic speech act on the other, a request, a promise, or a warning. In terms made famous by John Austin, the ritual language of magic consists of "illocutionary speech acts," or words that perform practical tasks.[28] In contrast, Frits Staal insists—for those who will listen—that the language of ritual is sound without meaning, like the chirping of birds (see chapter 15). Ritual language, on this theory, is affective in a biological, almost genetic, sense. In any case, rituals seldom use language without the manipulation of objects that place the words in a concrete situation. The objects used in the rite must be perceived interactionally or relationally, just as the magical world is perceived in the VR machine. Magical objects are touched, heard, seen, smelled, or eaten in order to be effective. The abstract idea of an occult force is never enough. The rite can resurrect the original experience of wholeness only by using ritual means that directly involve the senses of participants. It does this by simulating the world it is trying to heal and by removing the obstacles to participation in it. At the same time, the ritual objects are manipulated as symbols or icons. They become the elements of a language that furthers the cultural ends of the rite. This language is not true or false—as science claims to be—by reference of "objective" facts; it is felicitous or infelicitous, depending on how well it transforms the awareness of the ritual participants.

Magical experience—the perception of interrelatedness evoked by magical rites—seems to transcend the distinction between culture and nature, mind and body. In fact, however, it simply makes such distinctions irrelevant. This does not mean that we can ask of magic, How does it achieve supernatural goals? or, What is supernatural causality? Magical practice is not aimed primarily at an objective world where causes mysteriously produce effects. It seeks, instead, to recapture an original experience that is natural and extraordinary at the same time. Gregory Bateson was very close to the mark on this point when he remarked: "The real point of things like rain dances is to affirm a total complex of relationship between oneself and the weather and the supernatural powers that control oneself and the weather and so on."[29] The experience as well as the ritual are almost always couched in specific cultural terms, as we shall see later on for Banaras. But behind the distinct cultural forms is a universal and natural event.

NOTES

1. Quoted from Wayland Hand, *Magical Medicine* (Berkeley: University of California Press, 1980), p. 82

2. Konrad Lorenz, *Studies in Animal and Human Behavior* (Cambridge, Mass.: Harvard University Press, 1970–71); Desmond Morris, *The Naked Ape: A Zoologist's Study of the Human Animal* (New York: McGraw-Hill, 1967);

Edward O. Wilson, *On Human Nature* (Cambridge, Mass.: Harvard University Press, 1978).

3. David Marr, *Vision: A Computational Investigation into the Human Representation and Processing of Visual Information.* (San Francisco: W. H. Freeman, 1982).

4. Ibid., p. 91.

5. R. L. Gregory, *The Intelligent Eye* (London: Weidenfeld & Nicholson, 1970).

6. James J. Gibson, *The Senses Considered as Perceptual Systems* (Boston: Houghton-Mifflin, 1966), p. 3; see also *The Ecological Approach to Visual Perception.* (Boston: Houghton-Mifflin, 1982), p. 377.

7. Gibson, *The Senses,* p. 5.

8. The computational and ecological positions are nicely contrasted—with a computational bias—by Howard Gardner, *The Mind's New Science: A History of the Cognitive Revolution* (New York: Basic Books, 1985).

9. Jerome Bruner, *Actual Minds,* p. 28.

10. David Olson, ed., *The Social Foundations of Language and Thought* (New York: Norton, 1980).

11. William H. Calvin, *The Cerebral Symphony: Seashore Reflections on the Structure of Consciousness* (New York: Bantam Books, 1990), pp. 83–84.

12. Calvin, *Cerebral Symphony,* p. 270; Gerald M. Edelman, *Bright Air, Brilliant Fire: On the Matter of the Mind* (New York: Basic Books, 1992), pp. 81 ff.

13. Daniel C. Dennett, *Consciousness Explained* (Boston: Little, Brown, 1991), p. 135.

14. Aldous Huxley, *The Devils of Loudon* (London: Chatto & Windus, 1970), p. 322.

15. Rodney Needham, "Percussion and Transition," *Man,* (n.s.) vol. 2 (1967), pp. 606–14.

16. The most comprehensive recent work on the psychology of magic is Leonard Zusne and Warren H. Jones, *Anomalistic Psychology: A Study of Magical Thinking* (Hillsdale, N.J.: Erlbaum, 1989).

17. Eric R. Kandel and Robert D. Hawkings, "The Biological Basis of Learning and Individuality," in *Mind and Brain: Readings from Scientific American Magazine* (New York: W. H. Freeman, 1993), pp. 30–43.

18. See for instance, *The Essential Piaget* (New York: Basic Books, 1977), pp. 198–214, which includes a paper entitled "The First Year of Life of the Child" read before the British Psychological Society in 1927.

19. Mark Johnson, *The Body in the Mind: The Bodily Basis of Meaning, Imagination, and Reason* (Chicago: University of Chicago Press, 1987); George Lakoff, *Women, Fire, and Dangerous Things: What Categories Reveal about the Mind* (Chicago: University of Chicago Press, 1987).

20. Lucien Levy-Bruhl, *Primitive Mentality* (Oxford: Clarendon Press, 1923).

21. Georges Batailles, *Theory of Religion* (New York: Zone Books, 1989).

22. Lakoff, *Women, Fire,* pp. 269–70.

23. George Lakoff and Mark Johnson, *Metaphors We Live By* (Chicago: University of Chicago Press, 1980).

24. Lakoff, *Women, Fire,* pp. 54–55.

25. Keith Thomas, *Religion and the Decline of Magic* (New York: Scriber's, 1971); Thomas sustains a monumental Malinowskian study of 700 pages, which he wipes out with a Weberian stroke in the last fifty.

26. "Wicca's World," *Times Literary Supplement,* 6 January 1995, p. 24.

27. Bruner, pp. 56–57.

28. John L. Austin, *Philosophical Papers* (New York: Oxford University Press, 1979).

29. *Sacred Unity: Further Steps to an Ecology of Mind* (New York: Cornelia & Michael Bessie, 1991), pp. 70–71; other researchers think magic does try to do what it claims, and, in fairness, this position must be taken seriously: "Of course the Dinka hope that their rites will suspend the natural course of events . . . but instrumental efficacy is not the only kind of efficacy to be derived from this symbolic action." Mary Douglas, *Purity and Danger: An Analysis of the Concepts of Pollution and Taboo* (Routledge & Kegan Paul, 1979), p. 84.

◪ NINE ◩

Philosophical Issues

BODY AND MIND

Do we consider certain phenomena magical because we think of the body and the mind as distinct and separate? It seems possible that the extraordinary power attributed to so-called magical healing would be accepted as commonplace if we were to let go of the centuries-old habit of separating body and mind. Many writers on new medicine, "quantum healing" and the rest, feel that this distinction should be dropped. But if we abandon dualism, what is the alternative: materialism? mentalism? Some New Age scientists, Fritjof Capra for instance, have fallen back on an idealism that uses the idiom of contemporary physics but owes more to the ancient mystical philosophies of Asia.[1] Unfortunately, it is far easier to lament the sorrows of Cartesian dualism than to devise an alternative that will satisfy our commonsense and ideals. This chapter considers the various philosophical possibilities and their effects on how one can understand magic.

◪ ◪ ◪

Case 9.1

Bedouin Infertility Cure

An infertile woman finds a knowledgeable healer, usually an old woman, and the two take the following supplies: a water pot, firewood, blanket and towels, bread, coffee, and cooking utensils. At night, on the darkest among the last nights of the final month of summer, the two secretly set out on an indirect path to a "holy *dayek.*" [A *dayek* is a vertical crevice that resembles, from a distance, a colorful strip running down the mountainsides of southern Sinai.] The women boil the water under the *dayek* and prepare a meal. . . . After eating, the healer reads a few verses from the Fatha section of the Qur'an, and if she knows the prayers, she prays.

Following these ritual acts the infertile woman sits naked on a stone, while the healer places into the pot a fist-size stone which had been heated in the ambers of the cooking fire. The hot stone will cause the water to burble and hiss and infuses it with power. When the water becomes lukewarm the healer pours it over the client and recites: "May the water cure thanks to the prayer and thanks to God." The infertile woman then rubs her own body with this water, and dries herself with the towel. The two women gather the implements and return to their tents. They take the shortest possible path, each going separately. The patient must not stray from her path, she cannot greet anyone on the road or strike up a conversation. At the tent her husband will be waiting for her.[2]

As the woman sits naked on a rock in the dark desert and washes her body with lukewarm water, she becomes aware that hidden strings she had not felt before now connect her to this place. She perceives herself as and feels related to the desert, and she may become healed through this feeling of relatedness.[3] Her consciousness is somehow altered when she recognizes a connection linking the healer's words and actions, the desert spot, and her own womb. For her, and for her healer, this is the magic: It is a special kind of consciousness. But what does this mean? What is this expansive consciousness, and how is it related to her naked body undergoing the rite?

Imagine the woman sitting on the ground watching the fire burn while her meal is being prepared. She watches the flames leap and observes the healer cook, but she is not thinking about much. At least two things take place, or perhaps we could say that there are two ways to describe what is happening to her. First, her peripheral nerve endings are stimulated by the optical, thermal, and sonar energy produced by the fire. This energy travels afferently, in the form of biochemical signals, up the neural paths to the brain, where the signals are processed into perceptions. The woman, of course, has absolutely no awareness of this neurophysiological process, although without it she could not perceive the fire.

But we can also describe another process. As she sits staring at the fire, the woman sees it changing shape and color from one instant to the next. She feels its soothing warmth on her skin and enjoys its lulling rhythmic crackle. Everything around her has qualities that she experiences as subjective states: The fire's golden glow is reassuring, while the darkness behind it is vaguely threatening. The woman's feelings are always about something: She hopes for a child, fears the dark, admires the old woman. She experiences her emotions by means of the objects at which they are directed, as though these objects had an independent life in her mind.

We are describing two distinct events here—a biological-physiological process accessible to quantitative measurement and a subjective "mental" experience that can be described only in mental terms such as qualities and intentionalities. Both apply to the same person (or organism) at the same time under the same conditions. Which is "real"? If both are real, how are they related? Does the chemistry or the physics of the two bodies (fire and patient) cause the wonderfully nuanced and fleeting experiences of the woman? Are the two events independent? Parallel? Are they just two ways of describing the same thing in fact? Commonsense tells us that both body and mind are real, and this is precisely what makes the healing "magical": It bridges, or tries to bridge, a gap that we normally regard as insurmountable, the body-mind gap. But does it? What follows is a brief review of the philosophical positions on the dualism I have described. Some philosophers might feel that a real chasm exist between the Bedouin's consciousness and the physical event. Other philosophers maintain that the dualism is only apparent. We cannot hope to understand magical consciousness—the awareness of an interrelatedness that bridges body and mind—unless we give these questions some consideration. They are the questions that drove René Descartes (1596–1650) to formulate the problem of ontological dualism that still challenges us today.

Dualism

Descartes owed his scientific worldview to Gallilean mechanics and was committed to the idea that all phenomena can be explained in terms of mechanical and mathematical models by reference to the size, shape, and motion of bits of matter.[4] The one exception to this range of phenomena, he believed, is the mind—a radically different type of substance. While all other material substances have a spatial extension (*res extensa*), only the mind (*res cogitans*) does not extend in space and cannot be divided. All substances in space, including even the human body, can be doubted away—one can imagine them not existing. The mind cannot be doubted because the act of doubting is itself mental. The result is an absolute but troubled dualism between the mind—for Descartes, essentially thinking—and the rest of the physical world. In the case of the Bedouin woman, she sees and feels the changing qualities of the fire, while at the same time a separate physical process takes place involving her body and its environment. The first is a private subjective experience; the second is its public aspect.

Few philosophers today—notable exceptions are John Eccles, Karl Popper, and Tom Nagel—subscribe to Cartesian dualism.[5] Though it accurately describes our common experience, the theory is bunk. Gilbert Ryle has ridiculed it as the "dogma of the Ghost in the Machine."[6] Even superficial reflection, he claims, rebels against Cartesianism, with its implied "little man in the head" (homunculus) and its mysterious mind-body interactions.

Assume that there really are two distinct kinds of substance, body and mind, as you consider the powers of Rakesh. Rakesh is a young expert in Hathayoga who lives near Tulsidas Ghāt in Banaras. He is capable, with little preparation, of stopping his pulse, as measured at the neck. Though I was unable to determine whether his heartbeat also stopped, the pulse disappears for up to three minutes. Rakesh then restores his pulse in order to avoid "unnecessary risk." If mind and body are truly separate, how could they possibly interact? If the body has its own causality and the mind cannot pull its strings, in what way could the yogi's "mind" or consciousness force the heart to stop? The view that the human organism—the pineal gland for Descartes—contains somewhere "inside" it a nonphysical component, something above and beyond neurological processes even, is not only empirically unproven and unprovable; it is logically absurd, because it involves an infinite regression. In fact, it flies in the face of ancient Indian psychology and metaphysics. The experience we have of controlling our bodies, usually at will, is itself a mental phenomenon and therefore not self-validating, either. It swiftly leads down the slope of idealistic monism on which Fritjof Capra, Deepak Chopra, and other New Age thinkers have slipped.

The most influential dualistic position in recent years is that of the people who think that the mind operates like a computer program. The idea was conceived by Hillary Putnam, who formulated the brilliantly original thesis that mental states, such as pain, are functional states of the whole organism.[7] Early in his career, Putnam realized that mental states—thoughts, feelings, pain—are "compositionally plastic": There is no one physical state that makes any given mental state possible. Many "beings"—organisms or even machines—can be in the same mental state without any corresponding physical identity. What determines the similar cognitive states of a machine, such as a computer, and a human being is the way they they are organized to function as systems. This function is the "program" of the system at any given point of time, and it is independent of the "hard wiring" of the physical state.

Putnam has more recently given up his esoterically named "Turing machine-functionalism" because of his belief that mental states are much more plastic, fuzzy, or indeterminate than any machine could *in principle* reproduce. Perhaps he tired of listening to the devastating critique that the body—brain included—is not a machine but a biological organism that belongs to larger biological contexts. However, the view that the mind is a complex computerlike process still dominates the cognitive sciences, especially the field of artificial intelligence. The dualistic implications of so-called cognitive functionalism can be encapsulated in the following two principles:

1. The cognitive process takes place by means of manipulating "mental representations," a technical term designating abstract, nonconscious units of information, such as David Marr's geometrical shapes.
2. The representational level is independent of the biological and the cultural contexts in which cognition takes place. It is intrinsic to the functional relations within the information-processing system.[8]

The epistemological and psychological implications for cultural analysis are devastating. On the cognitive model the Bedouin woman who participates in magical events is simply engaged in a process that uses ritual and its implements as a syntax. The rite has no "meaning," properly speaking. The physical and affective properties of rocks and water are useful only as abstract representations—symbols—of an objective world. The "magical" quality of the rite derives from the fact that some of its steps are implicit and therefore mysterious. There is no point of speaking about a magical consciousness.

Monism

The obvious alternative to Cartesian dualism is a monistic view of the world. This view comes in two diametrically opposed modes: idealism and materialism. The first dominates ancient Indian metaphysics and asserts, when boiled down to a phrase, that the material world is an illusion.[9] Contemporary readers who do not practice mystical discipline will find this position either forbiddingly obscure or hopelessly tepid. It can contribute to the analysis of magic only by denying the evidence of our senses. The second mode, materialistic monism, is far more vibrant and pervasive in modern philosophical debates. Boiled down to its own bottom line, materialism states that the subjective experience we have of possessing conscious minds is an illusion or an "epiphenomenon" of the nervous system at work. The yogi who "controls" his heart is not an autonomous mind that extends its reach out to a body. He is a complex of neural circuits extended to link up with other circuits that monitor heart functions. The experience of control is perhaps a feedback feature of such a system.

Other versions of materialistic monism vie for the most thorough denial of the mental fact. The earliest of several roughly contemporary schools was behaviorism, which, led by John B. Watson, rebelled against one of Descartes's central and most influential ideas, introspection. Introspection was the methodological upshot of the doctrine that we possess a consciousness that is private, internal, and easily accessible to our own view. Behaviorism became a self-conscious revolt against the idea of mental and intentional control of action, in a word, of consciousness. It replaced consciousness with strictly conditioned environmental learning, which Watson discovered in Ivan Pavlov's experiments and which B. F. Skinner saw to its nadir.[10]

Behaviorism's methods of denying the existence of subjective mental states seem crude in contrast with the contemporary materialistic philosophy of the mind. Crude enough, in fact, to have inspired such jokes as this one about the behaviorist who asks her partner after a bout of lovemaking, "It was great for you; how was it for me?" In contrast with behaviorists, "identity theorists," "eliminative materialists," and other exotic birds make their living by either explaining subjective experience in material terms (J. J. C. Smart) or eliminating the subjective qualities ("qualia") of mental life altogether (D. Dennett). Some have sought halfway positions between the extremes (R. Jackendoff).[11]

Assume that the young Bedouin woman becomes pregnant. In her mind the experience she has undergone in the night—the sense of being connected to the desert environment and to the ritual process—has been efficacious. A philosophically naive researcher might then claim that the Bedouin's sense of magic results from her impression that something traveled across the boundary of mind and matter. The woman would be wrong, of course, but that is the source of magic for her, namely, the failure to distinguish two orders of being. In order to be taken seriously, such a magical belief would then have to be interpreted symbolically, as standing for another, nonoccult reality. Such a premise is false from the outset, the materialist would argue, even if the Bedouin did possess the conceptual tools attributed to her. Eliminate such confusing distinctions as *body* and *mind* from the anthropological toolbag, and the researcher would have to look for magic elsewhere. The occult nature of the naked woman's experience may perhaps make sense in terms that come from a different area of philosophy. This is an extremely useful insight that forces us to take materialism as seriously as dualism. Of course, the two approaches will finally lead to an impasse that only phenomenology and system theory can circumvent.

Nature and Culture

The magical experience, as we have seen, depends on both the awareness of interconnectedness and an actual intimacy with an ecology. I have talked, metaphorically of course, of a link based on hard and soft wiring. Considered on the level of the individual, this theory runs into philosophical obstacles of body and mind. But since magic is also a cultural fact, and is often a corporate affair, the question of body and mind extends to nature and culture. In the theater of human action, body and mind occupy different stages: nature and culture. The body, with its bones, sinews, and nerve cells, is our very own slice of nature, while the mind, with its holy books and Hollywood and everything else you can dream of, all that is culture. What does King Lear owe to DNA? What does the rain have to do with our personal or collective ambitions?

Evans-Pritchard recorded the following case: A man feels threatened by an oncoming rainstorm because he is building a hut. He knows that if anyone should beat the skin of a dig-dig, the rain would certainly come down, so he hides the skin to prevent this from happening.[12] Here is the problem: Beating the skin of a dig-dig is a cultural act, acquired and stored through oral tradition. Rain is a matter of humidity, temperature, barometric pressure, and saturation points. What does one have to do with the other? Is it a leap of faith only primitives are willing to take, or does some connection exist outside the mind of the drummer?

Some of those who practice magic claim extravagantly that the connection is real, objective. Above every other cultural boast—technological, artistic, or sacred—magic jostles our commonsensical views about human interaction with natural forces and about causality. Of course, one may simply follow Frazer's example and call magicians ignorant fools. Or, like Levi-Strauss, one may respect the claims of magic but only in the form of hidden signs. But the "magical experience" of Chapter 8 claims that a magical bond does in fact exist and that it somehow straddles distinctions of culture and nature. The audacity of such a thesis can perhaps be mitigated by looking at nature and culture in anthropological thought.

Beating the dig-dig to stop rain and lighting fires to bring it on are cultural acts that imply certain views *about* nature. But what is the ultimate basis of cultural action? Are humans distinct in principle from other animals, say higher primates, that also perform rituals? Is culture, which seems to separate us from other animals, autonomous from biological forces, or is it the expression of underlying material causes? These are important questions for a theory that argues that magic depends on a resonance between humans and nature.

Periodically since T. H. Huxley and Darwin took on the Cambridge Anglican establishment, the conflict between culture and nature has flared up and spread much heat in academic circles for a few years. There have been the nature-versus-nurture debates, those over eugenics and superorganicism and race and intelligence, to name a few. The latest conflagration was occasioned by Edward O. Wilson's simplistic and sensational *Sociobiology* (1975).[13] Wilson did not stray far from Darwin when he argued that "[b]y comparing man with other primate species, it might be possible to identify basic primate traits that lie beneath the surface and help to determine the configuration of man's higher social behavior."[14] Unlike the ethological writings of Konrad Lorenz, Robert Ardrey, and Desmond Morris, Wilson's theories never truly reached a nonacademic audience. But the academy, cultural anthropologists mostly, made up for this omission by swiftly and vocally excoriating Wilson's thorough materialism.

Marshall Sahlins responded almost immediately with *The Use and Abuse of Biology,* which elegantly and swiftly dispatched biological determinism.[15] "Vulgar" sociobiology, as Sahlins called it, makes a very easy target. It posits a necessary link between human needs and emotions and social relations. Since evolution operates on the individual brain and on genetic structure, the effects of biology on social life takes place through the mediation of the individual organism. This is where Sahlins drove his stake: "The idea of a fixed correspondence between innate human dispositions and human social forms constitutes a weak link, a rupture in fact, in the chain of sociobiological reasoning."[16] If, for instance, we take warfare as an expression of biological forces such as aggression and territoriality, simple reflection shows that this cannot apply to individuals who fight in wars. Men may fight out of a sense of honor, guilt, self-esteem, or even love and compassion. Therefore, Sahlins argued, "agression does not regulate social conflict, but social conflict does regulate agression."[17] In more general terms, human social behavior is determined by culture, which mediates between natural necessity and the relative freedom of conduct within the symbolic domain. Sahlins, and many other critics of sociobiology, do not deny the influence of nature and material needs on culture, but they refuse to recognize a direct natural determinism over the cultural realm, which is characterized by meaning and freedom rather than by order and natural selection. In fact, if there is any determinism at all, it must operate in the opposite direction. Levi-Strauss confessed, "I believe that there is always a mediator between *praxis* and practice, namely the conceptual scheme by the operation of which matter and form, neither with any independent existence, are realized as entities which are both empirical and intelligible."[18]

A. L. Kroeber, the leading American culturalist at midcentury, defined the cultural perspective as "superorganic" because it is separated from biological factors by an "unbridgeable chasm."[19] Because magic is a cultural activity that relies on language and rituals, cultural anthropologists like Stanley Tambiah own a larger toolbox for analyzing the phenomena of magic. And even when wrong, their theories make more interesting reading. Biological determinism, in contrast, adds little to the discussion of specific forms of magic, though it has enjoyed the appeal of simplicity. Even Malinowski did not escape the power of Darwin and the impact of evolutionary thought.

🔊 🔊 🔊

Case 9.2

Canoe Magic

After the prow-boards are put in, and before the next bit of technical work is done, another magical rite has to be performed. The body of the canoe, now bright with the three-coloured boards, is pushed into the water. A handful of leaves, of a shrub called *bobi'u*, is charmed by the owner or by the builder, and the body of the canoe [*waga*] is washed in sea water with the leaves. All the men participate in the washing, and this rite is intended to make the canoe fast, by removing the traces of any evil influence, which might still have remained, in spite of the previous magic, performed on the *waga*. After the *waga* has been rubbed and washed, it is pulled ashore again and placed on the skid logs.[20]

Reading Malinowski's account of Trobriand boat building, one cannot fail to be impressed with the technical proficiency of Trobriand craftsmen. The process, excluding the accompanying magical rites, is complex in itself: cutting the right tree, trimming it into a workable log, hollowing out the log, preparing boards, planks, poles, and sticks, piecing together the planks and prowboards, trimming them if necessary for a proper fit, piercing and lashing the outrigger, caulking and painting the canoe, fabricating the sail, putting in the ribs and planks, trimming and lashing them, attaching the float, and binding the outrigger frame and the platform. The Trobrianders do all this expertly and effectively. So why do they need magic? Biological determinism has to dredge up some psychological complex, which is perpetuated by genetic and environmental causes. It suggests, for instance, that the ritual may soothe an instinctive fear of land mammals going to sea, a fear that technology could never completely dispel, in the same way that ritual mating regulates aggression in some species. Magic, like other forms of culture, is adaptive behavior, though what makes it uniquely magical remains unclear.

In between biological materialism and cultural superorganicism are numerous shades of determinism. Cultural ecology, associated with Julian Steward, Andrew Vayda, and others, seeks out the environmental causes of cultural facts. In its stronger forms of environmental determinism, as articulated for instance by Leslie White or Marvin Harris, stark caloric calculations may be used to explain even such cultural values as the sanctity of the cow in India.[21] By "explain" I mean to say that these scholars *reduce* the religious ideas of the sacred to the calculation of calories or other considerations.[22] Such theories can be elegant and simple, but far from simplistic: Only a great effort of the imagination can link a sanctified act such as circumcision to a natural force like the climate of the tropical rain forest.[23] In principle, however, the more materialist and deterministic a theory, the duller its instruments for analyzing the specific forms of magical conduct. None of the authors cited as representing these deterministic approaches to culture are particularly interested in magic. Like religion, myth, and other cultural forms, magic is simply the visible evidence of deep material needs and implicit solutions. Magic is a way of expressing and performing ideas that are useful but unconscious. What makes magic unique, however, remains unclear.

NOTES

1. Fritjof Capra, *The Turning Point: Science, Society and the Rising Culture* (London: Flamingo, 1983).

2. Shabtai Levi (Shabo), *The Bedouines in Sinai Desert* (Tel Aviv: Schocken, 1987), pp. 254–5.

3. As in many cases of "infertility," there is no evidence that anything is wrong with her reproductive system. The rite, in turn, is not conceived as a "medical" procedure.

4. On Descartes, see Chapter 5.

5. Karl R. Popper and John C. Eccles, *The Self and Its Brain* (Berlin: Springer-Verlag, 1981).

6. Gilbert Ryle, *The Concept of Mind* (New York: Barnes and Noble, 1949).

7. Hillary Putnam, "The Mental Life of Some Machines," in *Intentionality, Minds, and Perception,* ed. H. Castaneda (Detroit: Wayne State University Press, 1967).

8. Howard Gardner, *The Mind's New Science: A History of the Cognitive Revolution* (New York: Basic Books, 1985), p. 6.

9. A vast traditional literature can be recommended on this topic. Readers may begin with the *Upaniṣads,* and move on to Śaṅkara's later commentaries, such as the *Brahmasūtras.*

10. John B. Watson, *Behaviorism* (New York: People's Institute, 1925); B. F. Skinner, *About Behaviorism* (New York: Knopf, 1974).

11. John J. C. Smart, *Philosophy and Scientific Realism* (New York: Humanities Press, 1963); Daniel C. Dennett, *Consciousness Explained* (Boston: Little, Brown, 1991), Ray Jackendoff, *Consciousness and the Computational Mind.* (Cambridge, Mass.: MIT Press, 1987).

12. *Witchcraft and Divination,* p. 473.

13. Edward O. Wilson, *Sociobiology: The New Synthesis* (Cambridge, Mass.: Belknap Press, 1975).

14. Ibid., p. 558.

15. Marshall Sahlins, *The Use and Abuse of Biology* (Ann Arbor: Univer-

sity of Michigan Press, 1977); sociobiology improved in response to its critics and became more sophisticated. Wilson later cooperated with Charles J. Lumsden on *Genes, Mind, and Culture: The Coevolutionary Process* (Cambridge, Mass.: Harvard University Press, 1981). See also Carl N. Degler, *In Search of Human Nature: The Decline and Revival of Darwinism in American Social Thought* (New York: Oxford University Press, 1991).

16. Sahlins, *The Use and Abuse*, p. 7.

17. Ibid., p. 9.

18. Claude Levi-Strauss, *The Savage Mind* (Chicago: University of Chicago Press, 1966).

19. *The Nature of Culture*. (Chicago: University of Chicago Press, 1952) p. 51.

20. Bronislaw Malinowski, *Coral Gardens and Their Magic* (New York: Dover, 1978), p. 135.

21. Marvin Harris, *Cows, Pigs, Wars, and Witches: The Riddle of Culture* (New York: Random House, 1974); See also *Cultural Materialism: The Struggle for A Science of Culture*. (New York: Random House, 1979).

22. "Reduction" is a necessary tool of all scientific explanation. But some restrictions apply to the ways it can be used. See, for instance, Richard Dawkins, *The Blind Watchmaker* (New York: Norton, 1987), p. 13.

23. John Whiting, "Effects of Climate on Certain Cultural Practices," in *Environment and Cultural Behavior: Ecological Studies in Cultural Anthropology*, ed. A.P. Vayda (Garden City, N.Y.: Natural History Press, 1969), pp. 416–55.

Systems, Mind, and Magic

Magical claims invariably run into insurmountable conceptual problems. Cartesian rationalism and positivistic empiricism have gored magic on the twin horns of mind and body. As a result, magical assertions are either rejected or reduced to symbolic speech. But there are alternatives: Phenomenology and system theory are the foundations of the "magical experience" described in Chapter 8. They offer a way out of the body/mind impasse. However, it is not an easy way.

SIMPLE SYSTEMS

One night in Banaras I took over the rowing of a boat whose oarsman was drunk. I had a long way to go upstream and plenty of time to reflect on feedback loops and systems, as mine were constantly failing. The boat was quite big, and the rower's station was improbably located at the front rather than the usual middle. There was a floor beam to brace my feet while I pulled the oars, but the seat was only a loose board placed on the front deck, in which a hole had been cut for the legs. The oars were long and uncomfortably thick tree branches, with flat planks nailed to the ends. Each oar was held in position by means of a rope looped to the side of the boat. The oars repeatedly slid up and down within the loops. I was rowing against the stream, which shifted direction and velocity every few minutes. As it was late at night, the river was submerged in darkness, and only distant lights at the rear of the boat could be seen clearly.

These, then, were the main features of the system in which I found myself participating, and, fortunately, my only witness was curled up on the floor of the boat. Of course, there was my body, too: Being right-handed, I expected that I would have to compensate by letting up a bit on the right oar every now and then. But I must have been overcompensating, because the boat was turning away from shore—to my right, or port—too often, and I discovered that a special effort was required to keep the boat straight. I suspected then that it had to do with the direction of the stream, which was curving in that area. But when the problem continued past the bend, I searched for another reason, until I discovered that my seat was not parallel to the floor beam. For some reason I had pushed harder with my right leg at the beginning of the journey, and now the left side of my body had a more effective brace and, therefore, more power.

Even after quickly correcting this imbalance, I still had to wrestle with other demons. The oars kept slipping through the loops, and the boat then veered in the direction of the oar that had slipped farther into the water. At some point I became conscious of a pulled muscle on the right side of my back; later my left knee became sore. All of these nags, and others too numerous or trivial to mention—though they hardly seemed so at the time—required full attention the entire way. The system, if you call the river, boat, and rower a system, never found a peaceful mode of existence: It was in constant flux and imbalance. The slow speed of the boat and the relatively leisurely reaction time I was allowed made most of my corrections deliberate. A few responses, though, such as shifting my hands on the oars at the sting of a new blister, happened spontaneously.

This unremarkable event provides a simple example of a system that involves both physical and mental elements. Surprisingly, in the consciousness of the participant it is often hard to distinguish where the physical ends and the mental begins. A master oarsman feels no conflict with the boat or the river—it is a natural context, an extension of his body and mind. How many of us have not flinched at the sight of a rock our car was about to straddle, as though our very bottoms would scrape? The system is actually a network of information that travels in every direction: from river to boat, from boat to my body to my mind and then back in the form of responses.

This network contains numerous "feedback loops," circular information channels consisting of signal-response-balance (stasis or homeostasis). Some loops pertain primarily to the boat in its environment; the design and the weight of the hull, for instance, respond to the direction and the intensity of the stream and tend to some form of self-correction, like the vaning of a wind-gauge or the self-correction of a plane when the control stick is dropped in the middle of a turn. Other loops take in wider aspects of the system and channel more information. The lights moving to my right gave me a visual cue that the boat was turning to port; the sudden pressure on the left oar indicated that it had slipped too far into the water. Feedback loops are "closed" when appropriate responses are made and the system returns to some balance, however temporary. In my case, many of these loops were happening slowly enough for my responses to be conscious and deliberate. Other systems, such as the physical movement of an Olympic diver, involve information loops with no feedback. They happen too quickly and rely on highly memorized or "programmed" sequences of behavior.

MIND AS SYSTEM

Considered as a system, or the property of a system, the mind's relation to the body no longer remains confined to the Cartesian straitjacket. Systemic thinking is phenomenological: It refuses to take either body or mind as exclusively real. Instead, both are equal actors on one stage, and the name of the play is "information," or what Gregory Bateson called "difference."[1] Recall your adventure in the virtual reality machine. Your magical experience was the product—the "emergent property"— of a system that included your body, your mind, and the machine.[2] In other words, the experience was not located exclusively in the machine, the body, or the mind. It emerged out of the flow of information throughout many circuits that crossed arbitrary conceptual boundaries. In fact, magic, taken as an experience rather than as a doctrine, is the very consciousness of an overall interactional system that defies the logic of composite parts. It is the "self"-consciousness of a system.

The philosophical and anthropological underpinnings of this claim can be found in part in the systemic thinking of John Searle in philosophy, Gerald Edelman in neurology, and Roy Rappaport in anthropology.[3] Searle explains that "consciousness is a higher-level or emergent property of the brain in the utterly harmless sense of 'higher level' or 'emergent' in which solidity is a higher level or emergent property of H_2O molecules when they are, roughly speaking, rolling around on each other (water)."[4] The precise relation of mind and brain is an empirical issue, and though far from understood at this time, understanding it is only a question of improved scientific methods and measurements.

But how is this possible *in principle?* Mental phenomena seem to be separated from physical processes by means of a conceptual barrier even to those who do not necessarily subscribe to Cartesianism. If Searle is right, the problem is based on a misunderstanding of the true issue: "The fact that a feature is mental does not imply that it is not physical; the fact that a feature is physical does not imply that it is not mental."[5] Our subjective experience of the mind as a nonphysical quality, as consciousness, does not contradict its physical nature in principle if we understand the notion of emergent property and the objectivist fallacy. The concept of emergent property explains the products of systems in terms of internal causal interaction. Mind, according to Searle, is such an "emergent property" of the system of neurons in the brain: "The existence of consciousness can be explained by the causal interactions between elements of the brain at the micro level, but consciousness cannot itself be deduced or calculated from the sheer physical structure of the neurons without some additional account of the causal relations between them."[6]

The "objectivist fallacy" is responsible for our mistaken view that the body is objective while the mind is subjective and that on account of this fact the two must be distinct and separate. The subjective qualities of mental experience are no less real than the system (of neurons) that gave them birth. The fact that qualities are experienced subjectively—and not as stuff—is simply not valid grounds for saying that they belong to a different order of being.

Gerald Edelman, a Nobel Prize–winning neuroscientist, has followed Searle's philosophical guidelines in trying to explain how a mind emerges from the brain. His theory, which he calls "neuro-Darwinism," tries to bridge physiology and psychology without resorting to the "little man in the head" or any other philosophical fallacy. The interest for students of magic in Edelman's brain theories is not hard to explain. If mind is an aspect of the brain's biological features and interaction with a natural environment, and if the magical experience is a unique awareness of the mind's systemic relation to the world, then a naturalistic theory of mind is a very valuable tool to own. Unfortunately, this hardly mitigates the difficulties of trying to understand Edelman's technical theory of selectional neuro-Darwinism.

Instead of paraphrasing Edelman's theory, I will illustrate the key points by means of a simple metaphor. Imagine a vast unfenced campus lawn that spreads out between the departments and schools of a large university. Students can go in any direction on the grass, but certain conditions favor a limited number of directions, so paths emerge. A pattern of paths could be imagined as a primary repertoire of neuronal pathways, one in front of the library, another in front of the chemistry lab across the lawn, and so forth. These are the anatomical structures or neural circuits in the brain. Individual patterns merge into maps, much as the haphazard patchwork in front of the school of liberal arts contrasts with the very precise lines in front of the school of sciences and the deeper cut grooves in front of the physical education complex. The maps, or groups of patterns, are "linked" by means of paths marked by students who frequent both the liberal arts departments and the physical education complex. But these cross-campus links are not really separate paths; they are parts of other patterns that students habitually use for a variety of reasons. In other words, these connecting links are no longer anatomical but functional. No new wiring is involved.

Now think of the different departments in this university as sense modalities and think of the administration as the hippocampus, basal ganglia, and cerebellum—the parts of the brain that control sensorimotor functions in response to survival needs. What happens next is the selectional event that leads to basic perceptions: There is no one map that "reads" the others, no university department that looks at the rest from above to read the universal patchwork of patterns. Also, there is no "hardwire" blueprint; students can move on any path. But natural selection establishes some order in this potential chaos. It turns out that the lawns are covered with patches of poison oak and potholes, parts are exposed to howling winds, and here and there a snake slithers. The students (like neurons) are entirely mindless, of course, but through a kind of Darwinism only those survive, and only those paths are reinforced, that enhance the survival of the university as a whole. This results in the linking of certain departments with other departments under given conditions, and so a limited number of possible perceptions develop. The survival needs of the university encourage certain perceptions that are coordinated under recurring conditions into perceptual scenes and categories. If, for instance, students going from the gym (touch) to the chemistry lab (smell) must always reroute via the art gallery (vision) because of a snake that takes its nap on the direct route, a specific scene will emerge that might combine the shiny skin of the snake showing through the high grass, the odor of the snake's favorite place, and perhaps a tactile recollection of pain.

In sum, if the mind—a neuronal selectional system adapted to the survival of the organism in an environment—is an aspect of a biological system, its contents and experiences must owe a great deal to the physical interaction with that environment. As a result, mental experiences often resonate with ecological conditions. The foods one eats, for example, can profoundly influence one's mental state, mood, concentration, and sensory perception. Authors of works of fiction such as *Like Water for Chocolate* may regard this as magical, but hospital dietitians and ethnonutritionists do not. Climate, altitude, seasonal changes, and many other physical features of the environment work with cultural factors in shaping our mental life. In the case of magical experiences, in which cultural factors are weakened, not strengthened, the naturalistic basis of the mind must be scrutinized even more carefully.

SYSTEMS, CULTURE, AND NATURE

Magic is both individual experience and cultural fact. The systemic theories that link the human mind to its natural context also illuminate the public and the functional aspects of magic. This can be seen in the work of Gregory Bateson and Roy Rappaport, among others. Rappaport traces his thinking to to general systems theory and defines a system as a "collection of specified variables in which a change in the value or state of any one will result in a change in the value or state of at least one of the others" without regard to the nature of the components.[7] These variables may be derived from cultural, biological, or inorganic phenomena; the systemic nature of the relationship is independent of such considerations.

The first feature of this nondeterministic cultural ecology is its systemic quality. The second feature is its cybernetic, or self-regulating, nature: "A regulating mechanism, control mechanism or homeostat is one that maintains the values of one or more of the variables included in a system within a range or ranges that defines the continued existence of the system."[8] In a closed ecological system, population size, for instance, will vary with other elements such as overgrazing or frequency of occurrence of the the sickle cell gene. If the population size becomes too small, reproduction cannot be sustained; if it rises too quickly, natural resources become scarce and overexploited, resulting in hunger and disease. This is a *natural* control mechanism of the system.

Cultural actions such as ritual slaying of pigs serve as a different type of control mechanism within the ecological system. Among the Maring whom Rappaport studied, pig populations must remain minimal if the returns from cultivating them are not to start diminishing rapidly. A well-controlled population of pigs is highly beneficial for the domestic life of Maring: Pigs keep the residential areas free of garbage and human feces, speed up the development of secondary growth by rooting among trees, and eliminate competition from relatively well-established trees by feeding on seedlings and tubers around them. If the pig population grows too large, however, the Maring must expend energy to keep them fed, thereby depriving themselves of needed resources.[9] So the Maring ritual cycle regulates the number of pigs, just as it controls other variables in the ecosystem, including human population density, warfare, amount of land in production, women's labor, and length of fallow. The function of ritual, then, is not to symbolize natural and economic forces but to coordinate participation in ecosystems:

> Religious rituals and the supernatural orders toward which they are directed cannot be assumed a-priori to be mere epiphenomena. Ritual may, and doubtless frequently does, do nothing more than validate and intensify the relationships which bind the social unit to its environment. But the interpretation of such presumably sapiens-specific phenomena as religious ritual within a framework which will also accommodate the behavior of other species shows, I think, that religious rituals may do much more than symbolize, validate and intensify relationships. Indeed, it would not be improper to refer to the Tsembaga and other entities with which they share their territory as a "ritually regulated ecosystem," and the Tsembaga and their human neighbors as a "ritually regulated population."[10]

Members in such ecosystems are not necessarily aware of the systemic effects of their actions, nor are they able accurately to measure calories, protein levels, and other units of information that are critical to the regulation of the system. What, then, is the conscious and explicit information that passes through the "circuits" of the cybernetic (self-regulating) system? How is this information picked up by humans and controlled in rituals?

According to Rappaport, rituals summarize in relatively simplified forms the quantitative information concerning such variables in a subsystem as the level of pig populations and translate this information into the simplest form of qualitative information. The simplest type of qualitative information is binary: yes-no—yes, the *rumbim* must be uprooted; no, the women must not garden. This simple control mechanism not only translates complex and fluctuating quantitative information to simple decisions; it also integrates numerous subsystems into a manageable single system in which the entire ecology can be regulated.

ℑ ℑ ℑ

Case 10.1

Rice Field Magic

One Perath account tells how the magician has a wood-knife stuck into the earth and can tell from the incision whether cultivation will prosper or not. He covers the hole with a coconut-shell full of rice-paste and fences it with sticks and brushwood. Next he cuts down a little undergrowth round the spot. A day or two later felling is begun. If the ceremonies were omitted, the earth-spirit would send fever, snake-bites, accidents from breaking branches or from premature fire.[11]

System theorists claim that sacred rituals are themselves an element in the regulation of the ecological environment. The symbolic information they transmit forms a loop in the general flow of information across different elements of the ecology. The stabbing of the field conveys information that is meaningful, in simple terms, to the magician, who understands his limited region of the overall ecology. His ritual actions and pronouncements therefore have an effect on the overall system, though he is conscious of only a small aspect. His actions and their consequences are perceived as magical precisely because only a small fraction of the entire system in which his actions take place is perceived. Douglas Hofstadter, in an altogether different context, put the matter succinctly: "Phenomena perceived to be magical are always the outcome of complex patterns of *non*magical activities taking place at a level below perception."[12] A ritual act is magical, on the ecological view, when it effectively transmits relevant ecological information in symbolic form but without an awareness of the overall system. The necessity of the Malaysian rite for avoiding snakebites and other dangers—its magical potency—expresses the interlinking of elements in a global system in which human actions have far-reaching, but not completely visible, implications. It is a cultural way of expressing the fact that the system extends across all boundaries, natural as well as human.

Notes

1. *Sacred Unity: Further Steps to an Ecology of Mind* (New York: Cornelia & Michael Bessie, 1991), p. 165.

2. For more on the notion of "emergence," see R. L. Gregory, "Emergence and Reduction in Explanations," in *The Oxford Companion to the Mind*, ed. R. L. Grerory (Oxford: Oxford University Press, 1989), pp. 217–8.

3. John R. Searle, *The Rediscovery of the Mind* (Cambridge, Mass.: MIT Press, 1992); Gerald M. Edelman, *Bright Air, Brilliant Fire: On the Matter of the Mind* (New York: Basic Books, 1992); Roy Rappaport, "Ritual, Sanctity, and Cybernetics," in *American Anthropologist* 73 (1971): 59–76, and *Ecology, Meaning, and Religion* (Richmond, Calif.: North Atlantic Books, 1979).

4. Searle, *The Rediscovery of Mind*, p. 14.

5. Ibid., pp. 14–15.

6. Ibid., p. 112.

7. Rappaport, "Ritual, Sanctity," p. 59.

8. Ibid.

9. Rappaport, *Ecology, Meaning*, p. 32; see also Anthony Leeds and Andrew P. Vayda, eds., *Man, Culture, and Animals: The Role of Animals in Human Ecological Adjustments* (Washington, D.C.: American Association for the Advancement of Science, 1965).

10. Rappaport, *Ecology Meaning*, p. 41.

11. Richard Winstedt, *The Malay Magician* (London: Routledge & Kegan Paul, 1961), pp. 43–4.

12. *Metamagical Themas: Questing for the Essence of Mind and Pattern* (London: Penguin Books, 1987), p. 174.

PART THREE

Magic in Banaras

❧ ELEVEN ❧

The Insider's View

❧ ❧ ❧

Case 11.1

The Exorcism of Rajakumari

Near the middle of November 1993, a small group of Swedish tourists was taken to the bank of the Ganges to watch an exorcism. They reached Assi Ghāṭ at 7:30 in the evening and strained in the dark to find the right spot. When they finally located their goal, the exorcism was about to begin.

Rajakumari was the twenty-year-old daughter of Bhagan, a weaver of the lowly Gaud caste, from the village of Rajatala. She had been pregnant once but had suffered a miscarriage. Now she was pregnant again and feared that her neighbor had thrown a curse on her to abort yet another child. Ram Prasad, the exorcist, laid out a wreath of marigold (*genda*) flowers in a circle about eight feet from the edge of the Ganges. Then he took three clay pots to the river. He filled one with water, the second with water to which he added wine (*dhār*) and the third with only wine. He arranged the pots between the circle and the river and informed Rajakumari that these were being offered to Mā Śaktī (Durgā). He put three lumps of camphor inside the circle and lit them. Then he proceeded onto the clove ritual, which was the main part of the exorcism.

141

Ram Prasad told the girl to spread her palms and keep them separate, then touched her head with the clove. He said, "You are the Goddess of Religion (Dharma), I will not stay here, I will not stay here, I will completely not stay here." Then he added, "I will tell you again, Mother of Religion, if she has any problem in her stomach or a headache or anything else, it will go out." (At this point he was touching her stomach with the clove.) Now, changing his voice to that of the goddess, he said, "I am finishing everything, it is completely clear (as milk of milk and water of water), you will be clear and pure like milk." Ram Prasad returned to his own voice and added that Rajakumari should have a strong appetite now and would be able to sleep well. "You will sleep like a horse," he said.

Now Ram Prasad pulled the clove away from the girl's stomach, making a guttural grunt, like the sound of something squeezing through a narrow passage. He said, "This sickness will be gone, look I am taking out the witchcraft." He added, "Calo mata, you have come completely. I have a fish, so I will put the clove inside the fish and throw it in the river, and the fish will swim like a horse." As he was repeating these words over and again in a singsong chant, Ram Prasad took the small fish his patients had brought and shoved the clove into its mouth. Then he released the fish into the river while repeating, "I will never come (again), I will never come." After the fish was gone and Ram Prasad ended the ritual, he told the girl to touch the river at the place where the pūjā (ritual offering to the deity) had been done.

At his house later, Ram Prasad performed a pūjā and chanted "It has gone completely" seven times. He offered wine to Mā Śakti and then another necklace of genda flowers. Then he put a divination rod on the floor and placed seven pieces of camphor on it and lit them. He performed a pūjā on behalf of the girl on the divination rod. Later he asked the rod whether the illness was completely out of the girl, and it indicated that it was. Mā Śaktī was present in the rod, according to Ram Prasad, and said that the illness was completely out. So he thanked the goddess. Finally he intoned, "We have done this very fast; if we made a mistake please forgive us."

The young Swedes had been told they would see an exorcism—the expulsion of a ghost or evil spirit—but they hardly knew what to expect.

Some of what they saw, such as the healer threatening the ghost to leave the body and enter the clove that he touched to the girl's stomach, and then the clove itself, loaded with the ghost, being forced down the mouth of the fish and sent off into the vast river, made sense to them in a basic way. These simple acts *looked* like the transfer of something from one place to another and its permanent expulsion. The Swedes could even understand the divination that took place after the exorcism, in which the diviner asked the divining rod simple questions: Is the ghost completely out? will the girl be well?, and the rod "responded" by turning this way or that. Most magical events are as easy as that to understand, like simple hand gestures in different countries.

But what is all the rest? The healer drew a circle marked with marigolds and placed three pots containing different items near the circle. He lit camphor sticks, used a boat nail for the divining rod, and performed a series of acts that looked suspiciously like the *pūjā* (worship) ritual the Swedes had seen earlier that day in a temple. Which is the magical act here, the simple transfer or the complex series of ritual acts? This is a question that all visitors need to ask and even scholars should consider carefully.

Freed and Freed recently published an immense study of ghosts in Northern India.[1] Their work, and similar projects in other areas of the world, draws on ethnography, medical anthropology, historical and textual analyses, psychology, and ecology to explain ghosts and exorcism. But these formidable scholarly efforts are no longer interested in one simple question that interests many lay readers: Where is the magic? Like the intimidating outer trappings of British judicial proceedings—hardly the substance of justice—magical events such as exorcism are clothed in thick layers of cultural actions and meanings that have little to do with magic. An observer who is interested in magic must learn to separate one from the other or must perhaps use the extravagant to decipher the essential.

With no discernable self-consciousness, Ram Prasad has mastered ancient techniques assembled out of half-known and mostly improvised traditions and ideas. He does not look like the pinnacle of a vast and vibrant healing tradition, but to his patients he is. A former attendant to the legendary Alain Daniélou—he displays sensuous photographs taken by the master of himself as a naked young yogi—he was close to eighty when I met him. Ram Prasad is a tiny man dressed inconspicuously, like a rickshaw driver or boatman. He seems to have compressed all his power into two huge brown eyes. They burn with with an odd paradoxical intensity, powerful and whimsical at the same time. Here, undoubtedly, is the source of his success as a healer, though the form of his rituals points elsewhere: to texts and oral traditions that a traveler would have to pause for very long in order to digest. Some of the traditions, beliefs, and social forces behind Ram Prasad's healing are summarized in this chapter in shocking abbreviation.[2]

BACKGROUND

India's diverse religious scene today reveals an extraordinary fact about its cultural history. As intellectual and religious trends arose and subsided, as foreign ideas arrived with invaders and traders, nothing was ever discarded as unworthy. India is an immense civilization with a bottomless basement full of old "stuff." Perhaps a better metaphor was coined by a professor who likened Indian cultural history to a lasagna made up of numerous layers, with the juice of each penetrating all the rest. The records of this history are more literary and mythological than historical, and much of what we know is speculative. Still, we know that these records date back to the end of the second millenium before the common era, to a time when the Aryan pastoral and warrior tribes came down from central Asia and began their conquest of the Indian subcontinent. The first cultural encounters with the indigenous populations took place immediately on the heels of military conquest and economic dealings. The pattern for later cultural encounters in Indian history was set at these earliest historic times. The Aryans brought a nomadic, patriarchal religion dominated by heroic male deities such as Indra and a complex fire ritual controlled by a class of specialists. The invaders encountered several forms of local societies, ranging from urban centers to agricultural settlements to primitive tribes. The local cults, if not entirely matriarchal, were often Earth-based and focused on sacred sites, usually attended by women serving female gods along with major male deities such as Rudra and Śiva.

The oldest text that gives some evidence of this early encounter, the *Ṛg Veda*, alludes to the militaristic qualities of the invading Aryans. They were led by Agni, the fire god, who burned down the cities and villages of his "enemies"—those who tried to slow down the southeasterly movement of the Aryans. Undoubtedly, the violent confrontation resulted in Aryan physical domination of large areas in the Gangetic plain. Many scholars believe that the enormously complex caste system owes its origins to the invasions and resulted from the integration of diverse populations. Others however, believe the system originated before the Aryans ever reached the subcontinent and had existed—at least in a triadic fashion—among the Aryans for a long time.[3]

If we compare the conquest by the Aryans of the indigenous Indian populations with other historic encounters—for instance, the Israelites in Canaan or the Muslim Arabs in North Africa—we discover a startling fact: On a cultural level, the victors did not win, and the losers hardly lost. The new civilization became an enormously complex patchwork of localized cults in which Aryan and non-Aryan elements blended in various proportions and manners. Outside the major Brahminical centers, which produced works on elaborate rituals and developed a legal and philosophical literature, the life of India's vast agricultural and tribal populations continued to focus on food, shelter, health, and the relationship between the sexes. Just as they do today, women set the tone in everyday religious activities, such as the home worship, local pilgrimages, temple activities, and vows, although the major religious occasions remained the domain of male Brahmins. The dominant gods in the pantheon after the mutual assimilation of autochthonous and invading cultures—Śiva, Viṣṇu, Kriṣṇa, Durgā, Kālī—were no longer the distant deities of the Aryan pantheon. Those older gods— Indra, Varuna, Agni—did not become mere relics but were relegated to a subsidiary role associated with specific rituals or limited social functions. Even the great Brahminical texts on dharma or the righteous life became colored with the local way of seeing things.

"Hinduism"—an imported concept coined by invading Muslims— developed into a rich tapestry of distinct cultures embodying a few central themes. Numerous cults and traditions existed side by side, permeating each other on some levels and coexisting peacefully or antagonistically on other levels. Little was ever relegated to the dumping grounds of old ideas and lifestyles, in the manner of Western civilizations. Two major ideas, representing extreme contrasts in world outlook, have existed at the two ends of this complex. At one end was the Aryan Brahminical religion with its Vedic sacrifical cults, which later evolved into abstract metaphysical speculations and otherworldly visions of salvation. The great German sociologist Max Weber regarded this as the normative mold of Hinduism and attributed to its "world-negating ethos" the failure of India to develop economically and technologically like the West.[4] But at the other end of the spectrum of religious life in India—and no less influential—were the various local cults, especially Tantric sects, accompanied by the worship of a multitude of local gods and goddesses for the purpose of gaining wealth and success. Here the vision of salvation was "innerworldly," emphasizing as it did health and prosperity and, on its more speculative levels, identifying the body of the worshiper with the cosmic powers he would eventually harness.

Obviously, for the Swedes who had just set foot in Banaras and for the reader who is unfamiliar with Indian history, no brief and sweeping generalization can convey the rich historic layering behind Ram Prasad's actions. Ram Prasad himself has reflected in only a very cursory way on the history and philosphy of Hinduism. He has little patience and less time for intellectual and speculative pursuits. His clients know even less, and though most of them talk about the goddess and about Tantra, they do so in the same way they talk about a distant relative and the functioning of a rickshaw motor. Still, on a given conscious level, the *pūjā* ritual Ram Prasad performs means something to the participants and observers. If we are to separate the magical event from the ritual context or identify the magical moment within the ritual act, we must understand a few basic facts about the *pūjā* and about Tantrism, even if this takes us slightly beyond the conscious awareness of the participants.

THE PUJĀ

Ram Prasad's healing procedure, which varies from patient to patient, takes on the form of a simple *pūjā* at several junctures.[5] In the case of Rajakumari, the young woman who had miscarried, three *pūjās* punctuated the evening: once at the river and twice later back at home. What exactly is a *pūjā*, and why does Ram Prasad practice it so often?

The meaning of the term *pūjā* is unclear, but we know that the rite has existed for a very long time. While the priests of the royal courts practiced the vedic ritual sacrifices (*yajña*), lesser priests and householders worshiped their gods in the home or in small temples, at nearby shrines such as rivers or sacred trees, or at work places. When unabridged, the rite can be quite elaborate and, for newcomers, difficult to decipher. But if you think of the *pūjā* worship as the hospitality extended by a householder to his honored guest, the ritual actions begin to make sense.

The rite usually begins with an invitation for the god or goddess to join the ceremony, and a "seat" is prepared. The god is then properly greeted. Like any other honored guest in ancient times, the god has his feet washed and is offered water for washing up and for drinking. Embodied in the form of his icon, a god is often actually bathed in order to cool down, though this is rarely done in the home, where the image is usually only a picture, as is the case with Ram Prasad's Durgā. Following the bath the god is clothed and perfumed, then garlanded—in Banaras, usually with marigolds (*genda*). Incense is lit for the guest's olfactory pleasure, and, in one of the central acts, a burning lamp is waved before the image, preferably tracing the shape (in Sanskrit) of the sacred syllable *om*. Then foods are offered and placed before the image of the god, and the worshipers bow in *praṇām* before it. In the final act, the god takes leave of his hosts, who are then free to eat the remains of the food offerings (*prasād*).

Temple *pūjās* are usually more elaborate than those performed at home, and the metaphor of the guest is best replaced with that of a resident who must be awakened and attended by his servants. No catholic standard sets the minimal requirements for a *pūjā*. This would have been inconsistent with the inclusive and flexible nature of the Indian imagination. However, there are universal standards of politeness and humility before a divine presence as before any respectable figure. Shoes must be left outside, and *praṇām* bowing of the head and joining of the palms are essential. But these hardly count as orthopraxy.

Ram Prasad's home *pūjās* are rudimentary. He invites the goddess Durgā with the invocation sounded out as a simple oral request, then offers her water. He seldom fails to present her with flowers and includes them always among the items his patients are to bring. Ram Prasad lights the incense sticks and performs the *āratī* with lit camphor cubes. At the river he offers the goddess some wine, and at home he often offers betel nut leaf, though he did not on the night he treated Rajakumari. All three *pūjās* performed that November evening were meant to invite the goddess to attend the healing ritual: once at the site of the exorcism and twice at his house, including one rite where the goddess was invited to enter the instrument of divination in which she could prognosticate. All present understood these basic facts and accepted the goddess's role in the healing procedure. But what is that role? Does she heal anyone, or is she just a witness? According to our common understanding of magic, the mere appeal to a god to heal a patient is not magical. The god may or may not respond, but the actions of the magicians are then not intrinsically healing. Some "force" intrinsic to the healing procedure must operate in a direct fashion in order for the procedure to count as magical. What is this force, and, if it exists, why is the goddess invited? In order to understand this problem, we need to look briefly at the Tantric elements that pervade this ritual.

TANTRA

The term *tantra,* which literally means "loom" or doctrine in the sense of woven ideas, is as old as India's earliest recorded history.[6] In this loose and open sense it has always existed alongside the mainstream beliefs and practices of Hinduism. Over the last ten or thirteen centuries Tantra has congealed into a more cohesive body of texts and ritual practices, which in many ways are distinct from the mainstream norms of Hinduism. The word *tantra* pervades the religious life of Banaras in both senses. In the strict sense many practitioners who identify themselves with Kashmiri Śaivism or with the Aghori center at Baba Kinaram Mandir and similar institutions are Tantrists.[7] They study medieval Tantric texts and follow Tantric practices, which can be antinomian and often include polluted or forbidden substances such as wine or meat and, in rare (and carefully concealed) instances, sexuality and necromancy. In most cases, however, Tantric unorthodoxy manifests itself in social service and communalism that flies in the face of caste distinctions and other forms of social hierarchy.

To most Banarsis on the street, those who visit magicians, Tantra is as vague and pervasive as Jesus is to most Americans. They use it in order to connote mastery over complex ritual secrets that are intrisically powerful, ancient, and dangerous in the wrong hands. There is a good deal of truth in this common usage of the term; secrecy, transmission by guru, and power are essential general features of the many Tantric traditions, along with another quality many Banarsis acknowledge—worldliness. The ritual practitioner applies his skills not only or even mainly for the sake of spiritual liberation but for mundane reasons such as as desire for wealth, financial success, and even the destruction of enemies.

These are very general observations, of course, and they tell us little about Tantric practices or the way Tantrism pervades mainstream Hindu behavior. As noted, Tantra is not a single tradition or doctrine, but a general term applied to numerous sects and traditions that share several basic features:

- Unlike normative (dharma) Hinduism, which is dominated by male deities such as Śiva, Viṣṇu, Kriṣṇa, or Gaṇeśa, Tantra—especially in its Śākta forms—is dominated by a goddess. The Śākta texts describe Pārvatī as she instructs her husband śiva on the secrets of the universe. The energy or force of the goddess (*śakti*) produces, supports, and reabsorbs the cosmos in its endless cycles. *Śakti* pervades the world and inheres in the smallest and most mundane forms. It may be tapped by those who are initiated into the secrets of Tantra by a guru.

- Many Hindus study under a teacher, a guru, but the Tantra aspirant becomes initiated through the secret guidance of a guru. Some of the healers I have met in Banaras refused to identity their gurus until some trust had been built between us and they knew their anonymity would be preserved.

- At the time of initiation the disciple receives a secret mantra, and throughout his training he memorizes additonal mantras that possess specific powers. A mantra, quite simply, is a verbal formula consisting of a few letters, words, or sentences (see Chapter 15). It may be nonsensical, or just a sound. The ancient Vedas used mantras in the performance of great public rituals, but mantras have come to pervade Hindu mysticism, as well as popular practices, through the prestige of Tantra. Underlying the pervasiveness of mantras is the recognition that the divine cosmic force that creates and sustains the world manifests itself as sound or word. This became a very elaborate philosophical doctrine in Kashmiri Śaivism, but all those who use mantras recognize it on this simple yet powerful level.

- A slightly less pervasive idea, but one closely related to that of mantra, is the visual representation of mantras in *yantras* and *maṇḍalas*. Tantric meditation frequently focuses on geometric symbols of the cosmos, which correspond to basic mantras. They are the visual equivalent of the auditory pattern of mantras, or, on a loftier level, the expression of the primordial cosmic power of sound as it manifests in space. Most Hindus never use them in this capacity, of course, but on a far more rudimentary level for the power contained within their form. For instance, according to several people I have met, a scorpion bite can be treated by drawing a five-point star *yantra* on the site of the bite. Many Banarsis wear amulets (*kavac*, literally "shield") that contain a *yantra* drawn on a minute scroll. Others use *yantras* or *maṇḍalas* to represent a household god for the purpose of worship.

- The concept of *śakti*—the all pervasive feminine cosmic force—animates the bond between symbols and what they represent. This extends even more forcefully to the human body, which corresponds to the cosmos on a variety of levels. The *śakti* in the body is the breath (*prāṇa*), and the manifestation of divine power is the upward unfolding of the *kuṇḍalinī* (coiled energy) along and through the *cakras* (planes) located in the "subtle body" of the spine. The cosmic power of the goddess plays in the body by means of this movement.

- The Tantra practitioner (*sādhaka*) does not necessarily strive for a blissful escape from this world but seeks a perfection of the extraordinary powers inherent in all humans. Such perfection is called *siddhi*, and it can be harnessed for worldly goals or for the control of spirits and invisible forces toward either good or evil ends. We shall look at *siddhi* in connection with another practitioner—Ram Prasad never claimed to have acquired it. Still, his healing is based on some of the most basic features of Tantra, aside from the mere fact that he describes his work as Tantric.

Ram Prasad heals with the powers of the goddess. He works at the river bank, where he hosts the goddess or her *śakti* in his own body, though he does not become possessed like other healers. Unlike shamans, who enter states of trance in order to diagnose or cure their patients, Ram Prasad does not depart his ordinary consciousness, but he slips in and out of roles at will. When the goddess speaks through him, his voice barely changes; it becomes singsongy and slightly more intense. He then interrogates the ghost, who answers, again through Ram Prasad, but this time in a grating gutteral speech that is hard to decipher. All this is possible, Ram Prasad claims, because the *śakti* of the goddess pervades him at his request during the *pūjā*. Earlier he had offered her wine—a Tantric substance—but he did not drink it himself at any stage.

Ram Prasad kept the identity of his guru a secret and demanded that I withhold that information in this account. He usually mumbles the mantras he had been taught, or else he silently moves his lips as many Tantrics do. He engages in a practice called *phutna:* While inhaling, he mumbles or whispers the mantra, then blows that air on his patient. The power of the mantra blends with the power of his breath (*prāṇa* permeated by feminine force), and this potent air is applied to the patient, who may or may not breathe it in. Many Banaras healers use the power of *phutna* in a variety of ways. They may, for instance, blow this "mantric" air on the water contained in a bottle the patient had brought from home. The "injected" liquid is taken home and drunk as medicine.

Ram Prasad's thriving—and free—practice represents the tip of an immense culture, and the few facts described here constitute only the most obvious features of his worldview. A cultural anthropologist, ethnographer, or Indologist could take apart Ram Prasad's sessions into the most minute details, then reassemble them as an elaborate symbolic language. This has been done repeatedly and with increasing precision for South American curanderos, Asian shamans, and African sorcerers. But where exactly is the magic in all of this? Is it the Tantric esoteric knowledge with its mantras and *śakti?* Or is it the unfailing invitation extended during the *pūjā?* Is magic a specific form of cultural behavior, a cosmology and a ritual in scientific jargon? If this is the case, then the magic of Ram Prasad shares nothing with the magic of a Bedouin healer except insofar as all ritual language uses the body as its symbolic instrument.

All known acts of magic are cloaked in cultural terms. "Pure" magic, like pure consciousness, is an armchair abstraction. The reality of living magic is messy and complex. One never knows exactly what participants know and which associations tie their knowledge to other, half-remembered, facts. So the distinctions between magical and cultural fact are always blurred in practice. But perhaps this point is moot. I have already shown in Chapter 8 that magical experience has to combine perceptual events with a meaningful form of communication. Symbols embedded in the magical objects resonate between perception and understanding like the two ends of one string. We see this in Ram Prasad's idiosyncratic—yet comprehensible—perfomance. The meaningful narrative of ghost expulsion, one that most Banarsis understand intuitively as an element of their culture, must be played out in excessively concrete and sensory forms. The narrative and the sensory participation, like script and performance, are both essential for a magical resonance. In the play acted that November evening, Ram Prasad became the stage, or at least the "sound system" for all the characters. As the ghost spoke through his chortling throat, Ram Prasad was touching Rajakumari. First he touched her head, then her stomach, both times using the clove to make contact. He touched her firmly enough in the stomach to make the clove disappear. Then, as the goddess, he glowered menacingly over the crouching girl, but suddenly his voice changed into an easy singsong. As the ghost departed from the stomach into the clove, Ram Prasad provided the sound effect, using the throaty, suffocated voice of one going through a narrow passage. Then he stuffed the loaded clove into the fish, which he released into the river.

Rajakumari and her relatives were spellbound by the play. Their mental participation was absolute, equaling perhaps the experience of audiences who first saw Alfred Hitchcock's "The Birds." They all felt the hands of the healer on the body of the young woman. They heard the goddess and the ghost; they saw, then heard, the ghost squeeze out of the stomach and end up in the fish. When a boy, who happened to come along just then, bent down to pick up the fish in the shallow water, they all yelled at him to release it. Their minds—imagination, thoughts, memories—were prepared by the ritual and by what they knew about Tantra, *pūjā*, Durgā, and the rest. Lacking such knowledge while observing Ram Prasad's play, the Swedes could only reduce the magic to a pantomime of some abstract formula—expulsion. But more was happening in other places. The senses of the participants were sharpened by the dark riverbank, the lapping of the great river, the creaking of the nearby boats, the feverish play of Ram Prasad illuminated in the flickering flames of the camphor, his touch. The family was made to *participate* in the expulsion of this ghost, at this time, with their whole beings. The cultural historian who ignores this contingent pole of the resonance loses something as essential as what the Swedes missed. The symbolic narrative of magical events is animated in the consciousness of participants *only* when the senses are engaged in a special way. This is why a learned Indologist merely reading an account of this affair might deny that anything extraordinary has taken place. Take away the living participation, and what's left is a distant report of magic.

NOTES

1. Ruth S. Freed and Stanley A. Freed, *Ghosts: Life and Death in North India* (New York: American Museum of Natural History, 1993).

2. It is easier to recommend too many specialized studies of Indian cultural history than to suggest enough adequate general works. The following are a place to begin: Stanley Wolpert, *A New History of India* (New York: Oxford University Press, 1982); Lawrence A. Babb, *The Divine Hierarchy: Popular Hinduism in Central India* (New York: Columbia University Press, 1975); Diana Eck, *Darśan: Seeing the Divine Image in India* (Chambersburg, Pa.: Anima Books, 1981); Mrs. Sinclair Stevenson, *The Rites of the Twice-born* (London: Oxford University Press, 1920); Alain Daniélou, *Hindu Polytheism* (New York: Pantheon Books, 1964).

3. For a summary of theories, see Louis Dumont, *Homo Hierarchicus: An Essay on the Caste System* (Chicago: University of Chicago Press, 1970), pp. 21–32.

4. *The Religion of India* (New York: Free Press, 1967).

5. Simple introductions to *pūjā* are found in Lawrence Babb's *The Divine Hierarchy,* and in C. J. Fuller, *The Camphor Flame: Popular Hinduism and Society in India* (Princeton, N.J.: Princeton University Press, 1992).

6. Tantrism is a rapidly growing but difficult area of research within Hinduism. A brief introduction, "Tantrism," was written by Andre Padoux for *The Encyclopedia of Religion*, ed. M. Eliade (New York: Macmillan, 1987). See also N. N. Bhattacharya, *History of the Tantric Religion* (New Delhi: Manohar, 1982); Sanjukta Gupta, Dirk Jan Hoens, and Teun Goudrian, *Hindu Tantrism* (Leiden: E. J. Brill, 1979).

7. Mark S. G. Dyczkowski has written extensively on these topics. See, for instance, *The Doctrine of Vibration: An Analysis of the Doctrines and Practices of Kashmir Shaivism.* (Albany: State University of New York Press, 1987).

TWELVE

Miraculous Powers and False Advertising

☙ ☙ ☙

Case 12.1

The Magical Rings

The Banaras court is a rambling, blood-colored building inside a four-acre compound. The area is dominated by huge banyan and neem trees under which hundreds of attorneys conduct the business of law. But other businesses are also licensed—at exorbitant rates—to operate there: Dentists (fifteen rupees per false tooth), eye doctors, Ayurvedic pharmacies, astrologers (nearly as many as lawers), and magicians. Among the latter, two brothers—this was only their stage relationship—had the audience spellbound one day in January. Surrounded by a very large group of mostly male spectators, the older man "hypnotized" his younger brother, who was lying on the ground. When a trance finally descended on the convulsing body, the older brother covered him with a brown sheet and placed a magical ring on the linen between his legs. This activated the sleeper, who suddenly broke into rapid chatter. His elder brother had to cover his mouth to stop the word flow, and then he began asking the younger man questions: What is the name of this man, what is the woman wearing who is now entering the courthouse, what is the file number for this man's case, and other similar questions. The young performer got it all correct. He identified the serial number on a one-hundred-rupee note, stated a few watch brand names, warned people of their enemies, and told them how to win their disputes. He made no errors and worked very rapidly. His older brother also kept a steady stream of chatter, paraphrasing the other or arguing with him, praising the wonderful ring that had made this possible, encouraging members of the audience to participate. The information was obtained by the older brother, who would approach a member of the crowd and ask him to whisper in his ear. The prostrate brother would then, or shortly after, repeat the information. As far as I could tell, they used a brilliantly simple, yet subtle, verbal cue system to communicate the information. For instance, if a man whispered to the older brother the name of his wife, Devi, then the next three words spoken (rapidly, distractedly) were "dekho vi ye" which is an ungrammatical way of saying "look at this." Phonetically, however, it provided an easy clue for Devi. Other bits of information were conveyed by other ways, and there may have been some sharp guesses, too.

The spectators were mostly villagers or low-caste people who found themselves at the courthouse on that day. None seemed to have too much cash, and the brothers did not demand money for the "show." Indeed, it was no show at all, but a demonstration of "Tantric" power—like the vendors in county fairs touting a wonderful electric bread knife. Here it was the powerful ring. Nearly half the audience, dozens of men, shelled out ten and twenty rupees to buy an exact duplicate of the powerful ring. The magician had proved that the rings were all equally effective by periodically replacing the ring on the brown sheet covering the prostrate partner. He claimed breathlessly that a husband-wife pair of rings would ensure full mental communication—no more secrets. These sold briskly.[1]

Some may explain magic in terms of the gullibility, ignorance, or infantile neuroses of its participants. But under the right circumstances, anyone is capable of experiencing a magical event, regardless of one's sophistication and maturity. In many cultures this experience is pervasive, and nowhere is it entirely absent. Like love and depth perception, it is the product of the natural mind. But for a variety of reasons, the topic of magic has become dominated by speculation about supernatural causality and miraculous achievements and, following closely on the heels of these, mischiefmakers and scroundrels. This chapter sorts out a few of the "occultist" topics, especially in relation to Banaras.

Some magicians in Banaras boast about miraculous acts they have performed or cures they have effected. One astrologer claimed to have saved a man's life with a timely warning; another healer brought a snake-bitten woman back from the dead. The magician's need to advertise locally, matched sometimes by a desire to impress a foreign scholar, is understandable. Miraculous claims therefore accompany magical practice as a matter of course. Furthermore, as we commonly understand and define magic, it goes hand in hand with the paranormal by its very nature. Both John Middleton and *Webster's New Collegiate Dictionary* define magic as an act or belief based on supernatural causality. A magical rite is judged effective by supernatural standards—whether it can leap across the gap that separates the ordinary from the fantastic. A miracle, in contrast, is an extremely unusual event that contradicts the normal course of nature. A successful magician, consequently, is the one who can either demonstrate or effectively advertise miraculous accomplishments. The simplest reason for associating magic with miracles is not truly intrinsic to either, but it is predictable. It is simple public relations based on sound business thinking. But like all overzealous advertising, it of course carries risks.

𒀭 𒀭 𒀭

Case 12.2

The *Ojhaini* Who Could Not Revive the Dead

In a small city in the state of Bihar lives a fifty-year-old *ojhaini* named Kishor Ganj Irgutali. She has enjoyed a strong reputation, which she nurtured with exaggerated reports about her powers. This helped her business of healing assorted ailments and exorcising ghosts. One day a restive crowd assembled in front of her house and shouted for her to come out. A young boy had died three days earlier, and his family was convinced that the *ojhaini* could bring him back to life. The calls were persistent and excited, so Kishor went outside. Pressured, then threatened, by the men to revive the boy, Kishor had to admit that she could not, that she had made up some of those stories about her powers. That only made the crowd angrier, and some began accusing her of causing the boy's death. The woman now felt she had no choice and agreed to try. A large procession followed her to the cemetery to exhume the boy. As the mob closed around her, the woman bent over the dead body and fainted.

She remained lying near the boy, and no one touched her. Everyone thought she had gone into a trance with the power of her mantras as part of the magical procedure. After some time, four policemen arrived and helped Kishor to her feet. They picked up the dead boy and carried him to the station along with the stunned *ojhaini,* followed by the angry relatives. Statements were collected, and tempers were cooled down. The police accepted Kishor's story that she had claimed she could revive the boy only to save her own life. She now also insisted that she herself needed medical attention, and under police guard she was admitted to the hospital. The boy was taken back for burial, also under police supervision, because the crowd began spreading word that for some reason the police did not want the boy revived. Kishor's life will probably continue to be in danger for far longer than the police could supply her with protection.[2]

Reputations for miracle working are not always self-propelled. They are often built on rumors spun by enemies, though seldom by detractors. A powerful enemy serves the practitioner very well as a way of rationalizing failure and explaining the persistence of certain nagging problems. Once obtained, a successful reputation continues to impress those who seek magical practitioners, even in the face of simple evidence to the contrary. Kishor's enemies chose to suspect her motives rather than discount her powers, despite her own confession. A Western reader who might quickly judge this behavior as ignorant superstition should reflect on the blind faith engendered by effective advertising in the West. How often is the appeal of a particular car model, brand of pop drink, or antacid based on direct factual information? If the boy's family members believed that he could be revived, they still thought this to be an unusual possibility and were motivated by profound grief. They never thought that Kishor herself possessed the power to revive the dead but believed that she had mastered a very effective method. Mantras or spells are impersonal forces and may be effective regardless of a god's will or the charisma of a magician. This sets magic apart from the religious rituals of the temple priest or the astonishing powers of experienced yogis.

One Hatha yogi I met, Rakesh, is able to stop his pulse, drag a car with a rope tied to his hair, walk barefoot on burning coals, and perform other impressive feats. Rakesh has attained mastery over a large number of nonvoluntary bodily systems. He claims—this I have not witnessed—that he can accelerate or retard the growth of his fingernails. Still, none of his displays shatters the safe boundary between mind and matter. They merely show that the effect of the will can extend beyond our usual expectations. In contrast to such demonstrations, a few reports recorded by Alexandra David-Neel that have never been properly verified make far loftier claims on behalf of Tibetan lamas.

श्री श्री श्री

Case 12.3

Weightlessness

The student sits cross-legged on a large and thick cushion. He inhales slowly and for a long time, just as if he wanted to fill his body with air. Then, holding his breath, he jumps up with legs crossed and without using his hands and falls back on his cushion, still remaining in the same position. He repeats that exercise a number of times during each period of practice. Some lamas succeed in jumping very high that way. Some women train themselves in the same manner.

As one can easily believe, the object of this exercise is not acrobatic jumping. According to Tibetans, the bodies of those who drill themselves for years by that method become exceedingly light, nearly without weight. These men, they say, are able to sit on an ear of barley without bending its stalk or to stand on the top of a heap of grain without displacing any of it." [3]

David-Neel's report differs dramatically from Rakesh's verified performances. While Rakesh stretches the bounds of our current physiological and medical models, he never seems to violate any basic law of physics. The lamas in Neel's secondhand reports reduce their body weights beyond any value tolerated by the known laws of mass. They contradict every physical explanation we could even imagine! No independent scientific observation, as far as I know, has ever confirmed these astounding claims.

But the recorded feats of yogis are hardly trivial. Some yogis demonstrate an astonishing mastery of the mind over the body. By consciously controlling a wide range of apparently nonvoluntary functions, they realign the commonsensical boundary between mind and body. This seems miraculous, but so do the discipline and perseverance necessary for attaining such mastery. In fact, yoga is neither miraculous nor magical, though it demands that we extend the limits of natural human potential far beyond the commonplace. If, after watching some of his training, you see a yogi submerge himself under water for thirty minutes, you may regard the feat as astounding but not miraculous. If a magician, untrained in breath control, were to claim that he could duplicate this feat through the power of a secret mantra, he would be staking a claim on the miraculous. Magicians are not extraordinary athletes. They possess a method or knowledge that brings about the types of result that some clients regard as miraculous. And unlike the hapless Kishor, a few have withstood the ongoing scrutiny of clients and enjoy a widespread reputation.

How can one explain powers and results judged by so many Banarsis to be astounding? Are there natural explanations for occult claims? Unfortunately, we find no relief in simple explanations. Variations in time and space concepts, nonverbal communication, effective information sources ("spies"), and numerous additional factors must be considered. And if the miraculous can still survive our skepticism, perhaps all the facts are not yet in.

🐍 🐍 🐍

Case 12.4

Sambho Under Water

Sambho, a Banarsi boatman who likes to drink, enjoys a grand reputation that is backed up even by the Banaras police. Sambho, everyone says, can stay under water for as long as one hour. He can do this on demand, with no preparation and using a secret mantra known only to himself. This is no small claim: It matches in extravagance the best of the yogis, and those men have undergone years of rigorous training. But Sambho is the man the police summon when someone disappears and interrogation reveals his whereabouts at the bottom of a deep well or the Ganges, with a rock tied to his neck. There is a direct correlation between Sambho's heavy drinking and the police work he is given. He is simply unable to stay sober for long after diving into a deep well and tying the police rope around the waist of a decomposing body.

I spent a great deal of time rowing with Sambho and decided one day to test his powers. It was a hot day, and he gladly agreed to plunge after a small red object thrown off our boat in the middle of the Ganges. The murky water made it hard to find, so Sambho had to surface three times before coming up with it. The longest stretch under water was forty-five seconds. During our conversation later, I asked Sambho how long he thought he had stayed under and he said fifteen or twenty minutes. I asked him how wide he thought the Ganges was at that point—directly across from Assi Ghāt it is about eight hundred meters—and he said four or five kilometers. My guide, Omji, who was in the boat with us, agreed with both of Sambho's estimates. He smiled with pleasure at the boatman's success.

No Western reader would think of a forty-five-second dive as a supernatural event. Even twice as long under water is commonplace. So how is Sambho's exuberance to be explained? Unfortunately, several factors complicate any simple explanation. He lives in a culture of water-shy bathers. Accepted reasons for entering the sacred water of the Ganges for Hindus are limited to ritual purification and cleansing. Most Banarsis, including Omji, do not engage in recreational bathing—they cannot swim at all—and seldom watch the few swimmers in the river dive underwater. The Ganges, of course, is not a swimming pool but a river of death—a crossing to the Other Side. Cremated and uncremated corpses are thrown into the water for their final liberation. Sambho's reputation in such a place feeds as much on his fearlessness as on his miraculous lungs. The hyperbole surrounding him may simply reflect a complex attitude toward the river.

On another level of explanation, I observed that Sambho and Omji possess a different sense of duration (and space) than most watch-wearing, schedule-bound, urban Westerners. Duration is the subjective perception of time that all humans experience independent of the clockmaker's chronology of yesterday-today-tomorrow following each other like a row of marching soldiers.[4] It is a flexible and capricious sense of interlocking mental states, sometimes sequential, sometimes merging in varying combinations and speeds, even changing direction. Duration is influenced by factors such as environment, climate, diet, mood, age, technology, and the role of cultural ideas, such as religion and mythology, in everyday life. Most people over the age of thirty have noticed the accelerating quality of their subjective duration: Every year passes by more quickly than the previous one. Similarly, vacations, school years, and other scheduled events seem to begin at a leisurely pace, only to accelerate toward the end. Under experimental conditions, blindfolded passengers in fast-moving vehicles have experienced time as passing much more quickly than those who have traveled for the same length of time in slow-moving cars. Numerous physiological and psychological theories explain such puzzling facts with hypotheses ranging from varying metabolic rates to simple boredom. But the basic fact remains: Duration and time are different. It should not surprise us, then, that Banaras duration differs from our own and that both Omji and Sambho may have experienced forty-five seconds as we might experience a longer duration. This means, of course, that time flows much more slowly for them than it does for us. Without precise psychological testing, we cannot be sure of the exact state of affairs. It may simply be that, free of the need to wear watches, many in Banaras simply do not share our meaning of the *terms* "twenty minutes" or "forty-five seconds." In this case, the entire matter collapses on linguistic grounds.

Measurement in space also varies individually and culturally. It may be influenced by ecological factors: Forest dwellers are accustomed to vertical scales and would have problems recognizing depth cues in wide open spaces.[5] City residents judge distance on the basis of receding geometrical shapes, while farmers do not. Technologically advanced societies deprive individuals of the natural cues for measuring distance, and other factors play additional roles. Since the perception of space and time are closely related in most contexts, Sambho's exaggeration of one was perhaps bound to be reflected in the other.

This complex, though incomplete, picture serves a warning that we must be very careful in evaluating extraordinary claims made in other cultures and comparing them with measured performance. Pride in such achievements may be due to elusive factors that are only implicitly embedded in the situation. We must be sure that we compare apples with apples and that we take into account as many factors as possible.

A subtler variation in time perception grows out of the narrative structure we give to events around us. In Chapter 8 I cited the work of psychologists on the social construction of the self and of philosophers on the complex structure of the stream of consciousness. The sense of self and the narrative that constitutes our perception of a meaningful sequence of events depend, according to writers such as Dennett, on endless splicing, editing, and revising of conscious experience. Our sense of time, the nature of memory, even the perception of cause and effect are in fact grossly oversimplified by cultural ideas and by a simple economy of effort. The true picture of the stream of consciousness is more closely akin to reading Joyce than Hemingway. But we are seldom aware of simplifying raw experience into a simple narrative. If we see a bird alight from a tree, followed immediately by a gun shot, we are likely to reverse the order of events in our minds and assume that the bird was startled by the blast. This quick and intuitive process takes place repeatedly during the day, most of the time without our being aware of it. Defense lawers in criminal trials feast on the distortions that presuppositions bring into our perceptions. Magicians, like conjurers, are also aware of the distorting effects of mind over the senses and either consciously manipulate or indirectly benefit by them. This is illustrated in the following case.

ॐ ॐ ॐ

Case 12.5

A Tantric Magician Gathers Information

A prosperous-looking woman came to see the Tantric baba who works near Naya Chowk. She was wearing a light blue sari and a richly embroidered woolen shawl around her shoulders. It was clear that she was not a widow, but something was distinctly bothering her. After four or five patients had been treated, she began to describe her problem. Suddenly, in the middle of her second sentence, Babaji turned away to a man sitting on his other side. The woman had only enough time to mention some nagging health problem of recent origin. She allowed her speech to trail without embarrassment or anger, then began to listen to the other man, as did most of the other people in the room. Meanwhile, two of the earlier patients were having a loud discussion with Babaji's assistant, who was preparing remedies. The fee was too high for what they felt they were getting, and they let him know. The small room echoed noisily with three simultaneous conversations. Then, just as suddenly, Babaji turned back to the woman and scolded her for not speaking. She began where she thought she had left off, and this time, after one or two sentences, Babaji said: "I know what your problems are. You are losing money in your business and having troubles at home. Recently you moved into a house which you bought unfairly. That house was built over the ruins of an old temple. That is the source of your problems. Bring me some dirt from under the house and I will tell you what to do." None of the patients in the room seemed stunned by the precision of this information, even as the woman nodded her assent. In fact, Babaji never paused after his diagnosis and swiftly turned to another patient, and another. His work was an ongoing collage of free-flowing information fed to him in halting bits, interrupted by his constantly swerving attention. It is very difficult for anyone who is not as focused as the perfected Tantric to keep track of who said what and when this was said. The Tantric, deep in concentration after repeating his mantra two or three thousand times before the session, has no such difficulty. By the time he made his diagnosis to the middle-aged woman, he had collected enough information to assemble a reasonable diagnosis. In the narrative formed by the minds of the witnesses, the conjecture preceded the woman's account. It was a successful divination. Of course, the ruined temple could be verified, but it is unlikely that anyone would find cause to try.

It is easy to see how flexible narratives can determine the interpretation of a situation. Magicians also rely on other factors such as unverifiable accounts, nonverbal reactions expressed as the practitioner is making his diagnosis, experience, and a sharp intuition for the lives and manners of his customers. During another session, for instance, two young men entered the room, which was very crowded. Babaji took one look at them and invited them to sit at the front. They both lowered their eyes uncomfortably. Then he said, "You came to test me, didn't you? You do not have any problem, I can see this right away, but you want to check out my powers." The young man sitting nearest the Tantric smiled wildly, as though in fear. The other one began to tremble. Babaji looked around the room at the other patients, who were studying the two men in amazement. Then he smiled and told them to get up and leave, and he added, "Take the third man who is waiting for you in the alley." He had read their faces, their clothes, their gestures of respect, which were staged carelessly—or perhaps too carefully—and they were an open book to him. But to the many patients and customers sitting in the room at the time, Babaji had seen directly into them. But this is saying the same thing.

Some cases of miraculous powers or achievements are impossible to examine because they depend on secondhand sources. Entire reputations are built on this fact, and it matters little how sincere the informants are. The following is a case in point.

शी शी शी

Case 12.6

Omji's Father

When Omji was about eighteen years old, he watched his father perform one of his divination feats. A nearby family had a son who, as a teenager, contracted smallpox and became critically ill. One day he lost consciousness, and his parents, believing he had died, put him in a casket and threw it in the river. Some holy men were passing downstream and spotted the box floating by. They fished it out and found the boy, who was not quite dead. Back at the ashram the boy regained his health under the nursing of the holy men. He decided to stay and joined the ashram several years later.

One day a number of astrologers gathered in the parents' town for a festival. The parents had by now recovered from the devastation of losing their son but decided to test several of the astrologers on the whereabouts of the boy. The astrologers consulted their charts and gave vague answers—understandably, under the circumstances. Omji's father did not use an astrological chart. He had a ten-year-od girl with him, on whose palm he had drawn a complex *yantra* diagram. He asked the girl questions based on the diagram, and she gave answers, which he passed on to the parents. In such a manner he informed these people that their son was alive and living in an ashram, which he then described. A few weeks later the boy was found and rejoined his family. [6]

Sociologists and psychologists do not care whether such a story is literally true. Only occultists and researchers of psychic phenomena (PSI) would investigate the facts of such accounts and claims. Banarsis take the truthfulness of these stories for granted, as long as the moral character of the narrator and the magician matches their achievements.

But why should we be interested in apparent paranormal events? Are they unverifiable curiosities, or do they teach us something valuable about the culture in which they happen? True or false, miraculous claims are taken by many residents of Banaras without the fanfare we have come to associate with the supernatural. They are not commonplace, but they are not "super" "natural" either—merely exceptional. Here is the lesson, then: A culture that does not insistently separate the mind from the body takes such achievements as possible *in principle.* Banarsis regard both body and mind as part of a "field"—an ancient concept that resembles system thinking. Without a Descartes in their intellectual baggage, Banarsis find no conceptual obstacle blocking the flow of information from body to mind and back or from both to the environment. Of course, the laws of physics, as we know them, are not suspended in India. But intuition, imagination, and empathy often extend far beyond the limits we have imposed on them in the West.

Conscious Deception

Some magicians engage in conscious fraud. They may practice conjurer tricks, collect information from third sources, or simply lie. The Tantric wholesaler at Hariścandra Ghāṭ does all three, according to the circumstances. One afternoon a couple arrived to treat the husband, who was suffering from headaches and sleeplessness. The woman spoke for her husband while he sat next to her pretending to be elsewhere. Prasad, the Tantric, noticed this, of course, and confronted the man about his skepticism. The man responded defensively: "You're just a man; why should I expect you to help me?" Prasad answered: "Yes, I am just a man, but with the power of the goddess I can do anything. Here, look at this." He produced a piece of rope about fifteen inches long and cut it in half. Then, directly in front of the couple he slid the rope through the palm of his hand, and it was whole again. They were impressed; the woman in fact was stunned.

The rope trick is an elementary conjurer's device, and Prasad did not perform it very well.[7] The short piece he had cut slipped out of his hand and fell in his lap, but the couple failed to spot this. I asked Prasad later why he uses *jādū* (sleight of hand) on his patients, and he did not deny it. He said he sometimes needs to build up faith in the power of the goddess to convince patients that they can heal. He does not take money for these services (though modest gifts are accepted), and nothing about his person suggests either wealth or immodesty. His deception is less about self-aggrandizement or profit than enhancing trust. It is a case of manipulaing the mind of the patient to remove mental barriers. This goal may be contrasted with many notorious cases of fraud in the West—for profit.

The most successful recent claim for the control of paranormal powers, one that swayed notable scientists (David Bohm, too, alas), was made by the magnificent trickster Uri Geller. Geller was a young Israeli conjurer who honed a number of standard routines but boasted that he was truly psychic. He was able to bend spoons, keys, and other metal objects, apparently without touching them. He could also project his own thoughts onto others, copy drawings he had not seen, drive cars while blindfolded, and perform other feats.[8] Geller came to the United States in 1972, having been exposed by Israeli scientists as a fraud. He was invited to the Stanford Research Institute (SRI) by Hal Puthoff and Russel Targ, who were studying paranormal phenomena there. In his autobiography, published a few years later, Geller professed fear of the "cold" and "threatening" laboratory, but he still succeeded in spinning his web around the two researchers. Describing one of the experiments, Geller feigned astonishment at the inexplicable power he possessed: "When they asked me to concentrate on a magnetometer, which tells how strong a magnetic field is, I was as surprised as anyone when the needle moved sharply without my having touched the instrument at all.

I concentrated very hard, though, to do it. They told me this was scientifically impossible, but I was able to do it every time they asked. They said my concentration was apparently able to produce a magnetic field that would register on the instrument."[9] The scientists were enormously impressed, and in their imagination the philosophical barriers between body and mind came tumbling down.[10] They recorded the experiments—the larger percent of which failed, incidentally—for future showing.

From the start of his American career, Geller was closely followed by James Randi. Randi was a successful conjurer with an unusual hobby: tracking down and investigating claims to paranormal powers. His trained conjurer's eye and unfailing skepticism allowed him to uncover Geller's game quickly. He managed to obtain a copy of the SRI film and, by his own account, nearly fell off his chair with laughter as he watched the "psychic" duping the scientists: "Geller is shown waving his hands about over a simple compass. We are solemnly assured that his hands have been carefully examined with a probe to be sure he has no magnets concealed. Nonetheless, the compass needle deflects! But it moves, not in rhythm with his hand movements, but in time with his *head,* and only when his head approaches the device! Open wide, Uri. What's this magnet doing in your mouth?"[11]

Randi's book was the definitive exposure of the young Israeli magician who claimed to be the real thing. All of Geller's "powers" were explained and convincingly duplicated by this conjurer whose starting position was a profound skepticism about any paranormal phenomena. Why did Geller cross the line between stage magic and psychic claims? The answer is simple: money. The wealth bestowed on a successful performer of miracles far exceeds the earnings of a competent conjurer. Geller's notoriety, spread by a few easily conned scientists, rewarded him with great wealth. But why do intelligent adults and millions around the world accept such exceptional boasts? Incidentally, Randi and other conjurers state that in their experience, better-educated and highly intelligent adults are easier to fool than simpletons. This may be due to the fact that they see with their mind's eye more habitually. They are easily conned by Geller's misdirections and verbal deceptions, which lay the ground for the quick sleight of hand.

Fraud is a familiar topic in the anthropological literature on magic and shamanism. Among the most interesting cases is the one retold by Levi-Strauss from Franz Boas about a young shaman in the Pacific Northwest.

🔊 🔊 🔊

Case 12.7

The Fraudulent Shaman

Quesalid (for this was the name he received when he became a sorcerer) did not believe in the power of the sorcerers—or, more accurately, shamans. . . . Driven by curiosity about their tricks and by the desire to expose them, he began to associate with the shamans until one of them offered to make him a member of their group. Quesalid did not wait to be asked twice, and his narrative recounts the details of his first lessons, a curious mixture of pantomime, prestidigitation, and empirical knowledge, including the art of simulating fainting and nervous fits, the learning of sacred songs, the technique for inducing vomiting, rather precise notions of auscultation and obstetrics, and the use of "dreamers," that is, spies who listen to private conversations and secretly convey to the shaman bits of information concerning the origins and symptoms of the ills suffered by different people. Above all he learned the ars magna of one of the shamanistic schools of the Northwest Coast: The shaman hides a little tuft of down in a corner of his mouth, and he throws it up, covered with blood, at the proper moment—after having bitten his tongue or made his gums bleed—and solemnly presents it to his patient and the onlookers as the pathological foreign body extracted as a result of his sucking and manipulations.[12]

At the end of Levi-Strauss's account, Quesalid came to recognize that, despite the fraudulent nature of shamanic healing, it is still magical and effective. And so he continued to practice his healing. This ending may reflect the French scholar's conviction that, from the shaman's point of view, magical power is identified with effectiveness, which does not depend on honesty or even purity of intention. Magical acts, Levi-Strauss argued, are human acts that "present the same necessity to those performing them as the sequence of natural causes, in which the agent believes himself simply to be inserting supplementary links through his rites."[13] The precision and the believability of the "fraud" manifest the natural laws that makes such rites magical. A well-executed sleight of hand is magical. Of course, Levi-Strauss's interpretation must be taken in the wider context of his understanding of nature and culture.

Most practitioners of magic in Banaras make no claims whatsoever in their own behalf. They merely possess the tools to help people who come to them for help. The terms for "supernatural" and "paranormal" do not even exist in the Hindi they use. The most that one may say in touting their abilities is that they possess "power" (*śakti*), and this too is due to the power of a god, a goddess, or a mantra.[14] Although such a power may become manifest through achievements a Westerner would term paranormal, Indians are equally impressed by other manifestations of this power. For instance, a healer who manifests the power of a mantra or goddess through his love of patients—regardless of caste, status, or appearance—is equally impressive in their eyes. We shall see later how the Kajjal Baba enjoys an astounding reputation for healing with love, with the force of an empathy extended to all who come for cure. Perhaps we should conclude by setting aside our obsessive interest with the paranormal and appreciate the near-miraculous effectiveness of empathy to initiate a process of self-healing.

If one regards magic as Frazer did, it must usually be judged as false. If magic is a rite or a belief that, with the help of supernatural causality, one can control forces of nature and spirits, then the investigation of paranormal phenomena bodes ill for believers. But when the focus of research shifts to the "magical consciousness"—to the experience of magical interrelatedness—then the question of miracles becomes irrelevant. The effectiveness of a magical rite is measured not by objective standards of success but by the quality of the experience engendered. This is an extraordinary experience, to be sure, but it is altogether natural.

NOTES

1. A detailed and entertaining study of street magicians in India is Lee Siegel's *Net of Magic: Wonder and Deceptions in India* (Chicago: University of Chicago Press, 1991).

2. "Dayanon ka Desh," 10 January 1994.

3. Alexandra David-Neel, *Magic and Mystery in Tibet* (New York: C. Kendall, 1932), p. 150.

4. The topic of duration or the experience of time in India is discussed in Ariel Glucklich, *The Sense of Adharma*, Chapter 2 (New York: Oxford University Press, 1994). Since its publication I have also found Akos Ostor, *Vessels of Time: An Essay on Temporal Change and Social Transformation* (Delhi: Oxford

University Press, 1993). A virtual encyclopedia of essays on time and duration was edited by J. T. Fraser, *The Voices of Time* (Amherst: University of Massachussets Press, 1981).

5. Jan Deregowski, "Illusion and Culture," in *Illusion in Nature and Art,* ed. R. L. Gregory and E. H. Gambrich (New York: Scribner's, 1973), pp. 161–92.

6. O. P. Sharma is the source of this narrative.

7. Sleight of hand has elevated mediocre yogis to stunning fame. In 1993 the Sai Baba was caught on video playing a common trick of conjuration on India's prime minister, P. V. Narasimha Rao. India's "skeptical inquirers," who call themselves "rationalists"—men and women like Prabhir Ghosh of Calcutta—relish their work of exposing holy charlatans. See John F. Burns, "Guru Busters Debunk India's Holy Charlatans," in the San Francisco *Chronicle*, 11 October 1995.

8. I saw Geller in 1970 in a small kibbutz dining hall. Some of his subjects were my classmates, all innocent of complicity. Geller was stunningly successful and left the kibbutz audience without a single skeptic.

9. Uri Geller, *My Story* (New York: Praeger, 1975).

10. This was precisely the attraction of a Geller for a scientist like David Bohm, whose implicate order theory was monistic. Bohm, as already noted, features strongly in the Process philosophy of David R. Griffin of the Center for Process Studies at the School of Theology at Claremont.

11. James Randi, *The Truth about Uri Geller* (Buffalo, N.Y.: Prometheus Books, 1982).

12. Claude Levi-Strauss, *Structural Anthropology* (New York: Basic Books, 1963) pp. 175–85.

13. Claude Levi-Strauss, *The Savage Mind* (Chicago: University of Chicago Press, 1966), p. 221.

14. In technical Sanskrit usage, the empirical results of an act or a ritual are "visible" (*dṛṣṭa*), while the religious or magical results are "unseen" (*adṛṣṭa*). These terms do not imply a supernatural causality. The Hindi adjective reserved for magnificant Tantric feats is *ādhisvābhāvik,* which connotes the expansion of human potential to its extreme limits.

🎐 THIRTEEN 🎐

Ghosts And People with No Boundaries

The road from Banaras to the village of Asapur, where Ramjanam exorcises ghosts from Hindu and Muslim patients, passes through lush farmland. As one looks out of the three-wheeled rickshaw, field follows field in glistening succession of mustard plants. Every now and then the yellow sea breaks up into islands of recently planted wheat fields, green stalks streaking against the rich brown soil. The fields are neatly divided by markers and by raised earthen boundaries. The rickshaw passes several banyan trees along the road, every large one also marked as a kind of boundary: Its ochre-painted trunk is surrounded by a round stone platform and a small shrine. A spirit or a minor deity resides there, serviced by a few local women. Throughout their lengthy history, Indians have shown a passion for marking space. The countryside has always been divided into regions, one field against the other, city against forest, mountain against river plain. This is the meaning of sacred geography here: The imagination shapes the natural world of space and is shaped in return by passage through it.

The same is also true for time. The Hindu calendar, which is based on the cycles of the moon, divides the year into separate zones. Holidays and festivals are set apart as sacred time. They are carefully observed with the aid of detailed calendars sold everywhere, at any time. In addition to observing the annual cycle of festivals, pilgrimages, and devotional days, Indians also mark boundaries in human life. Birth, naming, male initiation, marriage, and death are like field markers in the expanse of time. They separate and mark different stages of exis-

171

tence by means of carefully orchestrated rites of passage. One does not "naturally" become an adult or a married woman in India. The girl must be shaped into a married woman; upon marriage, she assumes a completely new persona. From a natural being—"girl"—she becomes a social being—"wife." This is a dangerous passage, and she must be led across with care, as the carefully ritualized wedding reveals.[1]

Even death does not mark the last passage; the temporal horizon stretches far beyond it. Cycles of death and rebirth continue their hold on the soul, and the traveler must continue to cross dangerous boundaries as a disembodied spirit. Meanwhile, the entire world also moves in endless cycles. On a mythical level, Hindus have long painted the life of the cosmos with vast strokes of time—eons or *yugas* consisting of tens of thousands of years each. In these enormous spans the gods play their grand roles, as the lavishly descriptive mythologies of the Puranas tell us. The changing of these eons from one to the next—from the golden age down to the Iron Age and back—usually bodes ill for humanity.

For a better view one travels with head sticking out the side of the rickshaw as it passes through the fertile landscape, along crowded roadside villages where life is lived outdoors. The residents are oblivious to the traffic as they cook and eat, bathe and do their toilet, play and work along the side of the road, as if it were a peaceful stream running through their village. A few miles ahead is Ramjanam the *ojhā* who works inside a small courtyard containing both a Durgā temple and a Muslim shrine. He sees both Hindus and Muslims, men and women who crowd onto the small veranda, squeezed together as they sit before him. They are not aware of touching one another, nor do they show any discomfort with having to share their problems with fifty strangers and a foreigner. There are no personal boundaries, one notes in amazement, and the paradox becomes immediately glaring. With all the boundaries and walls everywhere—between fields, homes, castes, sexes, holidays and regular days—how can one explain the total absence of personal space and sense of privacy here? The paradox is not easily explained and it forces us to look at another startling fact.

Indians, in traditional contexts such as villages or the older sections of Banaras, are connected to each other through bonds that go far beyond familiarity, intimacy, or even blood. In sociological terms, the basic social unit here is not the individual but the extended family. A man defines himself only in relationship to his family, caste, or village. A woman is either someone's wife, mother, or aunt. Even self-awareness, the very experience of personal existence, reaches beyond the skin to the web of family relations that constitute a larger "self." Individuality, as the distinguished French sociologist Louis Dumont has shown, is a modern Western notion we must avoid tagging onto Indians.[2] Relationship and bonding are the basic facts of social and psychological life, and they find expression in whom one can marry, touch, or share food with. A stranger is someone outside these circles of contact, not someone you do not know.

Even the religious ideas about the destiny of the individual—karma—is permeated by the reality of interrelationship. A man's life may end prematurely because of his wife's karma, or a child may become gravely ill because of something his grandfather did forty years earlier. Wendy O'Flaherty (Doniger) once wrote that karma is a metaphor for the interlocking grid of people's lives in India: an idiom of relationship.[3] Karma demonstrates, on a philosophical level, that human actions—the very notion of intention and consequence—can dissolve as the separation between people disappears. This is precisely what makes Banaras fertile soil for the magical experience. But the traditional situation is rapidly changing in urban India, and the same bonds of karma (and purity) that tie people to their relatives can also set them completely apart from strangers. In a society that is held together by the bonds of blood and food, karma can become a vicious metaphor for one's complete loneliness.

𑁋 𑁋 𑁋

Case 13.1

Hira Mani's Bad Karma

On the morning of January 27, Hira Mani's meager portion of luck gave out completely. She had left her parents' house early as usual and walked to the main railroad station in Varanasi. There she would find a spot to beg where no one would drive her away. She was new at begging, still fighting for territory. Hira was a twenty-six-year-old widow. Her husband had died unexpectedly the previous summer, leaving her childless. She shaved her head and returned to her parents' house. But they could not support her, and she began to beg. She was strong and optimistic and felt that some work would eventually materialize. She loathed begging and feared getting to her begging spot. Twice a day she had to cross the busiest intersection in Banaras, a convergence of a major boulevard with the trunk road.

That morning Hira made it safely across and sat on the high embankment. She had an old cloth bag that she would spread on the ground for the *paises* flung down by passersby. The bag fell off the curb, and she went after it, right foot first. A municipal bus was just then rounding the corner, the driver miscalculating his distance from the curb. Hira was struck by the bus, her right leg pinched against the concrete curb by the metal skirting at the bottom of the vehicle. Two seconds of searing pain midway between her foot and knee; then the bus was gone, and she fainted onto the embankment.

Five hours later a foreigner was passing under the bridge in a three-wheeled rickshaw. In the middle of Banaras's busiest intersection, lying on a raised embankment, he saw a woman in a torn pink sari and a crimson blouse. Her black hair was shaved in the manner of a widow. Through the thick traffic she could be seen writhing on the ground and waving her arms at passersby. Some stopped and bent over her, then shook their heads and walked quickly away. The foreigner told the rickshaw driver to stop and walked over to her. The woman had a compound fracture in her shin bone and a gash so deep the leg was almost severed. The blood had long since encrusted into a dark stain that covered her foot, the ripped sari, and the pavement. The foot was black and swollen into frightening proportions. Flies had settled on the woman's leg, too brazen to mind her weak movements. She was delirious with shock and dehydration but responsive. The sahib went to a tea stall and bought water for fifty *paise*—the boy chuckled—and gave Hira Mani a glassful. She drank it so quickly that she needed to be slowed down, but she refused another glass. The scene was now becoming a spectacle: A foreigner with a prostrate Indian woman on the street will draw a crowd. The traffic slowed to a crawl but made up for this with increased horn noise and fumes.

A bored police inspector, who stood chatting with a friend at the far end of the intersection, noticed the changed tenor of the traffic. He spotted the source of trouble and began to cross the road with the swagger of a needed man. The inspector looked down at this woman he had for hours assumed was just

crazy. He then looked up and asked the foreigner in amazement: "Why are you bothering yourself over this woman? Do
you know her?" The foreigner did not answer, and the inspector shook his head in frustration. Finally he commandeered a
reluctant rickshaw, and Hira was placed on the rear bench. The
rickshaw followed the inspector—he was riding a shining white
Enfield Bullet—to a government hospital.

After they admitted her into the emergency room—the two
beds were occupied, and she was placed on a stone slab—the
sahib made the mistake of giving the commandeered rickshaw
driver fifty rupees. The man became ecstatic. The first driver
muttered, "Fifty" with repulsion, and it suddenly dawned on
the sahib what was coming. He had just transformed himself
from an eccentric foreigner into a big philanthropist. As they
arrived home at Assi, the driver insisted on 250 rupees—an exorbitant fare. For ten minutes they stood and argued; then the
sahib threw 150 rupees onto the rear seat and walked away.

"You rich foreigners," the driver yelled at his back. "You
go out of your way for a stranger, but you will not pay me a
fair price."

The next day the foreigner found Hira lying on the balcony
of the government hospital in ward 6. She was covered completely in a red woolen blanket, standard issue. Everyone else
in the ward had several blankets, Hira, lying in the open air,
had just the one. He could make her out because of the new
cast sticking out of the blanket, the only part of her that was
showing. The patient lying next to her, a healthy-looking local
woman, said that no one had been to visit Hira; she had spoken
with no one and had not eaten. Government hospitals do not
provide meals for patients; their overmatched budgets simply
cannot accommodate a need that can be met by family members. Because no one knew where she came from, the doctor
brought her some bread and crackers, which she had not
touched. The sahib squeezed two hundred rupees into her
hand, hoping no one saw—it could too easily be stolen. That
evening he came back and placed two extra blankets over the
red one. He gave her some aspirin—it was her only pain medi-
cation—and, when no one was looking, he gave her more
money. She closed her eyes and covered her head in the blankets. Her hand clutched the money, but no other sign of recognition came from Hira. It was dinnertime, and everyone else in

the ward was sitting with family members, cooking or eating their vegetables and chapati. All he could do was give Hira money. Hira's karma, he thought, had to be tied to the actions of a foreigner.[4]

In a city where most healing is performed by magicians, without cost, and where magic depends on the absence of personal boundaries, the case of Hira Mani stands out. Hira was victimized into widowhood by either her own or her husband's bad karma. She then became "untouchable," not due to a state of impurity but because no one would dare link destiny with her. The concept of *ṛṇabandhana*, the bond of karmic debt, was just too powerful. Unlike almost every other person in Banaras, Hira was surrounded by a wall, one that only a foreigner could climb and then only with money, the currency most despised by magicians.

THE OPEN PERSON AND GHOSTS

The interrelationship of individuals in traditional societies such as Banaras manifests itself in a variety of phenomena such as the "open person" and the ever present danger of ghosts of departed relatives *(bhūt pret)*. The term "open person" is taken from the anthropologist McKim Marriott, who has spent the last two decades describing the traditional ways that Indians conceptualize their social life.[5] It is a striking term because it mixes a metaphor of space (open) with a psychological concept (person). One can almost visualize such a being. But perhaps this mixing of metaphors is appropriate. The term describes an empirical individual who lacks the sense of a rigidly enclosed body and a distinctly separate ego confined to that body. The open person, instead, possesses a "transactional" self, which is experienced in fluid terms as not entirely distinct from other such selves. One grows up to be an open person in societies that do not recognize the ideology of individualism, self-sufficiency, or separateness. More important, children are nurtured from infancy into becoming "open persons." They are held and touched for long durations by many people in the extended family. They are clothed loosely and allowed to relieve themselves freely. Such children experience themselves as a direct extension of a nonthreatening environment that can literally be felt. In the jargon of comparative psychology these children are "field-dependent." They develop no rigid boundaries that separate an "interior" space from the "outside" world. Inner moods and outer landscape become blended in their conscious awareness. Even cognitively, they develop along an alternative course. Erik Erikson, whose interest in Gandhi extended beyond the usual political and "spiritual" topics, made the following observation about child play in India:

> [Children create] a play universe filled to the periphery with blocks, people, and animals but with little differentiation between outdoors and indoors, jungle and city, or, indeed one scene from the other. If one finally asks what (and, indeed, *where*) is *the* "exciting scene," one finds it embedded somewhere where nobody could have discerned it as an individual event and certainly not as a central one.[6]

Erikson concludes that if he could choose one word to describe what takes place in the play space, as well as in the Indian street, that word would be *fusion*.

A culture that consists of people who experience themselves fused in relation to others will develop a distinct vocabulary for describing psychological events. Because interior landscapes make no sense, emotional states, mental disorders, and feelings cannot be described in personcentric terms. The boundaries of the external landscape are then experienced as the terrain of psychic experience. As one travels from city to forest across a river, an "inner" journey is also taking place that is—experienced in space. This is the meaning and the source of power of pilgrimage in traditional cultures such as India's. As the Indian psychiatrist Sudhir Kakar noted (see Chapter 5), inner states are described in mythical terms: Anger is a ghost, terror a ferocious goddess. But one should go further: Inner states are *experienced* in mythical terms because the boundary of inner and outer does not really exist. Therefore, the sudden and drastic change of moods experienced by a betrothed girl about to get married becomes "possession" by a ghost. The true danger of ghosts lurking all around Banaras and its district must be understood with the open person in mind, particularly in its relational aspect. In other words, the space in which one travels in and around the city holds the psychic energy of those who move in this space, open and vulnerable to possession.

GHOSTS

An hour after leaving the city, the rickshaw turns off the main road onto a short dirt path and stops. It is nearly noon on a Tuesday, and the compound is crowded with Hindus. Muslims prefer Thursdays, though no hard and fast rule separates them from Hindus. During our stay Ramjanam worked mostly on a rugged-looking man, who happened to be a healer, too, and who was possessed by a pair of ghosts. These ghosts, to make things worse, were married to each other. Babaji sang in ever increasing rhythm, his pitch and his emotion changed in a musical conversation between Durgā and the ghosts, who were taking turns speaking through his person. As Ramjanam exhaled, his voice was the voice of Durgā, and as he sang inhaling, it was the voice of the responding ghosts. The song was a request that the ghosts identify themselves and state their desires. To aid Durgā, Babaji called on three hero-spirits *(bīrs)* to enter the body of the patient and coax the ghosts out. Brahma Bir, Lohara Bir, Kedarya Bir, and Durgā took turns conversing with the dominant ghost who was then "playing" in the patient's body. It was a melee, a cacophony of spirits, gods, and ghosts working through the bodies of two men. The ghosts were given water and ashes as pure offerings, and then a lemon was sliced—a minor sacrifice that calls for the ghost to separate itself from the host's spirit and to speak.

Babaji's interrogation revealed that the woman ghost was low caste, while the male ghost belonged to a high caste, and that they were married. As a married couple, they could not agree on what to accept in order to leave. When he first heard this, the healer slapped the patient sharply on the face, then hit him on the back, but without anger. The two ghosts were Kashmira and Mari. Babaji was accusing them of accepting gifts while refusing to leave. The patient claimed that the ghost Mari was the soul of his guru, and Babaji said this was a lie and slapped him harder. The large man accepted his punishment meekly, his coarse body merely sagging as the ghost drew back inside.

The man had become possessed three years earlier by the Kashmira ghost, and the ghost had promised to leave in exchange for a platform built for it. The platform is an elevated seat for respected men such as teachers, healers, and elders. Being the younger, though more precocious, of two brothers, this villager could not directly demand what he felt he deserved. He was locked in a losing battle for status. Then he became possessed, and, sure enough, a platform was built for the Kashmira ghost. But his brother destroyed the platform, and the ghost came back. Later on, the one ghost was joined by another ghost, and the two became a couple. On the day of the treatment Babaji did not accomplish much, and he was tiring. He performed a *phutna* (blowing a mantra on the patient) and sprinkled the patient with water. Then he moved on to a woman sitting nearby.

The emotional impact of the session on the observers was overwhelming. Ramjanam's voice and rhythms mesmerized his patients, who swayed in synchrony with his songs. The incense, heat, and noise formed a thick screen that blocked out the intellect. Comprehension was out of the question at first. Still, the events in the compound are not difficult to explain, though far from obvious to the casual observer. They require a certain familiarity with the basic Banarsi ideas about death and the survival of disembodied spirits, who sometimes haunt the living.

DEATH

Banaras is a good place to die. Elderly men and women come from all over India to await their death here.[7] They live in hostels and ashrams that line the alleys of the old city, along the banks of the Ganges. After they die, they are cremated near the river and their ashes thrown into the flowing water. The signs of the death rituals are everywhere along the numerous *ghāṭs,* or bathing steps. Though only two *ghāṭs*—Hariścandra and Maṇikarṇikā—are used for burning bodies, rituals for the dead are performed somewhere along the river all the time. In Assi Ghāt, high in the branches of a huge pipal tree that towers above the steps, hundreds of healthy-looking crows observe the activities below. Ritual feedings of the dead are performed there. According to ancient mortuary texts, if the crows do not touch the leftovers of the rice balls offered to the recently deceased, this is a sign that the person has died with an unfulfilled wish, that, discontent with his present state, he may yet haunt survivors as a ghost.

The final passage in the human cycle, death is as complex and dangerous as any of the rest. The last breath in the present body signals the start of a new journey, which leads through several stations and requires the help of the survivors to ensure success. Death, at least of an older relative, is thus accompanied not so much by sorrowful mourning as by anxiety for making the journey complete. This has been true since the beginning of India's long recorded history, as seen in the following ancient verses from the *Rgveda:*

> [To the dead man:] Go forth, go forth on those ancient paths on which our ancient fathers passed beyond. There you shall see the two kings, Yama and Varuna, rejoicing in the sacrificial drink.
>
> Unite with the fathers, with Yama, with the rewards of your sacrifices and good deeds, in the highest heaven. Leaving behind all imperfections, go back home again; merge with a glorious body.[8]

In order to arrive at the world of the ancestors, or of the gods, the deceased needs a "body," because immediately after death his spirit wanders like thin air and will become a *bhūt-pret* (disembodied spirit, "has-been") or a *piśac* (ghoul) if it remains unfed. Balls of rice flour called *piṇḍas* are offered for ten or twelve days with water and sesame as part of the offering. The soul then takes a body called *bhojadeha*—a body for enjoying the rice balls.

The world, even within the sacred space of this holy city, is rife with disembodied spirits who are hungry and unsatisfied. People die unexpectedly and prematurely with unfulfilled wishes; they die of accidental or violent causes, commit suicide, die of black magic and Brahmins' curses, in anger, terror, resentment. According to the astrologers of Banaras, any person who dies before the indicated time on the astrological chart falls into this category.[9] He is not necessarily condemned to exist as ghost or ghoul, but if the body is not properly disposed of and the ritual feeding is not successfully completed, his odds take a dip for the worse. The miserable luck of the prematurely deceased becomes evident only after a relative becomes possessed with the deceased's ghost. Due to the subtle and disembodied existence of spirits, only a few people, mostly accomplished Tantrics and *ojhās,* are able to see them, though in reality they are said to be everywhere. This is the reason, for instance, that one must be careful where one urinates; the spirit in a tree might not take kindly to this act of disrespect. In fact, one can never be sure where possession will occur. A woman at Baba Bahadur, herself possessed, sang repeatedly the following popular song:

I was crossing the street, there she caught me.
I had gone to my relative's marriage, and she gave me a sweet.

Street crossings, isolated trees, and cremation grounds are some of the notorious places haunted by ghosts. A coin lying on the ground of a busy fair will be picked up only by a fool—it is an old way of passing on a ghost to a stranger.

In some popular accounts, ghosts are depicted as large-bellied, insatiable monstrosities that drink the vital force out of their hosts by means of their mosquito-like needle mouths. Once in place, a ghost will seldom depart spontaneously; it must be coaxed, threatened, or bought off if it is to leave its victim. Exorcisers (*ojhās* and *sokhās*) abound in the city and its surrounding area. The municipality requires registration and licensing of exorcists, and hundreds of practitioners have complied.

Ramjanam of Asapur uses many of the tools available to *ojhās.* He coaxes the ghost to "play" in the body of its victim, to make itself known through body gestures and voice. This playing of the ghost accounts for the tormented and sordid contortions one sees among the women at Baba Bahadur and for the inhuman, gutteral sounds coming out of their frothing mouths. Ramjanam himself becomes "possessed" with the power of the goddess Durgā. She speaks through him as he exhales during his rhythmic nasal singing. She forces the ghost to speak and negotiates a solution to the problem. Ramjanam also uses the spirits of three *bīrs* (heroes) to penetrate the victim. The *bīrs* were men of political and social distinction who met untimely deaths. A popular cult of *bīr* worship, aimed at honoring these men and benefiting by the powers of their helping spirits, has existed for centuries.[10] Like Durgā, the *bīrs* are charged with coaxing ghosts and intimidating them. *Bīrs* are better negotiators than Durgā, and expelling a ghost often boils down to haggling over price, an unfitting activity for a great goddess. Ramjanam's three *bīrs* are a formidable assembly, but he still felt six months might be needed to expel the married ghosts.

The exorcisms performed by Ramjanam and other *ojhās* are often accompanied by altered states of consciousness, ecstatic shamanic singing of sacred songs, ritual performances, and other extraordinary events. Ramjanam's throaty and rhythmical voice is hypnotizing, and mere bystanders find themselves losing grip on their self-restraint. But none of the events in Asapur meets the usual definition of magic because no "supernatural causality" is attributed to any ritual object or act. The disembodied spirit makes its presence known in response to direct inquiries initiated because of marked changes of mood or behavior in the host. The ghost's terms for leaving are also straightforward and can easily be explained in psychological terms. For instance, the ghost of one teenager who had recently graduated from high school demanded lipstick, nail polish, and jewelry in order to depart. The girl felt that her parents were confining her to a traditional life she was not prepared to accept after what she had learned in school. The price of evicting the ghost seemed like a reasonable compromise between parents and daughter, at least for the time being. A counselor or psychologist in Oregon might have recommended a similar solution. Yet the entire range of phenomena that falls into the category of ghost possession, namely death, the prevalence and subtlety of disembodied spirits, possession, and the rites of exorcism, are all made possible by the operation of the magical consciousness.

The magical consciousness—a direct experience of relatedness—is the thread that holds all these facts together. Ghosts are not the subject of *belief;* they are *perceived.* One perceives them in the same way that an American might comment on the connection made possible by genes: "Look, he has his father's nose!" So one says in India: "Look, she has her aunt's spirit in her!" An awareness based on perception and on the psychology of the open person in an interrelated society makes the occurrence of ghosts possible. The language of "repressed emotions," "neurosis," and "hysteria" simply does not apply to persons with no boundaries. Their emotional terrain belongs as much to the external world around them as to any unconscious cellar. They are part of a large emotional system that encompasses their entire physical world. Spirits and ghosts are simply disembodied forces that occupy this terrain as they do. The key word, again, is *fusion*. The phenomena of ghost possession simply represent fusion run amok.

Notes

1. Classical texts on the wedding ritual are listed and described in Glucklich, *The Sense of Adharma*, Chapter 6 (New York: Oxford University Press, 1994).

2. Louis Dumont, *Homo Hierarchicus*; Others have written on the corporate or relational self in India, including E. Valentine Daniel, *Fluid Signs: Being a Person the Tamil Way* (Berkeley: University of California Press, 1984). Perhaps most astute of all have been the observations of McKim Marriott in numerous works, including his edited *India through Hindu Categories* (New Delhi: Sage, 1990).

3. "Karma and Rebirth in the Vedas and Purāṇas" in *Karma and Rebirth in Classical Indian Traditions*, ed. Wendy Doniger O'Flaherty (Berkeley: University of California Press, 1980), p. 29.

4. Food, clothes, cigarettes, blood, semen, and other "stuff" are the currency of interpersonal exchange in traditional India. Money is the currency of loneliness. For more technical information on this topic, see McKim Marriott, "Hindu Transactions; Diversity Without Dualism," in *Transaction and Meaning: Directions in the Anthropology of Exchange and Symbolic Behavior*, ed. Bruce Kapferer (Philadelphia: Institute for the Study of Human Issues, 1976), pp. 109–42); see also R. B. Inden and R. W. Nicholas, *Kinship in Bengali Culture* (Chicago: University of Chicago Press, 1977).

5. "The Open Hindu Person and Interpersonal Fluidity," paper presented at the annual meeting of the Association for Asian Studies, Washington, D.C., 1980. The topic of the transactional self is hardly new and extends as far back as St. Augustine. See Jerome Bruner, *Actual Minds, Possible Worlds* (Cambridge, Mass.: Harvard University Press, 1986), ch. 4.

6. Erik Erikson, *Gandhi's Truth: On the Origins of Militant Non-Violence* (London: Faber & Faber, 1970), p. 40.

7. Jonathan P. Parry has published several articles on this topic. His most

recent work is *Death in Banaras* (Cambridge: Cambridge University Press, 1994).

8. Wendy Doniger O'Flaherty, tr., *The Rig Veda* (Harmondsworth: Penguin Books, 1984), p. 44.

9. The astrologer's prediction itself can profoundly influence the course of events, especially for a hapless believer. A splendid and humorous example is described by R. K. Narayan in "The Antidote," *An Astrologer's Day and Other Stories* (Mysore: Indian Thought Publications, 1974).

10. Diane Marjorie Coccari, "The Bir Babas of Banaras" (Ph. D. diss., University of Wisconsin at Madison, 1986).

FOURTEEN

Animal Magic

Banaras was slowly zippered between the Ganges at its one northbound turn and the lush farmland laced with ancient forests of banyan, nim, and ashoka trees. Unlike other cities its size, Banaras did not annihilate the life it displaced; it merely squeezed the farm and forest animals into its narrow alleys. The predators, excluding mosquitoes of course, are gone now, and so are the forest animals that could not adjust to cobblestone. All the rest gave up field and forest grazing for scavenging in garbage heaps. In a place where the interrelationship of all beings is conceived in terms of karmic bonds and debts, each animal life has been allowed to settle its own account. Humans do not interfere in this process, and the result is a kind of urban-karmic Darwinism that selects some for survival and many for death by starvation, disease, or traffic. And like humans—perhaps even better—animals are endowed with the perceptual apparatus to recognize and to absorb the invisible forces that permeate the city. Animals can sense ghosts, deliver good karma, and even become possessed. Some animals, birds for instance, serve as magnets to draw out the ghosts and are therefore common remedies for humans.

No clear demarcation line separates humans from animals in Banaras, either in theory or in practice. This means not that animals are confused with humans but that their respective qualities easily intermingle. As one chicken butcher put it when asked about the lives he takes, "These chicken give up their life for us. They sacrifice themselves to be eaten." The residents of Banaras do not classify the world according to zoological guidelines. Even those who climbed through the public schools and have heard of Darwin and natural species ignore objective natural categories. Just as Americans speak English with little reflection on rules of grammar, so Banarsis interact with animals directly and without the intervention of a scientific system of classification. Banaras residents cannot avoid interacting with animals, of course, because animals are everywhere. Humans and animals share a limited amount of space, so the simple fact of ongoing interaction, along with traditional norms, determines the "grammar" of this exchange, including the implicit classes of animals.

CLASSIFICATION OF NATURE

The rise of modern biological taxonomies, or classifications, in the seventeenth and eighteenth centuries reflected a vast change in worldview. Carl von Linne or Linnaeus (1707–1778) is credited with inventing the modern scientific method of biological classification. His *Systema Naturae* divided the world into large categories: Stars, Elements, Earth, Natural Law, and Nature. Nature, in turn, was divided into three Kingdoms: Animal, Vegetable, and Mineral. The Kingdoms were further subdivided into classes. For instance, the Animal Kingdom was divided into *Mammalia, Aves, Amphibia, Pisces, Insecta,* and *Vermes.* The classes were then further divided into orders, genera, species, and races. *Homo* is one of four genera in the order of Primates, which belongs to the class Mammalia. This genus contains two species, Homo Sapiens (with six races) and Homo Troglodytes (with just one race—Orangutan).[1]

In a similar manner, the full range of biological beings was divided on the basis of morphology (form), sexual behavior (ability to interbreed), and comparative analysis of morphological relations. In short, the method was based on objective observation. But in the process of classifying animals objectively—Linnaeus was actually preceeded in this by John Jonston in his *Natural History of Quadrapeds* (1657)—some essential subjective qualities of animals were permanently lost. As Foucault puts it: "The whole of animal semantics has disappeared, like a dead and useless limb. The words that had been interwoven in the very being of the beast have been unravelled and removed."[2] The mythical quality of animals, by which they were all related to the mythmaker, vanished. The earlier subjective way of classifying animals is demonstrated in a list attributed by J. L. Borges to a Chinese encyclopedia called *Celestial Emporium of Benevolent Knowledge:*

> On those remote pages it is written that animals are divided into (a) those that belong to the emperor, (b) embalmed ones, (c) those that are trained, (d) suckling pigs (e) mermaids, (f) fabulous ones, (g) stray

dogs, (h) those that are included in this classification, (i) those that tremble as if they were mad, (j) innumerable ones, (k) those drawn with a very fine camel's hair brush, (l) others, (m) those that have just broken a flower vase, (n) those that resemble flies from a distance.[3]

This apparently eccentric list expresses the cultural values that permeate and order "nature" in one traditional society. It is more an attitude than a taxonomy. Before Linnaeus, animals had always been classified according to a symbolic imagination that was shaped by social and ideological values, as well as by subconscious forces. In traditional cultures a class or a species represented the embodiment of the "ideal type," to a greater or lesser extent, among several individuals. Consequently, a society's classification of animals as totems, as sacred or defiled, edible or inedible, always revealed basic social facts, cultural values, or ecological needs. This was certainly true of classifications that dominated European sciences until modern times. Traditional, or even "primitive," modes of classification are not necessarily "unscientific," of course. Ornithologists like Ernst Mayr or Jared Diamond, for instance, have found that indigenous New Guinean methods of classifying the hundreds of bird species correspond with modern classification in 99 percent of cases.[4]

CLASSIFICATION IN BANARAS

India has always had both types of classification: the objective and the subjective-mythical. A vibrant medical and even veterinarian tradition produced hard-nosed empirical ways of organizing physiological facts and pathologies. However, as Brian Smith has noted, the only method of classifying the entire world according to one system was based on the rituals of the ancient Vedas.[5] These revered ritual and mythological texts—India's closest thing to a canon—placed archetypes at the center of a network of resemblances. Any particular being was related by analogy either vertically to the archetype or horizontally to another being or class of beings. This system of hierarchies must look familiar to anyone who reads about Darwin's struggle against ancient Aristotelian notions of species. Still, despite the fact that classes are defined by embodying ideal types ("archetypes"), this is not a capricious mode of classification because it is ruled by clear ideological and intellectual categories.

Banarsi folk-classification of animals, in contrast, is always implicit, and it resembles the archaic Chinese taxonomy in its subjective perspective. The deciding criterion is essentially the relation of animals to humans, or, as George Lakoff calls it, "the domain-of-experience principle." On these grounds animals are divided into at least five major classes: mythical, iconic, pets, zoological, and transmigrating.[6] Unlike the Linnaean or even the Vedic classification, these categories do not constitute mutually exclusive classes, and any given animal may belong to one or more, though seldom to all, of them; like any taxonomy, however, the classes are further subdivided into genera, or whatever one wishes to call the subclasses. Mythical animals, for instance, are divided according to the god with which they are associated or according to the myth or narrative in which they appear. The principle of classification is seldom based on morphological observation or on other scientfic methods, except in the case of the zoological class, which is limited to the professional and modernized residents of Banaras.

Mythical animals

Any animal—dogs, monkeys, peacocks, fish, rats—can be linked by an observer to one particular myth or another. India's mythology is vast and vividly populated with an immense variety of animals. Still, the act of linking a particular animal to a given myth is seldom a clear-cut intellectual act. Sociologists and anthropologists like to use such terms as *analogy, homology, symbolization,* and *instantiation* to describe the connection.[7] This daunting jargon simply means that collective cultural values are responsible for depicting the relationship between a specific living animal and its conceptual model. Members of that culture can relate to this animal only with the cultural tools at their disposal; the relationship is never completely natural. But in Banaras the connection between animal and myth is experienced in a visceral and free manner, as the case of monkeys may demonstrate.

The Durgā Temple is home to hundreds of rhesus macaques *(bandar).* The monkeys spread out in every direction in search of garbage or groceries, which they steal from shoppers. They leap from one rooftop to the next with ease, never failing to judge the distance accurately. One wonders how evolution has prepared them for such a task, which cannot be learned by trial and error. I asked several Banaras residents how they thought the infant monkeys acquired the ability to gauge leaping distances without making fatal errors. One of the priests at the temple said, "The monkeys have Hanuman in them." Hanuman, a great flier, was one of the heroes in the great epic *Rāmāyana,* and he is credited with helping Rāma save his kidnapped wife, Sītā. The story, familiar to every Indian, is one of the main pillars in the cultural edifice of Hinduism. The priest could not explain how any specific monkey— we spoke while a dozen *bandars* (a generic term for rhesus, but never langurs) sat above our heads—"contains" Hanuman. He said, "Hanuman resides *(rahta)* in each and every monkey." The metaphor of containment is used very loosely and with little reflection. As a mythical hero Hanuman is not just an individual monkey but a symbol for a quality they all possess to some degree. According to Brian Smith's archetypal model, the priest is expressing an abstract analogy in concrete, though hazy, terms. A specific monkey resembles the archetype (Hanuman) in some manner and therefore belongs to a class of Hanuman-like beings. This is undeniably true, but the attitude of the priest is more complex, even paradoxical. When the priest, or anyone else carrying a grocery bag, is attacked by a hungry monkey, he will kick the "thieving beast" as hard as he can. The priest, like everyone else in the area, keeps a stick in his apartment, and does not hesitate to use it when monkeys come to steal clothes hanging on a line. I had never seen any monkey treated like a member of an honored species related to Hanuman until I began nagging people with my questions. The mythologizing of the flea-plagued, aggressive macaques seems to be improvised and haphazard. It is also inconsistent with the ongoing turf war between humans and monkeys. In short, I believe that the intellectual reflections of the temple priest and others, in their explicit form, arose strictly from the need to resolve an intellectual dilemma posed by a foreigner.

The psychological and mental act of linking individuals to mythical (or ritual-totemic) classes has been studied thoroughly by anthropologists and sociologists since Louis Henry Morgan and Emile Durkheim. Levi-Strauss built his considerable reputation on such work. Myth and ritual seem to embody every known cultural relationship between humans and animals in traditional cultures. Every specific mode of interaction, including hunting and husbandry, finds its meaning in a broad symbolic spectrum that clearly encompasses magic. Given this dauntingly enshrined truism, one must summon quixotic resources to claim that the mythical and the magical are two entirely distinct types of relationship and that the Durgā temple priest is closer to the magical.

The common thread in the rich sociological analysis of symbolic animals is the arbitrary or conventional quality of human relations to nature. On birds used as divining instruments of good and evil omens, Levi-Strauss wrote:

"It is obvious that the same characteristics could have been given a different meaning and that different characteristics of the same birds could have been chosen instead. The system of divination selects only some distinctive features, gives them an arbitrary meaning and restricts itself to seven birds, the selection of which is surprising in view of their insignificance.

The bird features that serve a system of anthropomorphic qualities are selected and "the terms never have any intrinsic significance."[8] This analysis defines the mythical relationship to a world of animals according to a cultural reduction. The magical, in contrast, is never arbitrary because it depends on affection, not just effect—on intimacy with a concrete animal, even a snake, not just on the significance of an entire class of animals.

The Icon and the Pet

The iconic animal, for instance the cow, resembles the mythical class of animals. But few people in Banaras can point to any myth that explains their special treatment of cows. Fewer still can give any practical reason for the unique status that the animal enjoys. This, of course, is not the point. Marvin Harris, the ecological anthropologist, reduced the sanctity of the cow to a calculus of calories. He argued that living cows provide more calories in support of human needs than eaten cows. For that reason, cows are spared the butcher's knife. Sanctity is utility dressed up in its Sunday best. But the water buffalo, which is not a sacred animal, produces more milk and manure, and, in the absence of expensive bulls, also provides more muscle than cows. Yet buffalo are killed and eaten. There must be some cultural value that is embedded in the practices that favor the cow. Unfortunately, this value is mute. Like reasons given for the sanctity of the Ganges, every stated justification for the status of cows is bound to be tautological or circular: The cow is sacred because it is pure, because it has always been a revered animal, because it is a symbol for things we value (such as fecundity). The iconic type of animal, like the mythical, only *seems* to be an objective standard; in practice, its status is based on indeterminate factors. The point is that such a sanctity can never, by definition, be explained in historic, theological, caloric, or any other terms. It is an aspect—a face—of a unique human capacity to feel something toward another being. The reasons for this attitude's being directed toward one animal rather than another fail to explain the attitude itself.

That aspect depends on prolonged interaction, as one clearly sees in the case of pets. Banaras is a city of dogs in the same way that Pune is a city of rats. The dog accompanies Śiva in some of his familiar mythical roles, especially in his hideous beggarly aspects. The mythology of Śiva, in turn, determines much of what happens in the city of Banaras, which is the city of Śiva. Consequently dogs are allowed to breed and wander freely in the densely populated city. Dogs are everywhere, hundreds of thousands of pathetic animals in varying stages of decrepitude. Unlike the generic *bandars,* which represent a specific species, these are indescribable mongrels that Banarsis call *deshies* (locals). Most are ravaged by their own struggles with fleas, the hair ripped out and the crusty, blistery skin hosting flies. They subsist on garbage, competing with cows and pigs for a meager vegeterian diet. The females conceive at every round of ovulation, but the overall population is controlled by the inevitable death of most puppies.

The residents of Banaras do not seek these animals for punishment; they simply ignore them. The dogs are completely untouchable in the strictest sense. Although they are a mythical class in a sense, *deshi* dogs will never cross the line that separates the filthy from the human.

In stark contrast, pets are homologized animals. They are humanized conceptually and in practice by naming and by their admission into the home. A few wealthy families own purebred dogs that they keep in their homes, feed out of hand, and allow on the couch. In practical terms, these are not dogs, despite any objective way of classifying. They are not even Śiva's companion. But such pets are very uncommon. More common is the "adoption" of a dog by an entire neighborhood. In such cases the lines between the animal and humans—rather than gods or mythical beings—become blurred. These dogs are much better fed than the rest, and they enjoy rich and lustrous hair. But occasionally, especially during mating seasons, the blurring of the lines between domestic and savage is an embarassment to the entire neighborhood, and the beloved dog, in the middle of its painful coupling, may be stoned.

ANIMAL MAGIC

The Azazel Animals

The practice of touching an animal or bird, then releasing it to carry away disease or sin has been practiced around the world in a wide range of contexts. Leviticus 16.5–10 describes such a ritual in connection with the sacrificial rite on the Day of Atonement. Before a bull was sacrificed, two goats were chosen, and the high priest (Aharon in the passage) cast lots to see which would be sacrificed and which sent to Azazel. Aharon laid his hands over the head of the surviving goat and confessed the sins of Israel. The goat was then sent to the desert to carry away the sins or to atone before God.

According to Henri Hubert and Marcel Mauss, prominent scholars in the French *Annêe Sociologique* school, this ritual represents the most elementary form of expiation.[9] The contact and the expulsion symbolize the removal of an essentially religious element—sin. The animal, the touch, the release—all are incorporated into a broad sociological symbolism. The authors extended their insight, which was strongly influenced by their mentor, Emile Durkheim, to the healing rites of ancient India and the *Kauśika Sūtra*. The use there of animals such as yellow birds and black cockerel to remove jaundice and other diseases points to the same type of symbolism. Illness is a religious event, the sociologists claimed, the result of Rudra's anger. It is removed by transfer to birds, which is really an expiatory sacrifice, but, like the Azazel goat, the birds are released rather than killed.[10]

ॺ ॺ ॺ

Case 14.1

Releasing Fish in the Ganges

Tuma is an elderly Tibetan woman who owns a shop on Janpath Road. She takes care of her thirteen-year-old grandson, Tashunima, whom she rescued from the hands of an abusive mother (her daughter-in-law). She raised the boy for a few years, but then, several months before we met, the boy's mother took him from school, where he had been happy and healthy, in order to put him to work doing household chores. She prevented Tashunima from going to school. Whenever he objected, she would pinch him very painfully by rolling the skin between her thumb and forefinger. Tuma took him back after six months of this—he had lost much weight and all his playfulness and had become nearly mute. She enrolled him in DCS, a boarding school for boys, and has slowly been nursing him back to health.

She asked me to purchase fish in Banaras, as many as I could for one hundred rupees, and to free them in the Ganges while chanting, "For long life." She does this herself every Tibetan New Year but had no time now. She insisted I could do it for her, for the boy, but I had to use the money she gave me, not my own or a substitute. It had to be done on a Monday, the auspicious day for boys.

On Monday, March 7, I went to Daśāśvamedh Ghāṭ and bought one hundred fish—small catfish—that were put inside a bucket. I rented a boat and went into the middle of the river, where I released them slowly, repeating, "For long life" three times.

The residents of Banaras, especially fishermen or boat-owner castes, use fish in their rites of exorcism, as we saw in the case of Ram Prasad. But the animals they use in the Azazel manner are birds. The Bhalya Tola (hunter quarter) neighborhood in North Banaras is home to several bird sellers, most of them Muslim. The shops that specialize in nondomestic animals such as birds, rabbits, and monkeys are concentrated in one narrow alley. Khalil and Muhammed own one of the smaller shops, but they will not be bargained down on any of their fine pigeons. They are both Muslim and their family has been in the business for generations. Khalil's family got its license to sell birds from the British in 1883. In the past they sold their animals and birds while walking the crowded lanes of old Banaras. Shopkeepers were loyal customers because a bird cage at the entrance to a shop meant good business. These days, bird sellers are frequently harassed by the police or other merchants who despise the animals, so they stay put in their alley. Customers still manage to find them, often traveling great distances for a bird. But even in their discreet shops, Khalil complains, forestry people and a few animal-rights activists manage to disrupt their business. The merchants get the birds from trappers who work in the country, often capturing protected animals such as parakeets in state parks. The birds—parakeets, pigeons, sparrows—are kept in separate but crowded cages.

Red sparrows (*lāl muni*), which are caught in Banaras itself, attract many buyers because they are cheap, and the red color effectively removes evil forces. People usually come to buy them when someone in the house falls ill. They touch the patient on the forehead with the bird. As the bird is released, it takes away the disease.

Birds are also bought for other reasons. Customers hang their cages, especially with the ubiquitous green (Alexandrine) parakeets, at the doorway, where they "absorb" the problems or ghosts that try to enter the house. If an evil force enters the house, the bird will be the first to become ill. Parakeets are particularly popular because they can speak and warn the owner that something is wrong. As an added perk, Khalil says, they can greet people with "Ram, Ram."

According to Muhammed, langur monkeys are bought despite their exorbitant price because they are good for the health—like Hanuman. Throughout India Hanuman is revered for his healing powers, often in the form of Balaji. The langur, Muhammed claims, "contains" some of Hanuman's healing powers, though the animal cannot actually do anything. And unlike the birds, langurs are not to be set free. Household animals are effective in absorbing the evil forces that enter the house, but only the birds can actually remove them. "They fly close to God in the sky and can intercede for humans," Khalil explains, unknowingly echoing Leviticus.

Despite being Muslim, Khalil and Muhammed are entirely ignorant of ancient sacrificial motifs or sociological symbolism. Their awareness, in turn, does not figure in the theories of sociological explanation. Rites and symbols have their own life in the pages of scholarly books. One could easily argue against the French sociologists that the ethical dimension so pervasive in Semitic religions is not particularly prominent in ancient Indian conceptions of illness or that the sociological explanation fails to account for the relation between religious ideas and material manifestations of disease. But these are separate issues. For any ritual to be *magical,* a subjective awareness must be present. A relationship with the bird must be experienced directly and then accurately described in order to account for the magical quality of the rite. Whether the rite also happens to be expiatory or even medical is beside the point.

The Bagar tribals in Rajasthan practice a magical rite that is more closely related to the sacrificial motif than any of the practices I have observed in Banaras:

> When some dreaded disease, or epidemic, either ravages the country-side or is expected to do so [. . .] *kelu,* chana, a whole lemon and a piece of red cloth are placed in a wooden cart. To the chant of *mantras* a goat or fowl is sacrificed and its blood sprinkled on the cart, which is towed out of the village by the bhopa and fellow villagers.[11]

The use of animals, usually birds, to detect the stealthy arrival of ghosts may be connected with another practice—the reading of omens in the behavior of animals. The Korkus and the Nahals, both tribes in Madhya Pradesh, chase away every owl that enters their villages. The call of the owl, they feel, indicates that someone in the village will become grievously ill. The prolonged howling of a dog or a jackal also points to such an event. If a snake crosses one's path, it is necessary to spit onto its trail. One must then step on the spit in order to counteract the illness or misfortune that is sure to follow the encounter.[12]

Omens are never improvised intuitions or forebodings about untold possibilities. They reflect a far more profound view of the way the world is interrelated. Indian literature of every genre uses omens as a way of linking psychological and personal events with the world at large. The number of examples is staggering, but the role of omens in the medical literature is particluarly instructive in its use of animals. The *Suśruta Saṃhitā* (29.13) states that a physician on his way to a patient's house should consider it an excellent prognosis if he encounters "harmonious melodies of birds chirping on the boughs of healthy Kshira trees, bent under the weight of fruit, and looking gladsome with their dowry of beautiful blossoms and foliage, or notes of birds perched on the terraces of palace towers or on the tops of banner poles singing melodiously." With typical thoroughness the text lists *every* animal the doctor may wish to encounter or to avoid. The assumption, if these texts are to be taken literally (as they should), is that the world is a network of relations. Health is one aspect of humanity's place in the overall scheme, a sign of harmony. The singing birds do not constitute a cause in a chain of cause and effect, nor are they a sign in a semiotic sense. The happy singing is one loop in a complex system, like the warning light on a dashboard indicating the use of high beams. It is both a sign and a loop in the same wiring system.

The Healing Essence of Animals

Magical theories about the way animals heal humans usually take one of two forms. First, living animals remove illness by means of direct contact or by resembling aspects of the disease. Examples of this homeopathic approach are the frog that attracts fever because of its coolness or the yellow parrot that draws the yellowness away from a jaundiced patient. Second, animals contain certain "essences," which are seldom merely psychological, let alone symbolic, projections of human values but are distilled physical substances—products of a natural alchemy—and profoundly healing. Extracting such pharmaceutical essences often demands the life of the animal.

ଶ ଶ ଶ

Case 14.2

Curing Tuberculosis

A milkman told me that when he was just a boy, he fell with tuberculosis. He suffered from severe coughing and high fever and had spots all over his body. His parents did not call a doctor, though they were not far from the city. Instead, they tied a goat to the head of his bed and kept it there until the boy began to improve. He was given goat milk to drink and hen eggs to eat. A he-goat was slaughtered and cooked. The meat of the legs was removed and given to the boy. Finally he regained his health. The milkman claimed that the goat had cured him because of its ability to digest any kind of plant, including poisonous ones. The milk and the meat contain the strength that allows the animal to overcome illness, and their smells transmit this strength through the air. Hen eggs—here the milkman seemed to be entertaining popular Ayurvedic ideas—store "heat and energy" *(rajas)* and supplement the goat products.

The milkman's ideas about animals are revealed just as clearly by his actions as by his words. Along with his family he shares a narrow living space with two cows, a calf, and several chicken. The calf is free to wander in and out of the hut, and the entire courtyard, deep with mud and manure in the rainy season, serves as the family's kitchen and sitting room during the dry seasons. One day, as we sat on a bench in the courtyard and the milkman was stroking the calf, he talked about his animals.

"Do you name your cows?" I asked.

The milkman laughed at that question and said, "It depends on their color and behavior. A frisky cow may be called Frisky, but the name can change if her behavior changes."

"Do cows have different personalities?"

"This depends on their place of origin. Himacal cows, for instance are very mellow. But cows are not like people with different character."

"How do you get a bull to come to the cow?"

"You say 'Arrahoy, Arrahoy' [He demonstrated. The "r" was

lengthened. The bull will understand this wherever it is. It also responds
to "Durruhoy, Durruhoy," for the same purpose. This does not work
for calling the bull to eat or for anything else, only to mate. If you say
it even from a long distance, the bull still comes. The bull recognizes
this call because this is the sound the cow makes when it is in heat. The
milkman called this imitation (*anukarṇa.*)

"Do bulls respond to music?"

"Yes, like this: [he clicked his tongue several times]. Then too he
will come."

"Do these things work only during mating season?"

"Yes. Cow and buffalo also start giving this sound when they are
in heat. They stop eating and act fidgety, so you know they are in heat;
then you make this sound to call the bull."

"But why do you have to call the bull?, Doesn't he know when it
is season?"

"Yes, but this is quicker."

"What do you do when a cow is difficult to milk?"

"In her season a cow will stop giving her milk. Good milk returns
when she is pregnant. If she misbehaves, you just tie her with a rope."

"Do cow have souls?"

"Yes, all animals have a soul *(jīv).*"

"Must they be buried?"

"Yes. We used to put them in Ganga. This is against the law now,
so we dig a big hole in the ground, put them with cloth over the top,
and cover them with salt against smell. Or we give them to the Nath
caste, who skin them. Buffaloes and goats also."

"Why did you throw dead cows in the river when it was legal if it
is so far from here?"

"It helps the cow in future births."

"Now that you cannot use the river, why must animals be buried?"

"This is how it has always been."

[Some milkmen do dispose of dead buffaloes in the river—against
the law. They make no secret of it, however, and usually tie up the
traffic in a long procession that seems to be accompanying the beast on
its last journey.]

Extracting Essences. The use of essences or "juices" extracted from
particular animals reflects both a specific ecological intimacy with these
animals and universal principles. Healers of the Banaras fishing castes,
for example, use the oil of the rohu fish for healing an enormous range
of problems. The oil must invariably be rubbed under the sun. In con-

trast, Rajasthani healers, who come from arid environments, sell sanda lizard oil for the very same problems. According to Hakim Ali's brochure, the oil, when rubbed on the skin under the sun, will cure joint pain, gastric problems, blood clots, earache, asthma, itching, weight loss, bad dreams, and many other problems. The diseases read like signs of the time: Hakim Ali works outside the Jama Masjid in Old Delhi. But the power of familiar animals to heal is as old as India's oldest medical texts, and older.

The *Suśruta Saṃhitā* describes an illness *(Sita-putanā)* that is accompanied by "constant and frightened startling up, excessive shivering, comatose sleep, constant diarrheic stools and bloody smell of the limbs" (Uttara 27.11). A rich mixture is prescribed as medicine for this condition, which includes, in addition to numerous herbs, the urine of a cow and a she-goat, the dung of an owl and a vulture, and the cast-off skin of a snake (Uttara 34. 2). The disease and the cure always reflect an etiology, a science of causes and effects. But in Banaras, as opposed to the extremely sophisticated ancient texts, causes and effects are actually the give-and-take between animal and humans across transparent boundaries. The essence of the rohu fish is not an objective zoological quality. The fish is the most intimate natural companion a fisherman has, a source of nourishment and sustenance. Whatever healing power it has comes from direct observation. This conclusion is supported by a comparison of the way animals are used for healing in other cultures.

ॼ ॼ ॼ

Case 14.3

Healing in the Stomach of a Cow

On Sunday, April 9, 1995, Israel's leading daily, *Yediot Ahronot* ran the following description of a magical healing rite, which shook the country. In a slaughterhouse near Tel Aviv, infants and young toddlers were placed inside the largest stomach of a freshly slain cow. The children had been brought by ultra-orthodox Jewish parents who were desperate to cure different types of gross-motor disorders. The rituals had been taking place at this slaughterhouse, a place renowned among the orthodox communities of Jerusalem and Bnei Brak. *Yediot* described the procedure schematically in the paper: The children were brought early Friday morning and were made to witness the butchering and dismemberment of the cow. The large stomach, steaming with warm juices, was placed in a plastic tub and slit at one end, into which the infants were placed and kept for fifteen minutes. According to interviews with parents, the cow transmits powers to the child, having refined the powers through its digestion process into the form of juices. The parents firmly asserted that they could see improvement in their children. A week after the article's publication, the slaughterhouse was closed down and its owner charged with numerous sanitation infractions.[13]

A day after the story appeared, Salem Abu Siam of the Bedouin Cultural Center in Rahat was quoted as saying that this method of healing was Bedouin. The main difference, he continued, was that Bedouins use sheep and pass the infants seven times through the still warm hide of the freshly butchered animal. A reading of Wayland Hand, or even James Frazer, will quickly convince anyone that no single culture can lay exclusive claim on this universal practice.

Animal Bites

An immense number of cases can be collected throughout India or from its ancient texts to illustrate the use of animals in magical rites. Animals either cause several types of injury or provide the cure. They are often the patients or the medicine, helpers to the healer-shaman or allies to a sorcerer. In some cases animals are both culprit and cure: "When a person is bitten by a snake or scorpion the healer digs up some pulverized dirt mixed with the dirt from an anthill. He places the dirt in a fresh skin pouch and ties it as amulet around the skin of the victim. Then the healer gives his patient a drink of yellow curcuma and ghee mixed in water."[14]

Residents of Banaras have lost some of the intimacy with animals that typified the agrarian and pastoral communities of the area. The thoroughgoing naturalism of archaic magical practices, such as those reflected in the *Kauśika Sūtra,* has been displaced to some extent by ideas about spirits and ghosts. But even in the city, no impenetrable wall stands between humans and animals. The connection is still there in principle, if not as intensely. One can almost imagine a Vedic magician walking out of the distant past and setting up a very successful practice in Banaras today. He might think that the language of ghost possession is overwrought, and he would probably find some of his trusted medicines hard to obtain, but he would certainly be gratified by the familiarity of the magic practiced throughout the city. For a dog or a snake bite, or for scorpion stings, several options, which he would probably recognize, are available to residents of Banaras.

Aparnath Math, a Sadhu college near the Viśvanath Gali, is a renowned place for curing dog bites. The patient must bring some mustard oil in a container and give it to one of the disciples. The disciple takes the oil to a shrine for the dog of the Sadhu (Aparnath). It is a small shrine outside the temple, covered with colorful tiles depicting peacocks and Ganesh with a mouse. Silently, with no mantra recitation or any devotional appeal, the disciple pours the oil into a vat, in which floats a smaller vat, with yet another vat floating in it. All three concentric containers are filled to the brim with oil. At the tip of the big oil vat a wick is dipped and permanently lit. The disciple pours the oil into the outermost container until some overflows into the inner containers. Then he scoops a cup from the innermost vat and pours its contents into the patient's bottle. He instructs the visitor to rub the oil over the injury several times a day and promises that the injury will quickly heal. The young disciple—he seemed about seventeen—could not explain why three concentric vats are necessary. He claimed that the oil works because of the power of the holyman and that it would work regardless of the shape or configuration of the vats. However, he told me that he had been instructed to follow the exact routine each time someone comes with oil. When he himself had asked why, no answer was given.

In Himachal Pradesh, Omji relates, healers use ghur and clay to cure the effect of a dog bite. They refine the clay into powder by rubbing it over a stretched cloth. Out of this pulverized earth they make a clay ball and apply it to the location of the bite. Although dogs are not poisonous, the clay draws out the pain and the fever. The cure is accompanied by mantras. The healer also gives the patient sugarcane sugar to eat for the duration of the treatment.

ꕥ   ꕥ   ꕥ

Case 14.4

Curing Snakebite

Bal Karan is an old laborer who lives in Nagwa, a decrepit mess of mud huts situated where the Asi and the Ganges rivers meet. He enjoys a considerable reputation for curing snakebites and can back it up. On June 29, 1989, the *Svatantra Bharata Varanasi* newspaper displayed an impressive photograph of Bal Karan, along with a rave report on a cure he had performed to save the life of a woman. A few days earlier, this woman, also shown in the photograph, had been bitten by a huge female cobra. This happened during a musical concert in which Bal Karan was performing along with some of his friends. A snake charmer at the concert tried but failed to heal the shocked woman. The panic in the audience grew as the woman began to lose consciousness. Before Bal Karan knew what all the commotion was about, several people rushed her to a nearby hospital, but she was refused admission on grounds that she was too far gone. Only then, nearly an hour after the bite, was she brought to Bal Karan, who treated her in the following manner, as he told me in 1994.

He began by identifying the location and the severity of the bite by placing an onion on the alleged spot (the woman's right hand). The onion turned black, indicating a severe bite. Bal Karan took her pulse and found it extremely "weak."

With some help, Bal Karan stood the woman upright and poured water over her head to run down her entire body. This woke her up.

He then gave her Neem leaves to eat in order to find how much poison was still in her body (the more poison in the body, the less bitter the leaves taste). She refused to eat, so he used a mantra, and she quickly took a mouthful.

After she finished eating—the leaves were hardly bitter—Bal Karan repeated his mantra and performed *phutna* and *jharna,* the blowing of a mantra and the sweeping away of the poison. During that time he kept giving the woman Neem leaves until she vomited. She then started coming back to her senses. Bal Karan gave her ghee and milk, told her not to eat food or salt and to try not to sleep all night. He also told her to take cardamon seeds to Hanuman temple and to give them to beggars as an offering.

Bal Karan had learned this simple procedure from a woman *aghori* renouncer, who also had given him the powerful mantras. He said that the mantras are the chief source of the cure and that the water is used to cool the patient down. Two hours after he began the treatment, Bal Karan knew that the woman would get well.

In another incident, Hansraj, the milkman, told me of a scorpion treatment he uses, which involves tying the limb in a tourniquet above the bite, then using a mantra and sweeping out the poison in the direction of the end of the limb. Before doing this, the healer "fixes" a brass plate to the back of the patient by means of mantras, and it falls off only when the poison is all out. The screaming that invariably accompanies this procedure, according to Hansraj, is the sound made by the scorpion (or the snake) as it is being expelled. Healers also use some herbs mixed with water, and if the bite took place at night they do not let the patient sleep.

The sweeping or squeezing out of the poison along the bitten limb is a common practice. Mrs. Arti Divedi of Lucknow claimed that she could cure scorpion bites by means of a five-point star *yantra* that she draws above the the bite on the same limb. After she draws the *yantra,* she "sweeps" the poison out of the limb by lightly moving her hand over it in the direction of the extremity. Then she prepares an herbal concoction she learned from her mother that cures pain immediately.

This account, like those that of Bal Karan and Hansraj, could not be confirmed because snake and scorpion bites are rare and treated immediately. However, the procedure closely resembles the "cutting" of illness that many healers perform for backaches, headaches, and many troubles attributed to possession by outside powers. In such a way, or in a more basic way such as squeezing through narrow openings, the "sweeping" resembles cases of healing around the world by means of passing through holes. The basic healing paradigm goes beyond poison in the circulatory system to a nonspecific, but very concrete, experience of shedding. This is explained in Chapter 16 of this book.

NOTES

1. Murray J. Leaf, *Man, Mind and Science: A History of Anthropology* (New York: Columbia University Press, 1979).

2. Michel Foucault, *The Order of Things: An Archaeology of the Human Sciences* (New York: Vintage Books, 1970), p. 129.

3. J. L. Borges, *Other Inquisitions* (New York: Washington Square Press, 1966), p. 108.

4. Jared Diamond, "Stinking Birds and Burning Books," *Natural History* 2 (1994); Edward O. Wilson, *The Diversity of Life* (New York: Norton, 1992), p. 43.

5. Brian K. Smith, *Classifying the Universe: The Ancient Varna System and the Origins of Caste* (New York: Oxford University Press, 1994).

6. The absence of zoological classification in Banaras should not be construed as the sign of a primitive mentality. The simple existing taxonomies reflect an urban environment consumed by religious ideals. Primitive communities, in contrast, tend to possess highly refined natural classifications. See Brent Berlin, *Ethnobiological Classification: Principles of Categorization of Plants and Animals in Traditional Societies* (Princeton, N.J.: Princeton University Press, 1992).

7. Claude Levi-Strauss brought this notorious science to a pinnacle in *The Savage Mind* (Chicago: University of Chicago Press, 1966). The history of religions, especially in the works of Mircea Eliade, has been equally guilty of hiding behind such terms, along with "hierophany." See *Images and Symbols: Studies in Religious Symbolism* (New York: Sheed and Ward, 1969).

8. Levi-Strauss, *The Savage Mind*, p. 54.

9. Henri Hubert and Marcel Mauss, *Sacrifice: Its Nature and Function* (Chicago: University of Chicago Press, 1964), p. 53.

10. Ibid., pp. 54–55; René Girard, *Violence and the Sacred* (Baltimore: Johns Hopkins University Press, 1977). Girard's book was very widely read during the 1980s. It follows Freud *(Totem and Taboo)* in the assumption that religion springs from a primordial act of violence. Students of magic should find Girard's insistence on the primitive power of the senses appealing.

11. Pramad Kumar, *Folk Icons and Rituals in Tribal Life* (New Delhi: Abhinav Publications, 1984), p. 62.

12. Steven Fuchs, *The Korkas of the Vindhya Hills* (New Delhi: Inter-India Publications, 1988), p. 412.

13. The rule that the patient must witness the killing of the cow is particularly important. It creates a bonding that supports the magical event. This bond ("empathy") is discussed in Chapter 16.

14. *Kauśika Sūtra*, 32. 5–7.

☙ FIFTEEN ☙

The Tools of Magic

On the roof of my landlord's house on a mid-February evening I can sample the sounds of Banaras like a shopper in the Old Chowk-market. One concert is held near Tulsidas Ghāṭ, another in the opposite direction at the New Colony. Both are amplified by speakers located on numerous poles around the area. There are subtle string sounds that unfold gradually and require unwavering attention. But tonight they are lost in the explosions of electric guitars and the whining of a synthesizer-organ coming from another concert behind the Assi post office. Meanwhile, a local temple is sponsoring a public recitation of the great epic *Rāmāyaṇa*. The amplification here is the best of the lot. One can see older rickshaw drivers sitting attentively on the back of their cycles under phone poles with speakers. Entire neighborhoods squat under the poles, silently participating in Rāma's breathless adventures coming on the wings of a hoarse and earnest voice.

Spells and Mantras

The sounds that permeate the dry wintry air of Banaras remind me of the ancient Hindu theory that the world was created out of primordial sound.[1] The sound unfolded in ever more complex rhythms, pitches, and melodies, and in time a world emerged. It is still changing to the same music, but not in an obvious way. On this night the cacophonous strands of music come from paid musicians and recitors, each focused on his own audience. But far subtler wisps of sound rise daily from the mouths of magicians and healers who recite powerful words in order to move the world in a willed direction, or perhaps just to resonate with the rhythm of the world. The voices of magicians are rich with sacred power that is renowned as mantra. Magicians are practical people, impatient with theology and philosophy of sound. But they accept the fact that mantra encompasses manifest and hidden divine forces and holds recoiled magical efficacies that are released by experts.

Magical sounds are hardly limited to India, of course. "Abracadabra" and "hocus pocus" have become synonymous with magic itself. Malinowski may have been wrong that spells and incantations are essential to magic, but not by much. Just as the mantra is ubiquitous in India, spells, charms, and incantations are everywhere else around the world. And one explanation must account for them all—the Banaras street magician as well as Shakespeare's Macbeth:

> WITCH: Scale of dragon, tooth of wolf,
> witch's mummy, maw and gulf
> Of the ravined sald-sea shark,
> Root of Hemlock digged i' th' dark,
> Liver of blaspheming Jew,
> Gall of goat, and slip of yew
> Slivered in the moon's eclipse,
> Nose of Turk, and Tartar's lips,
> Finger of birth-strangled babe
> Ditch-delivered by a drab
> Make the gruel thick and slab.
> Add thereto a tiger's chaudron
> For th' ingredient of our cauldron.
>
> ALL: Double, double, toil and trouble,
> Fire burn, and cauldron bubble.

Spells always exist in a specific cultural form—language, symbols, functions. What would a Hindu see in the liver of a blaspheming Jew? But the act of reciting or chanting—word meanings aside—must be explained by reference to a general theory. A reductive explanation, like Frazer's imitative principle, must be applied to this strange, though universal, human behavior.

Banaras Mantras

The majority of those who practice magical healing in Banaras regard mantra as the most powerful tool in their bag. Sanskrit dictionaries define mantra as the part of the ancient Vedas that contains specific sacrificial formulas.[2] Mantra is also defined as a sacred verbal formula addressed to a god or goddess or as a mystical or magical sound—an incantation, charm, or spell. These broad definitions show that mantra is not only a magical device: The bathers in the Ganges at dawn recite mantras or hymns to the sun as it rises over the horizon. They mumble ancient Vedic words about creation and about righteousness, not magical chants. But elsewhere in the city magical mantras are used in order to heal or injure people, to attain success in business and love, or to give birth.

Mantras may have a rich history and an enormous body of metaphysical speculations behind them. But to practical magicians and single-minded patients, mantras are simple and powerful. They are perceived among magicians and patients as having come down from three distinct sources, each esteemed in its own way: Vedas, theistic cults (usually Tantra), and personal inspiration (or divine revelation).

Vedic Mantras. Vedic magical formulas are found mostly in the *Atharvaveda,* an ancient treasurehouse of powerful words for every occasion. Scholars are not certain whether such spells actually served specific rites, but the verbal formulas were apparently known to the anonymous authors of the near-contemporary text of practical magic, the *Kauśika Sūtra.*[3] The spells of the *Atharvaveda* are usually clear and direct, as illustrated by the following case. A person who suffers from the loss of hair may recite to the Nitatni medicinal plant: "You were born like a goddess on the Earth Goddess. We dig you up to strengthen the hair. Strengthen the old hairs and grow new hairs. Make the existing hair more luxurious"(6.136.1–2).

Early mantras were almost always meaningful; they made sense. Their words clearly stated the desired goals of the ritual that required the mantra, whether the ritual was magical, sacrificial, or devotional. A few mantras, however, were nonsensical, and the actual chanting of any given formula—even a meaningful one—always depended on rhythms and pitches more than on clarity of enunciation.

Tantric Mantras. In contrast to the relatively staid early formulas, medieval mantras recited by Tantrists can seem absurdly meaningless. For instance, someone desperate for wealth may find a quiet isolated spot and recite the following formula 21,000 times: "*Oṁ hrīṁ klīṁ śrīṁ namaḥ.*"[4] The words mean nothing in literal translation, except for the last one, which means *obeisance.* Over the centuries, the doctrine makers of various Tantra schools have developed elaborate theories to explain the origin and meaning of these sounds, as we shall shortly see. But the esoteric meaning of mantras is more of a meditative device than an instrument of communication. A phrase consisting of these five words is known as a "seed" mantra. It is an elementary vocalic building block that magical chanters can combine in various manners with other words to attain specific goals. For example, someone who gets passed over for a promotion may utter: *"Oṁ hrīṁ śrīṁ śrīṁ śrīṁ śrīṁ śrīṁ śrīṁ śrīṁ Lakṣmī mama gṛhe pūrya-pūrya cintā dūrya dūrya svāhā"* 108 times daily for twenty-one days. The sentence, again, "means" nothing, despite the fact that it holds a plea for Lakṣmī to make the chanter's household satisfied and his trouble removed far away. Most Tantric spells combine both the meaningless and the direct plea, but in constant repetition—the reader may try it—the sound drowns the meaning.

Inspired Mantras. Magicians do not recite the ancient Vedic mantras. These are either archaic or reserved for particularly sacred events officiated by special priests. The Tantric mantras, which are used with great frequency, are the secret property or tools of some magicians. They were handed down by the magician's teacher—the guru—at the time of initiation and, later, throughout the prolonged training. A Tantric magician, or one claiming to be, will not reveal the mantras to the uninitiated. But other magicians, or even those who follow Tantric practices on occasion, rely on mantras that come from other sources or some that may even be "invented." (No practitioner ever uses this terminology. The mantra is said to be revealed directly by a god during a dream or meditative state.) These mantras are easy to collect because their users enjoy sharing them. Among those I have recorded are the following two:

1. To get rid of particularly nasty enemies, one may recite the following:

Śānte Śān
Glory of Ali
Hit my enemy with a thousand arrows,
Whichever arrow you shoot, let it hit its target.
Let my enemy die
That week.
Give him a push
Ākūn, khākūn, ho, hā, he.

This mantra mixes elements from classical Sanskritic sources with Islamic terms and culminates, in typical fashion, with a series of nonsensical sounds.

2. To exorcise ghosts, whose mischief can cause a large variety of problems and diseases, one healer, an old *sokhā,* chants a very long mantra that includes the following lines:

> Kamaru and Ajmer Mari, High Court Mari,
> Meerut Mari, Jalawa Mari, Hari Ban Mari,
> Basti Ghar Mari, Chanarauti Fort Mari, Gate Mari,
> Janda Mari, Amkas Mari, Numberless Mari,
> Hawrah Bridge Mari, Court House Mari,
> Jail House Mari . . .
> Capture them and bring them everwhere
> Mari, Marayal, be there.

This quotation is just a small fragment of a repetitious fifteen-minute chant. The healer *(sokhā)* names several places followed by "Mari," a type of ghost that attaches itself to victims in one of those places mentioned. The portions of the mantra that I have omitted name other ghosts, places, gods, or benevolent forces that can help drive the ghost out. Naming the ghost starts the process of identifying, then addressing the agent of the patient's misery. A resonant verbal greeting, fortified by knowledge of the ghost's identity, invariably proves necessary for a successful expulsion. Over the course of many years the *sokhā* has assembled a growing list of local spirits to cover every possibility. His is an idiosyncratic roster, found nowhere else. He approaches his mantra with profound respect and repeats it with precision, until he adds new elements.[5] The pattern of vocalic repetition continues throughout the old man's nasal intonation: "Harasu Brahm, Kaleswar Brahm, Himal Brahm, Hari Brahm. . . ." On a warm day this monotony drones and lulls the listener into a comfortable drowsiness, though the ghost may suddenly rear its head and shatter the peace.

Traditional Hindu explanations for the power of mantras vary with different genres. Because mantras are powerful and make things happen, they must somehow be grounded in the creative forces that move the world. For the street magician, this may simply be the power of the goddess, who is summoned by means of her special sounds. For the ancient Vedic seer, the power of mantras may perhaps have been the mysterious or invisible effects it sought through the force of *brahman*— the sacrificial energy. Tantric theories are by far the most elaborate and elusive. They link the words or, better yet, the sounds of mantras to the mystical goals of the practitioner. The Tantric seeker after perfection— the *sādhaka*—becomes identified with various divine beings whom he places on his own body by means of esoteric practice, making them an effective part of his life. A correspondence between individual consciousness and mantric sound becomes reinforced through esoteric practices. In fact, the very heart of Tantric thinking is this notion of correspondence, or mediated opposites. Sexual symbolism lends itself neatly to express a profoundly abstract philosophy. Just as vowels animate consonants with power *(śakti)*, for example, so too the goddess quickens a passive god with dynamic energy. This correspondence pervades each and every mantra and accounts for its power. The mantra of ten "letters" (syllables)—*hrīṁ, śrīṁ, krīṁ, pa-ra-me-śva-rī, svā-hā*—is formed of both basic principles: male and female (consonant and syllable).[6] The effectiveness of this mantra derives from the sexual duality it exhibits in a symbolic sense. Many Banaras magicians who subscribe to Śākta Tantrism view mantra by means of similar simplifications of excruciatingly complex doctrines. For them mantra is a bridge between the goddess and the embodied consciousness of the practitioner, the access to her benevolent healing power. These magicians are not theologians, and they keep their mysticism to themselves. Their knowledge of doctrine is limited to basic principles, but their practice amply proves that mantras, for whatever stated reasons, are powerful words.

Mantra as Spell

India has produced magnificently subtle ideas about the psychology and the cosmology of sound. But in practice, the basic fact about mantra remains a universal one: Magical rituals in India, as anywhere else, are frequently accompanied by spells. The mantra is simply the Indian aspect of a much broader phenomenon. Traditional Hindu theories cannot therefore fully explain the meaning and function of mantras. Even the expert Indologist must go beyond indigenous theories, as Wade Wheelock and Frits Staal have done. Wheelock, like Tambiah and other scholars who implemented the ideas of Wittgenstein and Austin, claims that the word of mantras is an effective word, a word of action.[7] Mantras do not just convey thoughts; they transform the consciousness of the chanter and elevate the entire rite to another level of reality. The magical force of mantras comes from the symbolic identities they establish between cosmos and magician, identities that are rendered subject to personal experience. This is a quasi-mystical explanation, because it places the magician directly in the realm of the sacred. Jan Gonda, the Dutch Indologist, also claimed that mantra is a means of "coming into touch or identifying oneself with the essence of the divinity which is present in the mantra."[8] But this probably applies more closely to highly trained Tantric practitioners than to the average street magician who uses mantras.

Frits Staal, an Indologist and philosopher at the University of California at Berkeley, has led his controversial thinking on mantras to the outer reaches of the humanities and into the realm of ethology. Mantras, he has repeated over the years, are not speech acts. They are not even language, though they share a few secondary properties with language. Instead, mantras are a type of sound, like music or the chatter of birds, that "represents a remnant, vestige, or rudiment of something that existed before language."[9] Oddly enough, this apparent biological reduction is consistent with the view of traditional folklore in numerous locations. The following Inuit poem is a case in point:

MAGIC WORDS
In the very earliest time,
when both people and animals lived on earth,
a person could become an animal if he wanted to
and an animal could become a human being.
Sometimes they were people
and sometimes animals
and there was no difference.
All spoke the same language.
That was the time when words were like magic.
The human mind had mysterious powers.
A word spoken by chance
might have strange consequences.
It would suddenly come alive
and what people wanted to happen could happen—
all you had to do was say it.
Nobody could explain this:
That's the way it was.[10]

When mantras are used in a ritual, Staal argues, their meaning "does not lie in their language or even their poetic or metrical structure, but in the sounds, with their themes and variations, repetitions, inversions, interpolations, and the particular distribution of their elements."[11] Mantras represent the survival of a primitive biological principle—a temporal structure manifest as sound—in a human cultural form. Ritual is another such form, and it too is primitive enough to be shared with many animals at the time of mating, expressing aggression or marking territory. Although Staal refuses to speculate on the nature of the biological trait represented by the sound of mantra, he concludes emphatically, and to the chagrin of many culturalists who know his work, that both ritual and mantra are meaningless. They are pure pattern.

The biological argument sounds extreme, but it is not absurd. Neurologists have agreed that musical ability probably originated in the same neural circuits that account for language ability. Neither represents a strict evolutionary adaptation, but both may have derived as a secondary result of another adaptational success, for instance ballistic movement—the earliest human hunting skill.[12] Ethological research may eventually discover the connection between ritual chanting and biological drives. At this point the claim that language and music share neuronal circuits is too broad to contribute much to cultural analysis. If one wishes to be really speculative about the biological basis of sound, there is also the work of the geneticist Susumu Ohno and his wife, Midori Ohno. Susumu Ohno assigned musical notation to the substances that constitute DNA according to a fixed and consistent pattern. He then chose a key and rhythmic pattern. The result was a melody his wife further enriched with harmonies to produce music that even trained musicologists could not distinguish from that of the great composers.[13] Of course, this is a mathematical or logical game; the geneticist *simulated* the chemical properties of DNA with sound. It is not the same thing as claiming, as Hindus have over the centuries, that the physical world *is* sound.

Taken at their face value, many mantras are clearly meaningful: They command a ghost to depart, specify an enemy's lot, beg the fever to come down. The impulse to give such desires a voice may be primitive, but its voice is often a language. To be sure, no intrinsic and necessary connection links the language of mantras to magical acts. Nonmagical rituals such as bathing use mantras, while some magical rites do not. An essential link does, however, connect the magical consciousness and the primitive impulse behind the vocalization—the musicality—of mantras. Even "meaningful" mantras are musical, using rhythms, repetitions, inversions, and other devices. The musical quality, the esthetic temporal pattern, of mantras induces in participants a state of mind comparable to what I described in Chapter 8. The *sokhā* who repeats the names of all the Mari ghosts is not just being thorough out of a pedantic compulsion. The musical patterns and the prolonged singsong of the invented mantra, with its constant alliteration and endless repetitions, are mesmerizing. They alter the awareness, which has already been affected by the smoking of the hashish-like *bhāng* prior to the recitation. Sound and smoke alike are primitive. The essential connection between mantras, when used, and magic, therefore, defies both meaning and meaninglessness. It is the resonant musicality of mantras, and all spells, that transforms ordinary plans into magical connections. As Aldous Huxley once wrote: "If words had not first moved him, how could man have come to believe that they would move things?"[14]

One could argue that because different spells or mantras are used for obtaining different ends, their power must lie in the word meaning. If pure musicality were the source of a mantra's power, no semantic correspondence would need to exist between mantra and goal; any mantra could serve any purpose. To answer this challenge, one should note that since the words are often meaningless, the correspondence between a spell or mantra and its goal, in practice, are a matter of rhythm, pitch, and even the status of the mantra—a matter of convention—but not its literal meaning. Practitioners do not change the wording of the one or two mantras at their disposal every time they encounter a different patient. One mantra serves many needs because its magic is not so much a matter of isolating specific causes to specific diseases. Instead, the mantra seeks to reestablish the harmony or connectedness that was broken as the illness surfaced.

Any native theory can explain the correspondence between words and goals in one way or another, but theories are not the stuff of magical experience. Experience is a far more mundane and tumultuous affair. It nods to enshrined norms but follows the playful energy of living performance. Somehow experience rarely deceives, and its goal—wellness—is served better by sound than by words.

Oddly enough, many mantras in Banaras today are never heard because they are never voiced. They are whispered as the healer inhales, then blown out on the patient or into a bottle of water or other objects. This is called *phutna*—"blowing" or "breaking"—and it suggests that mantras can combine with air to create a powerful substance. The practice of blowing a mantra is associated, in varying degrees, with Tantric ideas about placing divine powers in the body of the mediator. The healer becomes a container of energy—*śakti*—through which the mantra passes before it is placed on the patient. Like every other practice associated with healing, this one too can be done with a magical attitude or indifferently. Unlike the chant or spell, which is heard, *phutna* is felt with the skin. In either case, the experience of magic has nothing to do with the meaning of the blown words, but everything to do with their "texture."

MAGICAL OBJECTS

Among the objects I have seen used in magical rites in Banaras are water, clay and metal pots, hammers, string, amulets made of numerous types of objects, stones, paper, coins, grains, knives, nails, quills, skulls, animals, diagrams, words, mud bricks, leaves, trees, hair, sticks, flowers, reeds, lampblack, oils, books, plates, handkerchiefs, fans, necklaces, various intoxicants, shells, feathers, lemons, images of gods, the limbs of the human body, and ponds.

The list is chaotic because any mode of organization would be completely arbitrary. Any object can be replaced with any other, and the determining principle is never an objective characteristic intrinsic to one item, let alone a whole class of objects. If one adds other objects used by magicians elsewhere around the world, the list would explode in size and disarray. In fact, every conceivable object would have to be included because, in one place or another during the course of four millennia, every available thing has been recruited into the service of magic.

How do magicians choose their preferred items, and how do these serve the magical event? Does each object have its own distinct explanation, or can one general principle encompass every object ever used in magic? A consistent and comprehensive theory of magic must answer these questions effectively. Tylor and Frazer claimed that magical objects either resembled or touched the goal or person at which they were directed. Hair, for example, could be used in a rite to injure the person from whom it came. Analogy and contiguity, the rules of sympathy, explained every magical instrument by means of such primitive ways of reasoning. This is an overarching, comprehensive principle, though it has now been rejected as simplistic. In contrast, Tambiah argued that objects become effective in magical rituals when they symbolize certain relations and thereby express the desired conditions the magician hopes for. Porcupine quills, for example, are regarded as effective in destabilizing the household peace of one's enemies only when taken from males and females of the species. The pair of quills is a powerful symbol because it comes from a pair of animals that display a distinct (quarrelsome) type of relationship. The symbolic principle, like sympathy, is comprehensive and consistent. It can explain the use of specific items in a given rite, but it also provides an abstract framework for the entire range of objects.

The theory of the magical experience (see Chapter 8) takes magic in a more literal sense once again. Magic is regarded as a unique experience that results from certain directly perceived relations. The tools of magic must be related to these perceptions in some way, whether direct or symbolic. In either case the objects must be incorporated into the experience, at least as symbols. To evaluate such a theory of magic, one must obviously look at its interpretation of magical objects. This job can be simplified by submitting the long list of "magical" objects to a few basic distinctions.

Rituals of magic seldom take place without some secondary implements such as tools, icons, musical instruments, or healing substances. Even the *ulṭā-janma* chiropractor, who only runs his foot down the back of the patient, must lean the correct hand on the correct shoulder. His magic depends on this precision, so both hand and shoulder become tools of the rite. If he accidentally leans on a chair with the other hand, the chair does not become a magical tool. If an image of Kālī happens to hang on the wall and the healer routinely greets it as he enters the room, the image may be more important than the chair, but it remains peripheral to the magical event.

The objects of magic are either essential or peripheral in any given context. This is a truism. But no fixed rule, universal to all the practitioners in Banaras, determines which object belongs to which category. The marginal in one case may become cardinal in another case, if circumstances warrant the change. The freedom to substitute resembles the freedom of the traditional musician to improvise on fixed themes. But as substitutions increase, both the theories of sympathy and of symbolism become inadequate. So while the distinction between essential and peripheral objects seems trivial, it draws attention to the limits of existing theories.

Nonessential objects are either cultural/religious artifacts or mere instruments of the ritual. The deities that often adorn the magical site, or even an entire temple, for instance, are seldom essential to the magical event. Similarly, the matches used to light the camphor cubes are instruments of the rite, like the flame, but, unlike the flame, they can be replaced with a lighter. They are nonessential instruments. But objects that seem irrelevant—a boat in the background, a bird call in the night, a brightly lit flame—all these can become essential to the mood that makes magical experience possible. The distinction, or rather the change, is subjective and not intrinsic to the object itself.

Essential tools are not limited to one type, either. Some are directly medicinal—herbs, for instance—while others are musical, symbolic, or social. The hammer used by the pundit to awaken a newly constructed boat is symbolic of the relation between the inanimate object and the craftsman who has given it a body. The raised sitting loft of the sorcerer is a social mark of status, but it also serves the ritual by establishing an appropriate mental attitude (awe) toward the practitioner. In short, the essential class of magical instruments is rich and complex, but it also owes its status to indeterminate reasons.

Symbols and Signs

Recall the ape in James Gibson's analysis of perception (see Chapter 8). The animal finds an item of food, say a skull, which it must shatter in order to eat. Next to the skull lies a rock. The ape turns to it, picks it up, and hurls it at the target. In what way, asks Gibson, does the rock "represent" a tool? Gibson claims that the rock possesses intrinsic qualities, such as "grabability" and "throwability," that are neither representational nor mental in any way. They are properties of the rock, which evolution has equipped the ape to perceive. Computational theories argue, in contrast, that the animal recognizes the rock as something other than what it is, as an instrument. The ape's ability to learn and to remember provides it with rudimentary forms of mental representation—symbolic thinking.

If this example seems a crude way to begin a discussion of signs and symbols, this may be a fair price to pay for the clarity with which it illustrates the central issue. A sign, according to C. S. Peirce, "is something that stands to somebody for something in some respect or capacity."[15] "Stands" carries an immense load because, as the case of the ape shows, it is unclear just how one thing stands for another. The two extreme positions cited in that example are the mental or ideational relationship and the behavioral response. If the person or animal who takes x to be a sign of y has an idea of y evoked by the object x, then the relationship between the two is mental. But if the object x only produces appropriate behavior relating to y—the mental component is unknown or nonexistent—then the "symbolic" relationship is behavioral.

This disagreement is the extreme form of a debate that goes to the heart of several psychological and philosophical disciplines. In the study of cultures, the debate revolves around the interpretation of cultural symbols, modes of classification, and thought. Rodney Needham, for instance, has developed a mental-culturalist interpretation of signs and symbols and rejects any physiological basis for traditional views on classification, right/left distinction, terms for basic colors, percussion, and others.[16] Brent Berlin and Eleanor Rosch, among other cognitive scientists, have shown, in contrast, that perceptual-physiological factors determine basic ways of classifying and knowing the world.[17] Although their position is far from behavioristic, it still explains cognitive processes in terms of a physical interaction with an environment.

Both approaches are vulnerable to criticism. In the case of mentalism, as Needham himself conceded, anything can stand for any other thing in a symbolic relationship.[18] This can render symbols trivial. Certain conditions have to be specified under which unique objects come to represent only other unique objects in order to make the symbolic relation meaningful. But this is not easy to do. Cultural historians have searched for such conditions—determinants—without always showing how a mental motive—an idea rather than an economic factor, for instance—actually brings contingent facts into a symbolic relationship. In many cases these scholars run afoul of historical materialists and, nowadays, postmodernists.

Behaviorism in its crudest forms is even harder to defend. It evokes the image of Pavlov's salivating dogs associating one object with another through harsh stimulus-response learning. In fact, many symbols summon ideas and emotions even though no corresponding behavior ever takes place. The sight of rain from inside a cozy house can result in either the opening or the closing of a window, depending on a variety of competing mental images in the mind of the beholder.

Behaviorism and mentalism are two ways of considering how a perceiver might take one thing as a symbol or a sign for another. But there are alternative ways of analyzing symbolic relations. Peirce divided signs into indexes, symbols, and icons. An index is a sign that refers to the object it denotes through a causal relationship. A thermometer is one example of an indexical sign that is causally related to the fact it signifies—temperature. A symbol, in Peirce's technical sense, is a sign that is related to its object by convention. A person's name or the elephant of the Republican party are two types of symbol. An icon, finally, denotes objects by virtue of its own characteristics. The floor-plan diagram of a magnificent cathedral represents the building because its own spatial proportions resemble those of the cathedral. The relationship is neither causal nor merely conventional. Some similarity between the characteristics of the icon and the object it signifies must exist.

Many signs contain mixed features and may be both iconic and symbolic or indexical and symbolic. Moreover, it is seldom obvious how other peoples in distant ages have understood symbolic relations. Researchers have assumed that primitive people take names and effigies as signs that are causally related to other objects and therefore can be manipulated as magical objects. In a similar vein, some Indologists have speculated that the forest in India's literature serves as a symbol for subconscious realms.[19] Freudian and occasionally even Jungian ideas have been used as navigational aides for charting the deep symbolic and iconic meanings of ancient India's vast texts. But indexical symbolism has been just as pervasive in India. Landscapes of immense forests and towering mountains have been perceived as *directly* powerful forces whose meaning often has depended on the way humans have interacted with their environment and shaped its contours by means of action and imagination. Unfortunately, no objective criteria exist for judging in what way an observer takes one object as standing for another. We risk confusing one type of rationality with another and losing track of the magical relationship altogether. Perhaps another example may illustrate the direction we need to take.

There are many ways to track humans or animals. Predators survive by developing habits that resonate with those of their prey. They also evolve effective camouflage. Above all, their senses are extremely refined in picking up the trail left by a moving animal. For the vast majority of species, this means a chemical trail in the form of scent. The predator does not need to differentiate mentally between the trace—the scent—and its source. The hunting skills of animals are not based on the interpretation of signs. To predators scent is an extension of the prey, an attractor in its own right, that is related biochemically both to its origin and to the nervous system of the tracker. In contrast, human trackers "read" the marks left on the ground or the broken twigs of bushes as signs of the person or animal they are tracking. Yosef Yarkoni, a Bedouin who assumed a Hebrew name while serving in the Israeli army, was a legendary tracker. His senses, intuition, and logic enabled him to spot and track smugglers and *Feda'ine* (terrorists) even months after they had passed through a landscape. Yarkoni's colleagues loved to boast about his powers. They claimed that if a man were to spit under a rock in the middle of the desert and Yarkoni were to pass by one hundred years later, he would be able to track that man to his grave and curse his soul for spitting on God's earth. Similarly, Jim Corbet, the renowned hunter of man-eating tigers in India, boasted that he could tell the sex of a distant tiger, its direction of travel, and whether it was hungry or not just by listening to the call of birds in the area.

Great human trackers rely on learning and reasoning, not on the conditioning and the genotypic advantages of animal predators. But that is not the whole story. The difference between an able tracker and a great one is intuition. When the habits of the prey become second nature to the hunter, or when the landscape becomes an extension of the hunter's personality, the tracks left behind—the indexical signs—no longer signify just by a logic that points to the prey's likely behavior. The tracker intuitively knows what the animal does because he knows, or feels, what he might do in its place. The tracks are "related" to both hunter and prey, almost as in the case of the nocturnal scent follower.

Many of the objects used in magical rites, when the magical consciousness is involved, signify in such a way. They are not only iconic or even indexical. They are like a trace that links prey to predator, because they link the object of the rite with its means through the perception and interaction of the participant. In fact, vision—the most "aloof" sense—is seldom enough in magical rites. The more primitive and immediate senses, like touch and smell, bring participants into intimate contact with the objects used. The use of amulets in ancient India may illustrate this point.

According to the *Kauśika Sūtra*, the mysterious skin disease called Kṣetriya is treated, among other means, by hanging an amulet around the patient's neck. The amulet is made of freshly killed animal skin in which the healer places mud, including mud from an anthill, barley straw, and sesame blossom. The amulet is kept on until the patient is healed (*Kauśika Sūtra* 26.43 and *Atharvaveda* 2.8).

The amulet acts as a layered therapeutic symbol. It contains dirt from the anthill because this dirt had been churned up from below the surface—or the skin—of the earth. The amulet leather shares a certain desired quality (transitivity) with the cure of the patient's skin. This is a case of iconic signification, so ably analyzed by Stanley Tambiah. But the amulet must also be made of fresh animal skin, usually deer. The emphasis on freshness indicates that the authors of the *Kauśika Sūtra* felt it important to preserve the living characteristics of the animal from which it came. The qualities of the animal or its skin can thereby "pass" on to the patient. Since fresh skin conducts living substances and liquids more effectively than dried or processed leather, the field-related contents of the pouch (the word *Kṣetriya* means agrological as well as uterine) can slowly percolate through the fresh leather to the patient. The magicians relied here on indexical thinking along with the symbolic and iconic modes.

This, in brief, is as far as theories of magic usually go. Objects used in magical rites and cures reveal a distinct way of thinking and acting; they encapsulate an implicit philosophy. When properly formulated, these theories are not only accurate but fascinating as well, because they illuminate the broader spectrum of cultural ideas in which magical symbols often participate. But magical experience is another matter. In order to be experienced magically, the amulet cannot simply signify. Every pendant, even expensive jewelry, signifies without necessarily being incorporated into a magical experience. The amulet must be perceived in the same way that the nocturnal predator sniffs its prey. And it is the task of the healer to see that this happens.

For this reason, the patient and the healer struggle to enter the subjective state of the magical consciousness by various means, including the use of mantras, music, and breathing techniques. The separate, symbol-reading self is stripped of its overriding authority in favor of a perceptual and interactive experience. Ordinary and separate events become transformed into magical relations. Anyone who has smelled fresh sheets after a long journey knows how deeply affecting such a simple sensation can be in contrast with the common routine of going to bed. The magical rite sharpens mundane sensitivities and directs them in a variety of ways in relation to the symbols magic uses. The amulet-pouch is felt to be transitive and its contents—symbols all—are felt percolating into one's body through the skin. If the subjective experience cannot be substantiated by means of biochemical analysis at the point of contact—for those who must have "objective" proof—it is still a neuronal reality, like the difference between seeing red and green or the pain of a phantom limb. Objective verification misses the mark if it does not take into account, as its primary fact, the consciousness of a relationship. Just as pain cannot exist without the awareness of pain, magic cannot exist without the awareness of a relatedness felt as osmosis. A magical object can be anything that becomes incorporated into such an event.

NOTES

1. This is a familiar idea to students of Indian music and religion. One recent work is Guy L. Beck, *Sonic Theology: Hinduism and Sacred Sound* (Columbia, S.C.: University of South Carolina Press, 1993); see also Robert Gottlieb, "Symbolism Underlying Improvisatory Practices in Indian Music," *Journal of the Indian Musicological Society* 16, no. 2 (1985): 23–36.

2. The topic of mantra is strewn with mines placed over three decades of pop culture. A good introduction to mantra is Harvey P. Alper, ed., *Mantra* (Albany: State University of New York Press, 1989); See also Paul E. Muller-Ortega, "Tantric Meditation: Vocalic Beginnings," in *Ritual and Speculation in Early Tantrism,* ed. Teun Goudriaan (Albany: State University of New York

Press, 1992), pp. 227–46; A more technical textual analysis of mantra can be found in P. V. Kane, *History of Dharmaśāstra* (Poona: ABORI, 1930–62), and Andre Padoux, *Vāc: The Concept of the Word in Selected Hindu Tantras.* (Albany: State University of New York Press, 1990).

3. Maurice Bloomfield, "The Atharvaveda and the Gopatha-Brāhmaṇa," in *Grundriss der Indo-Arischen Philologie und Alterumskunde* (Encyclopedia of Indo-Aryan Research) G. Bühler ed., F. Kielhorn, 1899, pp. 1–136; N. J. Shende, *The Religion and Philosophy of the Atharvaveda.* Bhandarkar Oriental Series No. 8 (Poona: BORI, 1985).

4. Like collections of prayers sold under the "inspirational" display at American bookstores, these old formulas are popularly available in books, magazines, and even comics sold by vendors in Banaras. See, for instance, L. R. Chowdhri, *Practicals of Mantras & Tantras* (New Delhi: Sagar Publications, 1990). In India, as elsewhere, religion has often been disseminated by means of "vulgar" popular media, which modern scholarship has now begun to take seriously.

5. Diane Coccari's version is different from my own in a few minor details, probably because two years or so went by between the two recitations.

6. *Mahānirvānatantra* 5.12.

7. "The Mantra in Vedic and Tantric Ritual," in Alper, ed., *Mantra,* p. 96; see also his "The Problem of Ritual Language: From Information to Situation," *Journal of the American Academy of Religion* 50, no. 1 (1982): 49–71.

8. "The Indian Mantra," in *Selected Studies.* (Leiden: E. J. Brill, 1975), p. 249.

9. "Vedic Mantras," p. 74,

10. David Guss, *The Language of the Birds: Tales, Texts and Poems of Interspecies Communication* (San Francisco: North Point Press, 1985), p. 10.

11. "Vedic Mantras," p. 58.

12. William H. Calvin, *The Cerebral Symphony: Seashore Reflections on the Structure of Consciousness* (New York: Bantan Books, 1990), p. 296; Calvin describes his theory in greater detail in *The Throwing Madonna: Essays on the Brain* (New York: Bantam, 1991).

13. Cited in Larry Dossey, *Meaning and Medicine: Lessons from a Doctor's Tales of Breakthrough and Healing* (New York: Bantam Books, 1991). pp. 140–41.

14. *Texts and Pretexts* (London: Triad Grofton Books, 1986), p. 197.

15. Charles Sanders Peirce, *Collected Papers.* 8 vols. (Cambridge, Mass.: Harvard University Press, 1931–58), 2:228.

16. *Circumstantial Deliveries* (Berkeley: University of California Press, 1981).

17. Eleanor Rosch, "Natural Categories," *Cognitive Psychology* 4 (1973): 328–50; Brent Berlin and Paul Kay, *Basic Color Terms: Their Universality and Evolution* (Berkeley: University of California Press, 1969), and Brent Berlin, *Ethnobiological Classification: Principles of Categorization of Plants and Ani-*

mals in Traditional Societies (Princeton, N.J.: Princeton University Press, 1991).

18. Needham, *Circumstantial Deliveries,* p. 32.

19. The most accessible (nonphilosophical) application of Peirce's categories to India is A. K. Ramanujan, "Is there an Indian Way of Thinking? An Informal Essay," in *India Through Hindu Categories,* ed. McKim Marriott (New Delhi: Sage Publications, 1990) pp. 41–58.

SIXTEEN

The End of Magic

For a variety of reasons, scholars of religions no longer find it useful to compare religion and magic. Although the old distinctions, dating back to the Victorians, are still deeply entrenched in the popular view, they mislead. According to the worst misconception, magic *compels* natural or supernatural forces to obey human will, whereas religion acts by *supplication* to a god who may or may not respond. With the rise of symbolical interpretations of magic, this distinction has stopped making sense. If the magical act is a form of expressive speech, which is not compelling but meaningful, then magic and religion become two types of one phenomenon: a symbolic rationality in relation to the sacred.

But there are better reasons for abandoning comparisons between religion and magic. The history of the term *religion* shows it growing out of European cultural and linguistic circumstances that rarely apply elsewhere.[1] Extending such a concept across cultural barriers results in a reification of diverse and fluid realities like faith and cumulative tradition. One may properly speak of the faith of Hindus or the cumulative traditions of Buddhists, but the abstract categories religion, Hinduism, and Buddhism ought to be abandoned or used in a very restricted sense. Not only are the terms empty intellectual containers, but they lead to false distinctions and set up boundaries between persons—the true subject of study.

These observations are doubly true for magic, which, more than even religion, is a distinct development of European cultural history. Of course, this does not mean that the phenomena we call magical do not actually exist around the world, only that the abstract substantive noun magic deceives when used away from its Near Eastern and European home. John Hick's summary of the situation with religion—"religion takes such widely different forms and is interpreted in such widely different ways that it cannot be adequately defined but only described"—is valid for magic as well.[2] Definitions are based on the objective properties of the thing defined. The object may be abstract, of course: One can define and compare two species of animals, not just a tiger and a cock. But the assumption that religion and magic are abstract, though objective, things like *Felis tigris* and *Gallus gallus* is false and misleading.

Unlike biological distinctions, no objective and universal criteria inform us when an act or belief is magical and when it is religious. When is submersion in a river a religious rebirth, and when is it a magical removal of pollution or disease? When is a pendant, say the Jewish *mezuzah* that hangs on doorposts, a religious object, and when is it—like the Muslim *hamsa*—a talisman? We gain little by even asking such questions, because the categories *religion* and *magic* have been recognized for the empty shells they are.

For these and similar reasons, scholars rarely use the term *magic*, except in reference to its specific cultural contexts in the European history of ideas. The diverse phenomena that have occupied students of magic—for example, alchemy, witchcraft and sorcery, and divination—are discussed only in the cultural and historical contexts in which they appear. They no longer serve as regional aspects of a universal category called *magic*.

So is this book a dangerous throwback to the mid-century and earlier studies of magic? The mere use of the word *magic* in the title might lead some among the current generation of students of culture to think so. However, the central thesis of this book is that a distinct and universal magical phenomenon does indeed exist, which I have called the "magical experience." It is not an objective category like religion or magic of old but a psychological quality like imagination. No action or object is ever intrinsically magical; it only becomes incorporated into a system of perceptions and responses that make it part of a magical event. The *mezuzah* can serve either as a religious object or as a magical talisman, just as it can serve as a door stopper if necessary. Considered in this way, magic—or the magical experience—begs to be distinguished from other states of mind, such as faith. The question of magic or religion is internalized and becomes a subject for a far subtler and more flexible distinction, for which we must listen to those who engage in both. The answer will be entirely subjective and embedded in the shifting contours of circumstances, moods, and states of mind. A snapshot rarely reveals enough.

र्ग्   र्ग्   र्ग्

Case 16.1

A Fertility Bath

Nothing matters more to the Hindu wife than fertility. The eternal life of her husband hangs on it. Unfortunately, nothing also is quite so uncertain as a successful pregnancy. More magic is practiced with this in mind than all the other reasons combined. I was drawn by this fact to Lolark Kund one Sunday morning. I went to observe women—for it was mainly women who acted as though the pool was powerful—taking their Sunday morning bath in it. Armed with notebook and tape recorder, I had to overcome the self-consciousness of a foreign voyeur in the company of bathers.

But there were only three women at the pool that early morning, an old woman and two teenagers. The old woman was bathing, a tiny bent figure inside her clinging wet sari. The two teenage girls were sweeping the steps around the pool, collecting dust and debris left by the previous week's bathers and *pūjās* into a pile, which they gathered in reed baskets. They did not seem to mind their work, or, rather, their work failed to interrupt their joking and laughter. The younger one, whose name was Sangita, as I later found out, suddenly pushed the other, Ranjini, into the water. Ranjini barely kept her balance and stumbled to the edge of the water, wetting the leg of her pants. She laughed loudly and squeezed her clothing, then pulled both her pants legs above her knees, showing smooth and muscular calves. She then turned around and noticed me, and her laughter became an embarrassed smile. I smiled back, and she quickly glanced at the old woman, perhaps expecting some rebuke.

But the old pilgrim was busy with other things just then. She was a Nepalese who had come to spend her remaining years in Banaras, and she lived in a distant neighborhood. Although her duties to her deceased husband and society had been fulfilled—she had three married sons—she still felt obliged to come and bathe "in order to avoid the diseases of old age." She was now in the middle of a *pūjā* to Lolarka, the sun deity who resides in the small shrine and makes the cold water of this pool so healing. The pilgrim offered two lemons, a few blades of holy grass, a rose, and a few *genda* flowers. Then she lit a lamp and traced seven circles in front of the icon, which was simply a circular stain of ochre paint with two eyes on the back wall of the shrine.

Ranjini was still in the cold water, showing no discomfort. She began sweeping the first few submerged steps. Clouds of dust kicked up and spread through the crystalline water. Sangita, the younger one, scooped a few handsful of water and vigorously rubbed her own calves, washing off the dust that clung to her feet. The girls were cousins and belonged to the low caste of the boat people. Ranjini's father had drowned in the river, but she had two older brothers. The two girls were in school now, but in a few years they would be married, and their lives would be devoted entirely to their husbands and their families. They would never know another man before then, but their glances and giggles showed they were maturing quickly.

The old woman was now silently reciting mantras, the bead necklace tucked—but not completely hidden—under a shawl indicated she was about halfway through her repetitions. By the time she finished, the dust in the pool had settled, and a serene calm was settling over the water. The girls, both dried now, turned away to go, satisfied that their job was perfectly finished, when suddenly the old woman flung her offerings into the water, where they landed with a splash. The lemons bobbed for a few seconds, then sailed deep into the pool and away from the leaves and blades of grass. The old woman gathered her belongings and began to labor up the steps. The two girls, baskets on their heads, grimaced with annoyance at the mess, then looked at each other, shrugged, and scampered off.

Accompanied by a woman assistant-interpreter, I returned to Lolark Kund many times in the following weeks and talked with the three women again. I asked them what made Lolark Kund so special. The old Nepalese knew all about Lolarka and the myths that surrounded the place. She claimed that her three sons were a gift of the sun, though she had never been to Banaras in her youth. "Lolark is powerful enough for anyone who believes, not only those who come here."

"Who is Lolark? I asked, and she told me the myth of the trembling sun who guards Banaras and burns away the sins of those who come to this place. She pointed toward the shrine at water's edge with the image of the sun on the rock and carefully said: "I try to come every Sunday (Ravivar) to bath and offer *pūjā* to Sun. I will do this as long as I can walk."[3]

The boat-caste teenagers also knew about the sun but did not seem to care much for his shrine. Pressed to explain the attraction of the place, they both said, "*toṭakā*" (magic) and laughed. On the special pilgrimage and bathing festival of Lolark Chath, thousands of visitors crowd the narrow space in and around the pool. Many bring fruits and vegetables, especially squashes, which are sent off on the water as husband and wife, clothes knotted together, take a bath. Other vegetables are pierced with needles supplied by the attendants of the boat caste. Saris are left in the water by women who change into new garments. The girls had seen these rituals because they are charged with helping clean up the flotilla of debris left by thousands of bathers. They knew that only someone of a low and polluted caste could handle such leftovers, but this failed to bother them. When I asked them why *toṭakā* made childless couples fertile, they had no answer. "We never talk about such things," they told me, "No one does. We just do what we are told." But I persisted: "Do you think the water is powerful, or is it the ritual action, or the sun? Will you have sons because you spend so much time in the water?" That last question was a riot, to judge by the outburst of laughter that followed. They never answered any of these questions, which they must have taken for misplaced curiosity.

Anyone who looks for clear and fixed criteria for separating magic from religion in the words and the actions of participants is likely to become confused. People—the proper subject for the study of religion or magic—are too complicated. Their beliefs and attitudes have no boundaries: Piety is mixed with greed, and superstition with purity. The objects of beliefs and aspirations have no life outside the imagination of believers; they show no Platonic clarity of form but are enmeshed in the ambiguities of daily existence.

Imagine that you have received a contract to edit an encyclopedia on magic. Or perhaps you decide to write a book on the history of magic in India, as I have. How do you divide the vast subject into manageable units? The encyclopedia might contain entries such as "astrology," "alchemy," "amulets," "exorcism (see possession)," "witchraft," and "spells." The book might discuss these topics in their Indian contexts and use the appropriate terminology and sources. But you quickly discover that this logical path is blocked by at least two major obstacles. First, magic, either as the "magical experience" (of Chapter 8) or as the commonly understood concept, permeates every aspect of life in many traditional societies. To be consistent, the encyclopedia will have to carry entries on farming, sex, fishing, sports, arts, crafts, warfare, and every other area of life. Second, the usual "magical" topics—divination, alchemy, and the rest—are no more intrinsically magical than any other area of life. An act, say a divination, performed without the magical frame of mind is no more magical than settling a legal dispute. In fact, conflict resolution, according to Victor Turner, is much of what divination is about.[4] The technique of identifying hidden culprits or diagnosing difficult ailments is not intrinsically magical. A diviner who comes into a college classroom to demonstrate her technique is not engaged in magic, because the essential mental component is missing. In contrast, the soccer player who carefully puts on his right boot first and touches the turf with his right hand, which he then kisses, is engaged in a magical act. On my definition, no act and no object are ever magical solely by virtue of being included in a certain esoteric tradition. The range of acts and objects surveyed in any work of reference will therefore be either limitless or arbitrarily limited to abstract theoretical categories such as "fetishism."

EMPATHY

Faced with extending their work on magic to cover every aspect of life or limiting magic to a few arbitrary topics, scholars have opted for neither. Instead, they have assimilated magic into their cultural histories or else ignored it altogether. Either way, magic expires.

Perhaps there is no good reason to revive the study of magic, despite some signs of life in 1995.[5] Maybe, instead of returning to hidden symbolic languages or deciphering abracadabra, a radically new approach is called for. Due to the fact that the magical experience can exist anywhere—a dentist's office as much as a hunting expedition—it is the subjective aspect of magic that should interest us most. Magical "empathy" can become the new subject of inquiry, the extension of the magical experience into daily life. "Empathy" should not be confused with Levy-Bruhl's quasi-mystical "participation," nor is it simply the moral concept of caring for someone. Moreover, the word *empathy* will jar those who study Indian society. Hierarchical societies, where castes and sexes are largely separated, have little use for empathy in its moral sense. Empathy contradicts purity, the ideology that organizes society into ranks from the pure to the impure. But the magical practices I have seen were often too urgent to be impeded by social considerations and ideologies. Sexes, castes, and religions mixed and even touched for the sake of health. A liminal space, set apart from other spaces, was dominated by a single goal and by the charisma of empathetic relations. At such times and places, empathy is a trans-subjective vicarious identification with another person, being, or object. Those who feel empathy participate in larger contexts without the limitations of a rigid social self or a detached intellect. The sense of self extends past the boundary of the individual person (or caste) to a system of relations—but not in a moral sense. In fact, the power of empathy can bring together a sorcerer and his victim as effectively as any healer and patient. I choose the word *empathy,* however, because the practice of magic can make sense only in a world of empathetic relations. A fragmented, atomistic world inhibits the experience of magic.

This is certainly true for our own world—with one possible exception. The monumental financial success of the Hollywood film industry can be credited to our unlimited capacity for vicarious identification, for empathy. Two-dimensional optical images on celluloid are converted into racing hearts and curdled blood. We sit in large dark halls with dozens of strangers and become transported—all of us in nearly the same way—into the life of an optical character. When the film is truly effective, we lose our sense of identity and become one with a simpleton like Forrest Gump, or even with a homicidal cyborg from the future. For two hours we participate in the modern idiom of the magical experience—in the movies.

The same complicated biological and psychological apparatus that made magic possible for Paleolithic cave artists—perception, imagination, and the rest—also animates the magical experience of both moviegoers and street magicians in Banaras and their customers. This magic becomes manifest as empathy, a simple term for a rich tapestry of interlinking beings. The heart of empathy and the key to every magical relation is a powerful sensory experience. Though magicians may substitute symbolic objects and even reinvent new procedures and spells, they leave one feature alone—the sensory bond of empathy. Touch, sight, sound, smell, and taste are the essential ingredients for participating in magical events, if not for interpreting them.

श्री श्री श्री

Case 16.2

Samoan Massage

Only in a few cases, connected with the administration of treatments for illnesses in which supernatural agents were impli-
cated, was there any instruction as to the timing of the administration of the medicine. In the medicine for an illness known as
"*ea saaua*" or "*ea fasia,*" for instance, the healer is required to
use

> Leaves of the *matalafii (Psychotria insularum).*
> An even number, in this case 20, should be beaten and
> mixed with water and the compound rubbed gently on the af-
> fected area.
> The treatment should take place when the locusts sing in
> the evening or at night. It should not be carried out during day-
> light.[6]

The strict emphasis on an even number (20) and the clearly specified
time of application read like the essential magical components of the
rite. But the one can be a pharmaceutical measurement, while the other
may be based on astute circadian observation. They may only seem
arbitrary—and therefore magical—to a Western scholar. The massage,
however, does not seem intrinsically magical; after all, the medicine
must be applied directly. There is nothing surprising about the ambigu-
ity, or rather the duality, of these applications. The vast majority of
magical rites, certainly all the rites I have witnessed, combine symbolic
action with a direct manipulation of the senses.

As a result, the vocabulary of magical empathy should not be just
a catalog of symbolic objects, nor should its syntax be limited to occult
ritual acts. Empathy—the experienced effect of magic—comes more
commonly from a massage, squeeze, rub, brushing, heating, cooling,
wetting, drying, pinching, or striking, to name just a few tactile manipulations. And touch seldom occurs alone. The magical rite is often a
cleverly orchestrated harmony of stimulated senses, accompanied by an
aroused imagination. Still, as the most primitive sense, touch is also the

most immediate and effective instrument of magical empathy. Of course, both touch and its effects are a mere starting point. In actual performance, matters become complicated very quickly, as the following cases of snakebite remedies show.

        ह्मी   ह्मी   ह्मी

Case 16.3

Snakebite Remedies

W. H. R. Rivers described specialists among the Todas, who make a cord out of women's hair and bind it tightly in three locations on the bitten limb. A mantra is recited during the tying of the cord. The cord is kept on for two or three days, during which time the mantra is repeated two or three times per day. The patient is prevented from crossing a stream, but if he must travel, he is carried above the water.[7]

Among the Jaunsaris of Uttar Pradesh, crossing also becomes a matter of taboo. According to Rizvi, the patient is not allowed to cross the door, the house cannot be swept with a broom, and the corner of a woman's saris—its border—is not allowed to touch the patient. The cure itself consists of eating *bhāng* (hemp) and drinking *bhāng* fried in clarified butter. Meanwhile, a cobra is killed and decapitated, then buried until it rots. After eight to ten days, a small portion of decomposed snake mixed with earth is cut out in the shape of a square frame (that resembles the shape of a snake's head) and washed with milk. The head is wrapped in a new cloth and placed on the bitten limb at the site of the bite. The cure consists of several additional practices, including the use of purgatives such as Dattura leaves. But even this brief sketch is enough to engage the interest of anyone who compares this case with others from unrelated locations.[8]

The Kethi and the Mutheu of Kenya insist that the biting snake be found and killed. The head of the snake is cut off and dried, then pulverized into powder that is applied to the wound. At the same time the venom is sucked out.[9] The Rama Indians of Nicaragua also use the pulverized head of a snake that has bitten someone. The snake head is mixed in a powder of leaves and roots collected by a specialized healer. The biting snake, according to the Ramas, must be killed, or the patient will not recover. However, it cannot be killed with a gun.[10] The patient is given a root to chew until he returns home, the only place he can be healed. The members of his family must hug him and stay with him, but he is quarantined and separated from everyone else. He must not even look at strangers, especially pregnant women. He is swathed in blankets and made to sweat. His diet is vegetarian and unspiced, but he also chews roots and powders that help him vomit the poison.

These treatments show how far the therapeutic imagination reaches, even when magic is reduced to empathy. In all these cases, touch (tying, hugging, swathing, sucking) is very important, but visual imagery seems to dominate the cure. The head of the snake in some simulated fashion is the essential component of the medicine. This imitation—recall Frazer's homeopathy—combines touch (the substance must actually come from the biting snake's head) with analogy, which is a visual concept. Furthermore, the patient's isolation among the Rama is defined as the taboo against making eye contact. Social taboos compel us to rely on sociological theories or at least to look at collective ways of thinking about such ideas as body temperature, substances, cooking, intentionality and fault, and crossing boundaries. These ideas are both collective and influential, but they transcend empathy. Or rather, they define the cultural parameters of empathy, not its experiential terrain. The existential force of a magical event comes from the engagement of actors in actual circumstances. A survey of simple sensory manipulations—most descriptions of magic unfortunately leave them out—needs to accompany social and cultural analysis in order to reclaim for magical experience its rightful place in the humanities.

The history of magic should consist first and foremost of a taxonomy of physical acts connected with the magical rite: tasting, pointing, beating, stepping, inhaling, exhaling, blowing, and many others. Which are the senses used, how does pantomime convey information, how are ideas integrated with manipulations of the body and other objects? These are some of the questions that the study of ritual in general confronts. In fact, ritual and magic overlap in several important respects. But magical rites are special. The uniquely magical dimension of such rituals emerges from the way sensory manipulations create a system of experienced relations.

The events of the rite are more important than the meaning of its symbols. Exorcism, for example, always requires touch, either with the hand or some other object. It is touch, above every other aspect of the ritual, that creates a healing relationship between patient and healer. Even expiation, a profoundly religious ritual, may contain powerful magical moments. An immersion in cold water or the self-infliction of pain accompany the symbolism of sin and regret. What is the relation between the experience of pain and the sense of moral purity that follows expiation, and how is pain incorporated into cultural symbolism? In the hands of a capable French structuralist, symbols can answer these questions with dexterity and finesse. But symbolism is a hired gun—it answers too much and becomes a law unto itself. The clove in the hand of an *ojhā* symbolizes one thing, the cane in the hand of a priest another. But both practitioners must touch their "patients." Both create a relationship of empathy. This is such a basic fact that it seems trivial.

To give an example that does not directly involve a human patient: The construction of a new house must begin with a *pūjā* in which a clay pot full of water from the Ganges is buried three feet under the cornerstone. The pot also contains *genda* flowers, a piece of silver, and a stone. It is impregnated with mantras before being buried. Magic is never an abstract plea. The house will not be protected merely by means of mental control of supernatural forces. Instead, the owner must fetch the water, place objects in the pot, bend over the hole, and reach down with pot in hand while lying on the pile of excavated earth. The ritual is a theater, with the owner playing a major role. He must participate because the magical event expresses his relation to the house. The rite creates empathy: It places house and owner in one network of relations that also includes every other force that can ever enter or possess the house.

As a unique discipline, the study of magic has to focus on such topics and then ground its material in specific cultural and natural settings. The inaugural building rite has a magical component and an institutional component, both with interlocking histories. A simple history of institutions and ideas without the theater would touch magic only tangentially. The study of magic must combine the history of embodied experience—the ground of interrelatedness—and its articulation in concrete cultural forms.

NOTES

1. Wilfred Cantwell Smith, *The Meaning and End of Religion* (San Francisco: Harper & Row, 1978).

2. John Hick, *An Interpretation of Religion: Human Responses to the Transcendent* (New York: Yale University Press, 1989), p. 5.

3. The Lolark Kund is discussed extensively by Ratnesh K. Pathak and Cynthia Ann Humes, "Lolark Kund: Sun and Shiva Worship in the City of Light," in *Living Banaras: Hindu Religion in Cultural Context*, ed. Bradley R. Hertel and Cynthia Humes (Albany: State University of New York Press, 1993), pp. 205–44; a briefer description is given by Diana Eck, *Banaras: City of Light* (Princeton, N.J.: Princeton University Press, 1982).

4. Victor Turner, *Ndembu Divination: Its Symbolism and Techniques* (New York: Humanities Press, 1961).

5. The XVII International Congress of History of Religions hosted a Magic Symposium in Mexico City, August 1995.

6. Cluny and La'avasa Macpherson, *Samoan Medical Belief and Practice* (Auckland: Auckland University Press, 1990), p. 204.

7. W. H. R. Rivers, *The Todas* (Jaipur: Rawat Publications, 1986), p. 267.

8. S. N. H. Rizvi, *Medical Anthropology of the Jaunsaris* (New Delhi: Northern Book Centre, 1991).

9. Charles M. Good, *Ethnomedical Systems in Africa: Patterns of Traditional Medicine in Rural and Urban Kenya* (New York: Guilford Press, 1987), p. 169.

10. Franklin O. Loveland, "Snakebite Cure Among the Rama Indians of Nicaragua," in *Medical Anthropology* ed. Francis X. Grollig, S. J., and Harold B. Harley (The Hague: Mouton Publishers, 1976).

🐚 CONCLUDING REMARKS 🐚

There is no such thing as a magical plant, a magical pond, a magical stone. There are curing plants, healing ponds, protective stones. These things become magical for some people at certain times. Anything can become a talisman, amulet, or even elixir under the right circumstances; conversely, even the most healing mineral spring can be reduced to a mere commercial spa. Magic is never an abstraction: It exists as a force only in the minds and bodies of people. If you wish to understand it, you must meet those who live by magic. This is what I have done, and these are some of the people I have met: healers and patients, astrologers, boat builders and construction workers, farmers, rain makers, Hindus, Muslims, Christians, Tantrics, atheists, believers, and scoundrels. All spin magic. Of course, people are messy. They say and do conflicting things, or they say one thing today, another tomorrow. They tell you too much, or not enough. They make it hard to classify things neatly, reducing a scholar to fits of neurotic classification withdrawal. We want to divide magic into neat categories: fetishes, taboos, exorcism, sorcery, and the rest. Instead, we have to watch and listen quietly, avoid pigeonholing the complex experience we encounter, and finally, when we are ready, participate in magical events.

But the raw data of magical rituals is too chaotic for simple description. The participants are often interested in matters that a researcher of magic might consider peripheral. Their descriptions seem to disperse the focus across a wide spectrum of events; their stories about magic, when we listen to them, can easily deceive. I found myself immensely entertained by many of these stories, but sometimes for the "wrong" reasons.

𝔖 𝔖 𝔖

The Sādhū and the Woman

A fake sādhū came into a village where some women were sitting. He began to read the palms of the children and women and was very successful. The women of the village were awed and showed him great reverence. One woman was very beautiful, and the sādhū decided to seduce her. As he read her palm, he informed her that she was very sick but assured her that he had the proper cure. "Give me some of your hair," he said. "I will make a *yantra* with it, which you can wear around your neck to regain your health." But the young woman was knowledgeable in the arts of Tantra and cures, so she knew what he was up to. She said, "Fine, but I must go inside to cut my hair." Once inside the hut, she found a goatskin gourd and cut some hair off it. She brought this to the sādhū, who took the hair to the edge of the village and discreetly performed his ritual. When he was last seen leaving the village, a black goatskin gourd was chasing the sādhū amorously.

𝔖 𝔖 𝔖

Piss Alchemy

In 1941–1942 during the hot season, a Banarsi Muslim named Shah (who told me this story) went with a friend to Daśāś-vamedh Ghāṭ. It was early morning but hot when two sādhūs came by. They asked for some water to drink, but Shah's friend decided to invite them to his house, where he gave them sweets and cold water. The holy men were deeply moved by this hospitality and asked for some aluminum. Shah and his friend did not understand this request, and they inquired how much they should bring. They were told to bring as much as they wanted. The two friends went to the market and bought 250 grams of aluminum for a few rupees. They brought the metal to the sādhūs, and one put the metal in a clay pot and peed into it. The aluminum melted. The sādhūs covered the pot and took it to the ghāṭ, where they put some herbs in it. When the holy men returned, they told their hosts to let it sit for four hours and wait for them to return, and they left. Two days later the sādhūs had still not come back, so Shah and his friend opened the pot and found 250 grams of silver in it.

As it turns out, both of these tales fascinated the Indians who heard them for the moral twist of the plots. A scoundrel got his comeuppance in one, and two good men were rewarded in the second. The supernatural incidents were barely noted, let alone celebrated by the narrators. This is typical for Banarsis, especially those who encounter magical events often. But the city of Banaras teaches another, equally valuable lesson. In the urgent practical need to seek out magicians, the townfolk set aside their social and ideological distinctions. Muslim and Hindus, high caste and low, men and women sit together—often even touching—before the healer. Religious beliefs are never discussed, and the power of the healer holds everyone in that special place.

The End of Magic is an effort to understand this unique experience. The book describes magic as a phenomenon that stands apart from the culture in which it is grounded. In order to understand the special bond between magician and client, one must always go beyond the cultural forms of the ritual performance to the universal nature of magic. This is a stereoscopic task: One eye is kept on the rich forms of cultural expression in Banaras, while the second remains focused on experience itself. Some sections of the book have described the traditions of my Banarsi acquaintances, while others have described theories of magic, mind, and language. Theory and description were interwoven throughout the book in a resonant interplay between reflection and observation. But this dance revolved around a unitary and consistent theme: Magic is the sensory experience of interrelatedness that emerges when individuals develop a unique intimacy with natural and social environments. Magical events are often experienced as extraordinary, and even occult, phenomena. But reports of such experiences are neither mystical nor strictly religious. They combine the mundane practicality of a noisy street with a lofty sense of belonging to an intimate world.

A word of caution to the impatient reader who has skipped directly to this conclusion: No single section, or even chapter, can recapture a complex experience that was teased out gradually over the course of the entire book. The explanation of magic must be as rich and as vivid as the phenomenon itself. It must hang on the twin pegs of description and explanation and sway from one to the other. The best way to profit by this book is to follow right along.

◙ BIBLIOGRAPHY ◙

Alland Jr., Alexander. *Adaptation in Cultural Evolution: An Approach to Medical Anthropology.* New York: Columbia University Press, 1970.

Alper, Harvey P. "The Problem of Ritual Language: From Information to Situation." *Journal of the American Academy of Religion* 50, no. 1 (1982): 49–71.

Alper, Harvey P., ed. *Mantra.* Albany: State University of New York Press, 1989.

Austin, John L. *Philosophical Papers.* New York: Oxford University Press, 1979.

Babb, Lawrence. *The Divine Hierarchy: Popular Hinduism in Central India.* New York: Columbia University Press, 1975.

Bacon, Francis. *The New Organon and Related Writings.* New York: Liberal Arts Press, 1960.

Bateson, Gregory. *Steps to An Ecology of Mind: Collected Essays in Anthropology, Psychiatry, Evolution and Epistemology.* New York: Ballantine Books, 1972.

——.*Sacred Unity: Further Steps to An Ecology of Mind.* New York: Cornelia & Michael Bessie, 1991.

Battailles, Georges. *Theory of Religion.* New York: Zone Books, 1989.

Beck, Guy L. *Sonic Theology: Hinduism and Sacred Sound.* Columbia: University of South Carolina Press, 1993.

Berlin, Brent. *Ethnobotanical Classification: Principles of Categorization of Plants and Animals in Traditional Societies.* Princeton, N.J.: Princeton University Press, 1992.

Berlin, Brent, and Paul Kay. *Basic Color Terms: Their Universality and Evolution.* Berkeley: University of California Press, 1969.

Bhattacharya, Deborah. *Pagalami: Ethnopsychiatric Knowledge in Bengal.* Syracuse: Maxwell School of Citizenship, 1986.

Bhattacharya, N. N. *History of the Tantric Religion*. New Delhi: Manohar, 1982.

Bloomfield, Maurice, ed. *The Kauśika Sūtra of the Atharva-Veda*. (Delhi: Motilal Banarsidass, 1972).

Bohm, David. *Wholeness and the Implicate Order*. London: Routledge & Kegan Paul, 1980.

Borges, J. L. *Other Inquisitions*. New York: Washington Square Press, 1966.

Brown, Slater. *The Heyday of Spiritualism*. New York: Hawthorn Books, 1970.

Bruner, Jerome. *Actual Minds, Possible Worlds*. Cambridge, Mass.: Harvard University Press, 1986.

Calvin, William. *The Cerbral Symphony: Seashore Reflections on the Structure of Consciousness*. New York: Bantam Books, 1990.

———.*The Throwing Madonna: Essays on the Brain*. New York: Bantam Books, 1991.

Capra, Fritjof. *The Turning Point: Science, Society and the Rising Culture*. London: Flamingo, 1983.

Coccari, Diane Marjorie. "The Bir Babas of Banaras: An Analysis of a Folk Deity in North India." Ph.D. diss., University of Wisconsin at Madison, 1986.

Crumley, Carol L., ed. *Historical Ecology: Cultural Knowledge and Changing Landscapes*. Santa Fe: School of American Research Press, 1994.

Daniel, E. Valentine. *Fluid Signs: Being a Person the Tamil Way*. Berkeley: University of California Press, 1984.

Daniélou, Alain. *Hindu Polytheism*. New York: Pantheon Books, 1964.

Darwin, Charles. *The Descent of Man and Selection in Relation to Sex*. London: Murray, 1871.

David-Neel, Alexandra. *Magic and Mystery in Tibet*. New York: C. Kendall, 1932.

Dawkins, Richard. *The Blind Watchmaker*. New York: W. W. Norton, 1987.

Degler, Carl N. *In Search of Human Nature: The Decline and Revival of Darwinism in American Social Thought*. New York: Oxford University Press, 1991.

Dennett, Daniel C. *Consciousness Explained*. Boston: Little, Brown, 1991.

Deregowski, Jan. "Illusion and Culture." In *Illusion in Nature and Art,* edited by R. L. Gregory, and E. H. Gombrich. New York: Charles Scribner's Sons, 1973.

Descartes, René. *A Discourse on Method*. New York: E. P. Dutton, 1951.

Desmond, Adrian, and James Moore. *Darwin*. London: Penguin Books, 1992.

Dossey, Larry. *Meaning and Medicine: Lessons from a Doctor's Tales of Breakthrough and Healing*. New York: Bantam Books, 1991.

Douglas, Mary. *Purity and Danger: An Analysis of the Concepts of Pollution and Taboo*. London: Routledge & Kegan Paul, 1979.

Dumont, Louis. *Homo Hierarchicus: An Essay on the Caste System*. Chicago: University of Chicago Press, 1970.

Durkheim, Emile. *The Elementary Forms of the Religious Life.* New York: Free Press, 1965.

Dyczkowski, Mark S. G. *The Doctrine of Vibration: An Analysis of the Doctrines and Practices of Kashmir Shaivism.* Albany: State University of New York Press, 1987.

Eck, Diana. *Darsan: Seeing the Divine Image in India.* Chambersburg, Pa.: Anima Books, 1981.

———.*Banaras: City of Light.* Princeton, N.J.: Princeton University Press, 1982.

Edelman, Gerald. *Bright Air, Brilliant Fire: On the Matter of the Mind.* New York: Basic Books, 1992.

Einstein, Albert. *Relativity: The Special and General Theory.* New York: Holt, 1920.

Eliade, Mircea. *Images and Symbols: Studies in Religious Symbolism.* New York: Sheed and Ward, 1969.

———.*Occultism, Witchcraft, and Cultural Fashions: Essays in Comparative Religions.* Chicago: University of Chicago Press, 1976.

Eliade, Mircea, ed. *The Encyclopedia of Religion.* New York: Macmillan, 1987.

Elwin, Verrier. *Leaves from the Jungle: Life in a Gond Village.* New Delhi: Oxford University Press, 1992.

Erikson, Erik. *Gandhi's Truth: On the Origins of Militant Non-Violence.* London: Faber & Faber, 1970.

Evans-Pritchard, E. E. *Witchcraft, Oracles and Magic Among the Azande.* Oxford: Clarendon Press, 1937.

Fichman, Martin. *Alfred Russel Wallace.* Boston: Twayne, 1981.

Firth, Raymond. *Man and Culture: An Evaluation of Malinowski.* London: Routledge & Kegan Paul, 1957.

Forbes, S. A. "The Lake as a Microcosm." *Illinois Natural History Survey Bulletin* 15 (1925): 537–50.

Fornell, Early Wesley. *The Unhappy Medium: Spiritualism and the Life of Margaret Fox.* Austin: University of Texas Press, 1964.

Foucault, Michel. *The Order of Things: An Archaeology of the Human Sciences.* New York: Vintage Books, 1970.

Fraser, J. T. *The Voices of Time.* Amherst: University of Massachussets Press, 1981.

Frater, Alexander. *Chasing the Monsoon.* Calcutta: Penguin Books, 1990.

Frazer, James G. *The Golden Bough: A Study in Magic and Religion.* New York: Macmillan, 1935.

Freed, Ruth S., and Stanley A. Freed. *Ghosts: Life and Death in North India.* New York: American Museum of Natural History, 1993.

Freud, Sigmund. *Totem and Taboo.* New York: W. W. Norton, 1989.

Friedman, Alan J., and Carol C. Donley. *Einstein as Myth and Muse.* New York: Cambridge University Press, 1985.

Frisancho, Roberto A. *Human Adaptation: A Functional Interpretation.* Ann Arbor: University of Michigan Press, 1981.

Fuchs, Steven. *The Korkas of the Vindhya Hills.* New Delhi: Inter-India Publications, 1988.

Fuller, C. J. *The Camphor Flame: Popular Hinduism and Society in India.* Princeton, N.J.: Princeton University Press, 1992.

Fürer-Haimendorf, Christof von. *Life Among Indian Tribes: The Autobiography of an Anthropologist.* New Delhi: Oxford University Press, 1991.

Gardner, Howard. *The Mind's New Science: A History of the Cognitive Revolution.* New York: Basic Books, 1985.

Geller, Uri. *My Story.* New York: Praeger, 1975.

Gibson, James J. *The Senses Considered as Perceptual Systems.* Boston: Houghton Mifflin, 1966.

———.*The Ecological Approach to Visual Perception.* Boston: Houghton Mifflin, 1982.

Girard, René. *Violence and the Sacred.* Baltimore: Johns Hopkins University Press, 1977.

Glucklich, Ariel. *The Sense of Adharma.* New York: Oxford University Press, 1994.

Gonda, Jan. *Selected Studies* (Leiden: E. J. Brill, 1975).

Good, Charles M. *Ethnomedical Systems in Africa: Patterns of Traditional Medicine in Rural and Urban Kenya.* New York: Guilford Press, 1987.

Gottlieb, Robert. "Symbolism Underlying Improvisatory Practices in Indian Music." *Journal of the Indian Musicological Society* 6 (1985): 23–36.

Gregory, Richard L. *The Intelligent Eye.* London: Weidenfeld & Nicholson, 1970.

Gupta, Sanjukta, Dirk Jan Hoens, and Teun Goudriaan. *Hindu Tantrism.* Leiden: E. J. Brill, 1979.

Guss, David. *The Language of the Birds: Tales, Texts and Poems of Interspecies Communication.* San Francisco: North Point Press, 1985.

Hand, Wayland. *Magical Medicine.* Berkeley: University of California Press, 1980.

Harris, Marvin. *Cows, Pigs, Wars, and Witches: The Riddle of Culture.* New York: Random House, 1974.

———.*Cultural Materialism: The Struggle for a Science of Culture.* New York: Random House, 1979.

Hertel, Bradley R., and Cynthia Humes, eds. *Living Banaras: Hindu Religion in Cultural Context.* Albany: State University of New York Press, 1993.

Hick, John. *An Interpretation of Religion: Human Responses to the Transcendent.* New York: Yale University Press, 1989.

Hofstadter, Douglas. *Metamagical Themas: Questing for the Essence of Mind and Pattern.* London: Penguin Books, 1987.

Horton, Robin. "Tradition and Modernity Revisited." In *Rationality and Relativism,* eds. M. Hollis and S. Lukes. Cambridge, MA: MIT Press, 1982.

Hubert, Henri, and Marcel Mauss. *Sacrifice: Its Nature and Function.* Chicago: University of Chicago Press, 1964.

Huxley, Aldous. *The Devils of Loudon*. London: Chatto & Windus, 1970.

————.*Texts and Pretexts*. London: Triad Grofton Books, 1986.

Huxley, Thomas H. *Man's Place in Nature and Other Anthropological Essays*. New York: D. Appleton, 1902.

Hyatt, Harry Middleton. *Hoodoo—Conjuration—Witchcraft—Rootwork*. Hannibal, Mo.: Western Publishers, 1939.

Inden, R. B., and R. W. Nicholas. *Kinship in Bengali Culture*. Chicago: University of Chicago Press, 1977.

Jackendoff, Ray. *Consciousness and the Computational Mind*. Cambridge, Mass.: MIT Press, 1987.

Johnson, Mark. *The Body in the Mind: The Bodily Basis of Meaning, Imagination, and Reason*. Chicago: University of Chicago Press, 1987.

Jung, Carl Gustav. *The Structure and Dynamics of the Psyche*. Princeton, N.J.: Princeton University Press, 1975.

————.*Basic Writings*. Princeton, N.J.: Princeton University Press, 1990.

Kakar, Sudhir. *Shamans, Mystics and Doctors: A Psychological Inquiry into India and its Healing Traditions*. New York: Alfred A. Knopf, 1982.

Kandel, Eric R., and Robert D. Hawkings. "The Biological Basis of Learning and Individuality." In *Mind and Brain: Readings from Scientific American Magazine*. New York: W. H. Freeman, 1993.

Kane, P. V. *History of Dharmaśāstra*. Poona: ABORI, 1930–62.

Kinsley, David. *Ecology and Religion*. Englewood Cliffs, N.J.: Prentice-Hall, 1995.

Kittredge, George Lyman. *Witchcraft in Old and New England*. New York: Russel & Russel, 1956.

Kroeber, A. L. *The Nature Of Culture*. Chicago: University of Chicago Press, 1952.

Kuhn, Thomas S. *The Structure of Scientific Revolutions*. Chicago: University of Chicago Press, 1970.

Kumar, Pramad. *Folk Icons and Rituals in Tribal Life*. New Delhi: Abhinav, 1984.

Lakoff, George. *Women, Fire, and Dangerous Things: What Categories Reveal about the Mind*. Chicago: University of Chicago Press, 1987.

Lakoff, George, and Mark Johnson. *Metaphors We Live By*. Chicago: University of Chicago Press, 1980.

Leaf, Murray J. *Man, Mind and Science: A History of Anthropology*. New York: Columbia University Press, 1979.

Leeds, Anthony, and Andrew P. Vayda. *Man, Culture, and Animals: The Role of Animals in Human Ecological Adjustments*. Washington, D.C.: American Association for the Advancement of Science, 1965.

Levi, Shabtai (Shabo). *The Bedouines in Sinai Desert*. Tel Aviv: Schocken, 1987.

Levi-Strauss, Claude. *The Savage Mind*. Chicago: University of Chicago Press, 1966.

————. *Structural Anthropology* (New York: Basic Books, 1963).

Levy-Bruhl, Lucien. *Primitive Mentality.* Oxford: Clarendon Press, 1923.

Lorenz, Konrad. *Studies in Animal and Human Behavior.* Cambridge, Mass.: Harvard University Press, 1971.

Lovejoy, Arthur O. *The Great Chain of Being.* Cambridge, Mass.: Harvard University Press, 1936.

Lovelock, James E. *Gaia: A New Look at Life on Earth.* Oxford: Oxford University Press, 1991.

Lukes, Steven. *Emile Durkheim, His Life and Work: A Historical and Critical Study.* New York: Harper & Row, 1972.

Lumsden, Charles J., and Edward O. Wilson. *Genes, Mind, and Culture: The Coevolutionary Process.* Cambridge, Mass.: Harvard University Press, 1981.

Macpherson, Cluny, and La'avasa. *Samoan Medical Belief and Practice.* Auckland: Auckland University Press, 1990.

Malinowski, Bronislaw. *Magic, Science, and Religion and Other Essays.* New York: Doubleday Anchor Books, 1954.

———.*Sex, Culture, and Myth.* New York: Harcourt, Brace & World, 1962.

———.*Coral Gardens and Their Magic.* New York: Dover, 1978.

———.*A Diary in the Strict Sense of the Term.* Palo Alto: Stanford University Press, 1989.

March, Robert. *Physics for Poets.* New York: McGraw-Hill, 1970.

Marr, David. *Vision: A Computational Investigation into the Human Representation and Processing of Visual Information.* San Francisco: W. H. Freeman, 1982.

Marriott, McKim. "Hindu Transactions; Diversity Without Dualism." In *Transaction and Meaning: Directions in the Anthropology of Exchange and Symbolic Behavior,* ed. Bruce Kapferer. Philadelphia: Institute for the Study of Human Issues, 1976.

Marriott, McKim, ed. *India through Hindu Categories.* New Delhi: Sage, 1990.

Maurice, Klaus, and Otto Mayr. *The Clockwork Universe: German Clocks and Automata 1550–1650.* New York: Neal Watson Academic Publications, 1980.

Maxwell, James Clerk. *Scientific Papers.* William Davidson Niven, ed. Cambridge: Cambridge University Press, 1890.

McElroy, Ann, and Patricia K Townsend. *Medical Anthropology in Ecological Perspective.* Boulder, Colo.: Westview Press, 1989.

McLuhan, T. C. *Way of the Earth.* New York: Simon & Schuster, 1995.

Merchant, Carolyn. *The Death of Nature.* New York: Harper & Row, 1980.

Morris, Brian. *Anthropological Studies of Religion.* New York: Cambridge University Press, 1984.

Morris, Desmond. *The Naked Ape: A Zoologist's Study of the Human Animal.* New York: McGraw-Hill, 1967.

Muller-Ortega, Paul E. "Tantric Meditation: Vocalic Beginnings." In *Ritual and*

Speculation in Early Tantrism, ed. Teun Goudriaan, Albany: State University of New York Press, (n.s.) vol.2, 1992.

Needham, Rodney. "Percussion and Transition." *Man* 1967.

———.*Circumstantial Deliveries*. Berkeley: University of California Press, 1981.

Newton, Isaac. *Mathematical Principles*, 1686. Berkeley: University of California Press, 1946.

———.*The Principia*. Amherst, N.Y.: Prometheus Books, 1995.

Odum, E. P. "The New Ecology." *Bioscience* 14 (1964): 14–16.

O'Flaherty, Wendy Doniger, ed. *Karma and Rebirth in Classical Indian Traditions*. Berkeley: University of California Press, 1980.

O'Flaherty, Wendy Doniger, tr. *The Rig Veda*. Harmondsworth: Penguin Books, 1984.

Olson, David, ed. *The Social Foundations of Language and Thought*. New York: W. W. Norton, 1980.

Ornstein, Robert, and David Sobel. *The Healing Brain*. New York: Touchstone, 1988.

Ostor, Akos. *Vessels of Time: An Essay on Temporal Change and Social Transformation*. Delhi: Oxford University Press, 1993.

Padoux, Andre. *Vāc: The Concept of the Word in Selected Hindu Tantras*. Albany: State University of New York Press, 1990.

Pagels, Heinz R. *The Cosmic Code: Quantum Physics as the Language of Nature*. New York: Bantam Books, 1990.

Parry, Jonathan P. *Death in Banaras*. Cambridge: Cambridge University Press, 1994.

Peirce, Charles Sanders. *Collected Papers*. Cambridge, Mass.: Harvard University Press, 1931–58.

Pelletier, Kenneth R. *Mind as Healer, Mind as Slayer*. New York: Delta/Seymore Lawrence, 1992.

Piaget, Jean. The Essential Piaget. New York: Basic Books, 1977.

Plotkin, Mark J. *Tales of a Shaman's Apprentice: An Ethnobotanist Searches for New Medicines in the Amazon Rain Forest*. New York: Viking, 1994.

Putnam, Hillary. "The Mental Life of Some Machines." In *Intentionality, Minds, and Perception*, ed. H. Castaneda. Detroit: Wayne State University Press, 1967.

Ramanujan, A. K. "Is There an Indian Way of Thinking? An Informal Essay." *In India through Hindu Categories*, ed. McKim Marriott. New Delhi: Sage Publications, 1990.

Randi, James. *The Truth about Uri Geller*. Buffalo, N.Y.: Prometheus Books, 1982.

Rappaport, Roy. "Ritual, Sanctity, and Cybernetics." *American Anthropologist* 73 (1971): 59–76.

———.*Ecology, Meaning, and Religion*. Richmond, Calif.: North Atlantic Books, 1979.

Richards, Robert J. *The Meaning of Evolution*. Chicago: University of Chicago Press, 1992.

Rivers, W. H. R. *The Todas.* Jaipur: Rawat, 1986.

Rizvi, S. N. H. *Medical Anthropology of the Jaunsaris.* New Delhi: Northern Book Centre, 1991.

Rosch, Eleanor. "Natural Categories." *Cognitive Psychology* 4 (1973): 328-50.

Ryle, Gilbert. *The Concept of Mind.* New York: Barnes and Noble, 1949.

Sahlins, Marshall. *The Use and Abuse of Biology.* Ann Arbor: University of Michigan Press, 1977.

Searle, John. *The Rediscovery of Mind.* Cambridge, Mass.: MIT Press, 1992.

Shannon, C. E. and W. Weaver. *The Mathematical Theory of Communication.* Urbana: University of Illinois Press, 1949.

Siegel, Lee. *Net of Magic: Wonder and Deceptions in India.* Chicago: University of Chicago Press, 1991.

Skinner, B. F. *About Behaviorism.* New York: Alfred A. Knopf, 1974.

Smart, John J. C. *Philosophy and Scientific Realism.* New York: Humanities Press, 1963.

Smith, Brian K. *Classifying the Universe: The Ancient Varna System and the Origins of Caste.* New York: Oxford University Press, 1994.

Smith, Jonathan Z. *Map Is Not Territory: Studies in the History of Religions.* Leiden: E. J. Brill, 1978.

Smith, Wilfred Cantwell. *The Meaning and End of Religion.* San Francisco: Harper & Row, 1978.

Stevenson, Mrs. Sinclair. *The Rites of the Twice-born.* London: Oxford University Press, 1920.

Talbot, Michael. *The Holographic Universe.* New York: Harper Perennial, 1991.

Tambiah, Stanley Jeyaraja. "The Form and Meaning of Magical Acts: A Point of View." In *Reader in Comparative Religion: An Anthropological Approach,* ed. William Lessa and Evon Vogt. New York: Harper & Row, 1979.

———.*Magic, Science, Religion, and the Scope of Rationality.* Cambridge: Cambridge University Press, 1991.

Thomas, Keith. *Religion and the Decline of Magic.* New York: Charles Scribner's Sons, 1971.

Turner, Victor. *Ndembu Divination: Its Symbolism and Techniques.* New York: Humanities Press, 1961.

Tylor, Edward Burnett. *The Origins of Culture.* New York: Harper Torchbooks, 1958.

Wall, Patrick D. "The Placebo Effect: An Unpopular Topic." *Pain* 51 (1992).

Wallace, Alfred Russel. *Natural Selection.* London: Macmillan, 1875.

———.*My Life: A Record of Events and Opinions.* New York: Dodd, Mead, 1906.

Watson, John B. *Behaviorism.* New York: People's Institute, 1925.

Weber, Max. *The Religion of India.* New York: Free Press, 1967.

Whiting, John. "Effects of Climate on Certain Cultural Practices." In *Environment and Cultural Behavior: Ecological Studies in Cultural Anthropology,* ed. A. P. Vayda, Garden City, N.Y.: Natural History Press, 1969.

Wiener, N. *Cybernatics*. Cambridge, Mass.: Technology Press, 1948.

Wilson, Edward O. *Sociobiology: The New Synthesis*. Cambridge, Mass.: Belknap Press, Harvard University, 1975.

———.*On Human Nature*. Cambridge, Mass.: Harvard University Press, 1978.

———.*Biophilia*. Cambridge, Mass.: Harvard University Press, 1984.

———.*The Diversity of Life*. New York: W. W. Norton, 1992.

Winstedt, Richard. *The Malay Magician*. London: Routledge & Kegan Paul, 1961.

Wittgenstein, Ludwig. *Philosophical Investigations*. Oxford: Oxford University Press, 1953.

Wolpert, Stanley. *A New History of India*. New York: Oxford University Press, 1982.

Woolf, Fred Alan. *Taking the Quantum Leap*. San Francisco: Harper & Row, 1982.

Zusne, Leonard, and Warren H. Jones. *Anomalistic Psychology: A Study of Magical Thinking*. Hillsdale, N.J.: Lawrence Erlbaum, 1989.

☙ INDEX ☙